高等院校公共事业管理专业"十二五"规划教材

公共事业管理专业英语

李 丹 编著

English for Public Services Management

清华大学出版社

北 京

内 容 简 介

本书以公共事业管理专业知识为核心，系统梳理了西方公共事业管理相关理论的发展过程、主要流派及其代表性观点。用英文全面介绍了中国主要公共事业，包括教育、科技、文化、卫生等管理的相关内容。此外，本书着眼于理论与实践的有机结合，在内容上创新性地增加了与公共事业管理实践密切相关的实用英语，如：党和国家主要机构的英文介绍、与中国国情密切相关的政治、经济英文词汇、专业英文文献的查阅与整理方法、毕业论文写作中英文翻译技巧以及就业过程中的面试英语、英文商务信函的写作等。本书既注重专业性与学术性，也突出实用性与趣味性，对于实现"用英语深化专业知识"与"通过专业学英语"的有机结合，提高公共事业管理人才的专业素养与英语运用能力具有重要的现实价值。

本书适合作为高等学校公共事业管理、行政管理、社会保障等公共管理类相关专业的教学与研究用书，也可作为广大公务员和社会组织人员以及任何对公共事业管理专业英语感兴趣人士的学习参考用书或培训用书。

本书配有课件，下载地址为：http://www.tupwk.com.cn。

图书在版编目(CIP)数据

公共事业管理专业英语 / 李丹编著. —北京：清华大学出版社，2016（2024.7重印）
（高等院校公共事业管理专业"十二五"规划教材）
ISBN 978-7-302-42520-5

Ⅰ．①公… Ⅱ．①李… Ⅲ．①公共管理—英语—高等学校—教材 Ⅳ．①H31

中国版本图书馆 CIP 数据核字(2015)第 299991 号

责任编辑：施　猛　马遥遥
封面设计：常雪影
版式设计：方加青
责任校对：牛艳敏
责任印制：宋　林

出版发行：清华大学出版社
　　　　　网　　　址：https://www.tup.com.cn，https://www.wqxuetang.com
　　　　　地　　　址：北京清华大学学研大厦 A 座　　　邮　　编：100084
　　　　　社 总 机：010-83470000　　　　　　　　　邮　　购：010-62786544
　　　　　投稿与读者服务：010-62776969，c-service@tup.tsinghua.edu.cn
　　　　　质 量 反 馈：010-62772015，zhiliang@tup.tsinghua.edu.cn
　　　　　课 件 下 载：https://www.tup.com.cn，010-62794504
印 装 者：三河市龙大印装有限公司
经　　销：全国新华书店
开　　本：185mm×260mm　　　印　　张：13.75　　　字　　数：292 千字
版　　次：2016 年 2 月第 1 版　　　印　　次：2024 年 7 月第 6 次印刷
定　　价：48.00 元

产品编号：057632-02

前　言

伴随着经济全球化和文化全球化的发展，语言全球化的趋向也越来越明显，英语成为大多数非英语国家的第一外语。在全球经济和文化交流日益频繁的今天，英语教学也受到越来越多的关注和重视。

在国外，专业英语又称为科技英语，在许多国家已成为现代英语的一个专门领域，在语法结构和词汇方面均形成了特有的习惯用语、特点和规律。据了解，英、美、日、德等国以及第三世界许多国家，都已建立起科技英语的教学和研究机构，出版了许多丛书、期刊和专著。

在我国，专业英语是大部分高校非外语专业开设的区别于基础英语的必修课程，课程一般设置在大学生修完基础英语和部分专业课程的高年级阶段。作为专业教育的重要组成部分，专业英语的作用主要是完善专业课程体系，提高学生利用英语表达和交流专业知识的能力，以及通过互联网和专业英文期刊等信息渠道获取国外本专业领域知识的能力。同时，专业英语也将为部分学生进入研究生学习和出国留学奠定良好的基础。

1998年，教育部将公共事业管理专业列入《普通高等学校本科专业目录》。1999年秋季，东北大学、云南大学两所高校在全国率先招收公共事业管理专业本科生。多年来，公共事业管理专业取得了飞速的发展，公共事业管理专业英语教学也受到越来越多的关注。但是，目前国内并没有专门针对公共事业管理的专业英语教材。因此，本书的编写与出版，对于填补国内公共事业管理专业英语教材的空白、提升公共事业管理专业教学质量、提高公共事业管理专业学生的专业英语能力具有重要的现实意义。

总体而言，本书注重突出以下几方面特点。

一是专业性。本书以公共事业管理相关理论为核心，强化专业英语训练，使学生掌握本专业的基础词汇和专业理论，熟悉本专业理论的发展过程及主要理论流派，能够阅读专业文献，了解专业文书的写作，为以后的学习研究和工作打下坚实的基础。在介绍经典理论和文献时，特别提炼或节选各理论流派的主要观点和核心理论，并附以中文翻译，避免学生因难度过大而丧失学习的兴趣。

二是实用性。专业英语教学的最终目的是学以致用，培养学生在工作、生活中运用英语的实际能力。因此，本书特别注重理论与实践的结合，在内容上创新性地增加了与公共事业管理实践密切相关的实用英语，如：党和国家主要机构的英语介绍、专业文书的英语写作、商务信函的英语写作等内容，提高学生应用专业英语的实践能力与技巧。此外，还编写了与公共事业管理专业学习相关的实用英语，如毕业论文写作中涉及的英文翻译、英文文献的查阅整理等，为学生的专业学习提供帮助。

三是趣味性。为拓宽学生的知识面并提高其学习专业英语的兴趣和积极性，本书还特别附上了与我国国情密切相关的政治、经济词汇，如"中国梦"(Chinese Dream)、"小康社会"(moderately prosperous society)等。

本书既可作为高等学校公共事业管理、行政管理、社会保障等公共管理相关专业的教材，也可供任何对公共事业管理专业英语感兴趣的人士学习参考。

本书由李丹统稿。参加编写的有：李丹(第一章、第二章、第三章、附录)、张晓杰(第四章、第五章)、李兴超(第六章)。

本书为东北大学本科教育教学改革研究项目"公共事业管理专业英语"课程建设研究、东北大学研究生教育科学研究计划项目的研究成果之一，并得到了入选"万人计划"第一批教学名师的娄成武教授设立的"教学改革研究项目"资助。在编写过程中，得到了清华大学出版社施猛编辑的大力帮助与支持，在此表示衷心的感谢。同时，本书引用了国内外诸多专家和学者的观点，在此一并表示深深的谢意。

由于编者的学识有限，书中难免存在缺陷和纰漏之处，敬请广大学术同仁和实际工作者提出宝贵意见。反馈邮箱：wkservice @vip.163.com。

李丹

二〇一五年八月于东北大学

目　录

Chapter 3　The Essence of Classics in Public Service Management ········· 38

Chapter 4　Political Party and State Organ ····························· 84

Chapter 1
Introduction to Public Service Management

1.1
What Is Public Service?

1.1.1 Definition of Public Service

Public services are essential to the functioning of our economy and our society. A strong and effective public service is recognized as a source of competitive advantage for any country.

Public service is a kind of service which is provided by government or non-governmental organizations (NGOs) to the public, either directly (through the public sectors) or by financing provision of services.

In China, public service is the supply of quasi-public and some public goods provided by public service units or institutions for the economic and social development.[1]

1.1.2 Characters of Public Service

The characters of public service can be refined to the following four points: firstly, public service is based on the requirements of public interests; secondly, public service aims at providing survival care and meeting the basic demands and development of the public; thirdly, the public can not achieve the aim above by themselves without the help of government or public organizations; finally, the government provides public service via exercising public power directly or indirectly.

1.1.3 History of Public Service

Historically, the widespread provision of public services in developed countries usually began in the late nineteenth century, often with the municipal development of gas and water services. Later, governments began to provide other services such as electricity and healthcare. In most

---

[1] LOU Chengwu, LI Jian. Introduction to Public Service Management[M]. Beijing: Renmin University Press, 2006.

developed countries such services are still provided by local or national government. The biggest exceptions are the U.S. and the U.K., where private provision is more significant. Nonetheless, such privately provided public services are often strongly regulated, for example (in the U.S.) by Public Utility Commissions.

⚙ Vocabulary

non-governmental organization (NGO)	非政府组织
quasi-public goods	准公共物品
public service unit	事业单位
institution	事业单位
healthcare	卫生，保健
regulate	管制，规制

👤≡ FURTHER READING

China Sets Up Special Fund for Public Service Ads

China has set up a special fund worth more than 10 million yuan (1.6 million U.S. dollars) to support public service advertisements.

Radio and TV programs, roadside billboards and banners have long played a key role in promoting good values and providing knowledge on a range of topics, from furnace safety to giving up bus seats to the elderly.

A total of 132 projects chosen from more than 500 applications have been covered by the fund, the State Administration of Press, Publication, Radio, Film and Television (SAPPRFT) said on Friday.

Completed projects that have already aired include one by the Beijing Media Network calling for patience in parenting, as well as an anti-speeding ad by a radio station in east China's Zhejiang Province.

Figures from the administration show that central and local television groups made 16,000-plus public service ads under the organization of SAPPRFT as of late November, with total air time of some three million minutes.

SAPPRFT vowed to increase financial investment to boost the production and airing of public service programs.

Source: available at
http://news.xinhuanet.com/english/china/2014-12/26/c_133881181.htm

1.2 Publicness of Public Service

1.2.1　Academic and Practical Research on Publicness of Public Service

In both the academic and practical discourse on public administration, the publicness of public service used to be a common concern, especially with regard to its possession of unique public qualities compared to business management. There also emerged critical observations regarding certain inherent obstacles to this publicness of public service, including its accumulation of excessive power, lack of accountability and representation, indifference towards public needs and demands, official secrecy and inaccessibility, and role in depoliticizing the public sphere (Garnham 1990; Haque 1994). Recognizing such limitations of public service to be a genuine public domain, some scholars became interested in exploring alternatives to enhance its publicness (Thomas 1999; Ventriss 1989), Coursey and Bozeman(1990, 532) went further to make the following comment: "There is no more important concern to public organization theory than the nature of 'public' in public organizations."

However, in recent years, the concern for ascertaining the status of public service as an authentic public domain seems to have diminished worldwide under the emerging market-driven mode of governance. Public service itself has undergone businesslike transformation, especially under the influence of current global context characterized by the triumph of market forces and the reorientation of state policies toward deregulation, privatization, and liberalization (Haque 1996). The examples of such businesslike reforms in public service include initiatives such as Public Service 2000 in Canada, Next Steps in the United Kingdom, Renewal of the Public Service in France, Financial Management Improvement Program in Australia, Administrative Management Project in Austria, Modernization Program for the Public Sector in Denmark, and Major Options Plan in Portugal (OECD 1993). This new genre of administrative reforms, often generalized as New Public Management, can also be found under various titles in countries such as Belgium, Brazil, Finland, Germany, Italy, Jamaica, Japan, Malaysia, Mexico, the Netherlands, New Zealand, Norway, the Philippines, Singapore, Sweden, Switzerland, Turkey, and Zambia (OECD 1995).[1]

---

[1]　M. Shamsul Haque. The Diminishing Publicness of Public Service under the Current Mode of Governance [J]. Public Administration Review, 2001,(61):65-82.

1.2.2 Obstacles in Pursuing Publicness of Public Service

There are many challenges or obstacles in pursuing publicness of public service, such as the eroding public-private distinction, narrowing composition of service recipients, weakening means of public accountability, shrinking role of the public sector, and rising challenge to public confidence. Despite cross-national and inter-regional variations in the intensity of these challenges, the common global trend is toward this diminishing publicness, which has critical implications for public service, especially for its identity, motivation, and legitimacy.

1.2.3 Suggestions and Solutions

Suggestions to meet these challenges include the following: firstly, academics and practitioners should try to introduce serious critical studies and debates on the use of private-sector concepts, values, structures, and techniques in public service that pose a challenge to its publicness in terms of the eroding public-private distinction. Secondly, the policy makers should reexamine the rationale that market-centered reforms in governance expand the base of ownership, ensure better allocation, and facilitate "popular capitalism" (Hamilton 1989, Okumura 1994). Thirdly, determine the nature and extent of the public sector role on the basis of objective criteria rather than market-based assumption that the public sector is inefficient and ineffective in comparison with the private sector (Clements 1994; Haquee 1996). Fourthly, although one of the common rationales behind the recent market-oriented reforms has been increased the responsiveness and accountability of public service to its customers, certain basic features of these reforms (such as privatization, contracting out, public-private partnership, and autonomous agency) tend to pose a new challenge to accountability, because these business-like features may render the traditional democratic means of accountability, including parliamentary debates, legislative committees, and internal administrative controls, ineffective. There is a need for redesigning the existing accountability measures and introducing new ones.[1]

⚙ Vocabulary

public administration	行政管理，公共管理
publicness	公共性
public service	公共服务
accountability	责任
representation	代表

---

[1] M. Shamsul Haque. The Diminishing Publicness of Public Service under the Current Mode of Governance [J]. Public Administration Review, 2001,(61):74.

market-driven	市场驱动
governance	治理
transformation	转型
reorientation	再定位
deregulation	分权
privatization	私有化
erode	损害
identity	身份
motivation	动机
legitimacy	合法性
rationale	基础理论
facilitate	促进
responsiveness	回应性
contracting out	(公共服务)外包
public-private partnership	公私合作模式
legislative committee	立法委员会

👤 FURTHER READING

Public Service 2000: The Renewal of the Public Service of Canada

The Public Service 2000 (PS 2000) White Paper set out a new management philosophy, with precepts grouped under innovation, service to the public, people, and accountability (the precepts are listed in the Appendix to this report).

The White Paper portrayed improved service to Canada and Canadians as the central theme of PS 2000. It argued that money saved by simplifying resource management and administration could be spent improving service delivery. Improved service would also feature new ways of interacting with Canadians—more effective consultation with stakeholders, for example, and partnering with other levels of government and other sectors of society. Since most services are provided in the regions, and most public servants work there, the greater authority that would flow to departments was to be delegated "wherever possible" to the regions—and to the management levels closest to the front lines.

Decentralization and increased delegation of authority would strike a new balance between the need for control and the desire to provide responsive, efficient and effective service. This would require the much more systematic management and development of public servants, with a greater emphasis on individual, or personal, accountability. Deputy ministers and public service managers and supervisors would be more clearly accountable for the way they used their authority and the way they managed and developed their staff, and for the results they produced.

The key to achieving the kind of public service that PS 2000 envisioned would be not just different practices but a fundamental change in attitudes about managing employees. The belief was that empowered public servants could better serve Canada and Canadians. The intent, as the Prime Minister said in announcing the initiative, was to foster a public service that "recognizes its employees as assets to be valued and developed." The public service was to adopt a culture of continuous learning, with greater emphasis on both the training and development of public servants and their career planning and mobility. The reform proposals recognized the key role of employees in meeting the organization's objectives; a more vibrant and creative workplace could attract and keep the best-qualified people who were in growing demand by other employers.

The fundamental changes envisioned for the corporate culture called for a long-term process of reform (the name—PS 2000—recognized that it would likely take 10 years). And it would be a dynamic process: the White Paper recognized some of the challenges of aspects of the reforms (for example, developing a culture of continuous learning) but did not offer much guidance on them; lessons learned by experience and the change of mindsets were expected to generate added reforms.

Source: available at

http://www.oag-bvg.gc.ca/internet/english/meth_gde_e_10222.html

1.3

Public Service in the Development of Public Administration Science

In the development of public administration science, there are at least several approaches to bringing excellent public services into reality such as Old Public Administration (OPA), New Public Management (NPA), and New Public Service (NPS).

1.3.1 The Old Public Administration

The elements showing the characteristic or the mainstream view of the Old Public Administration(OPA) include the following:

(1) Government provides the direct delivery of service through its agencies.

(2) Public service provision is administered through hierarchical organization with top down system.

(3) OPA approach is more centralistic. In addition, the role of government is so big or even as single player in giving service to the public.

1.3.2   The New Public Management

The New Public Management is based on concept from market mechanism and professional management. In public operation, there are seven main points of the NPM:

(1) Give precedence to professional management, focusing on freedom of administrator in using discretion of administrative decision for deftness and success.

(2) Emphasize clear objective making and fix the aim of operation in obviously. Therefore, for the public operation to be accountable of the result more than give precedence to the rule and process of the government.

(3) Connect practice and resource management in government sectors and create the prize system, making the administrators and the workers have motivation in practice, which is the highest success of the organizations.

(4) Improve the organization structure and operation system, with smaller structure for deftness operating in potential. Shift from a unified management system to a decentralized system in which managers gain flexibility and are not limited to agency restrictions.

(5) Promote to have the competition system on public service management for the government and the other organizations to improve efficiency and quality of public service management.

(6) Change the administrative methods to have more modernity and support technology using and also the techniques of private management in the government sectors.

(7) Promote discipline of finance, emphasize on economical spending and worthiness of public resource using that is limited to the highest profit for the public sectors.

1.3.3   The New Public Service

The continued paradigm was New Public Service (NPS). NPS was proposed by Janet V. Denhardt and Robert B. Denhardt through their book entitled *"The New Public Service, Serving not Steering"* published in 2003. The book was started with the statement of "Government shouldn't be run like a business; it should be run like a democracy". Running bureaucracy is similar to running democratic system. Therefore, there are differences between the two paradigms. NPM emphasizes on the 3E economic values (efficiency, economy and effectiveness). Whereas, NPS focuses on the political values namely: equity, democracy, equality, etc. That is a classical issue in the public administrative science.[①]

Therefore, the interesting point between the two paradigms is the role of society in public service provision. In NPM, there is no involvement of the society. Society is only customers who have responsibility for taking and paying for public service provided for them. In the mean time, in the NPS, society should actively be involved in the process of public service provision (particularly in term of policy formulation or deciding of society needs).

From explanation above we can conclude that the differences among OPA, NPM and NPS exist in the involvement of the actors for public service provision. In the OPA, government is a single actor responsible for conducting all of the process of public service provision. While in the NPM, government or bureaucracy was strived to involve in the process and use economic and private management in the process of public service provision to achieve public service efficiency and effectiveness. However, because of the weakness in the provision, NPS was emerging. In this paradigm, society has a wide range of participation in the process of public service provision, particularly in deciding the society needs. Therefore, in this paradigm, it is not only government and the private are involved in the public service provision, but also society. These are the important differences among OPA, NPM, and NPS.[②]

⚙ Vocabulary

Old Public Administration	传统公共行政
New Public Management	新公共管理
New Public Service	新公共服务
hierarchical organization	阶层制组织
market mechanism	市场机制
discretion	判断力
deftness	灵巧
objective	客观的
efficiency	效率
paradigm	范例
democracy	民主政体

① Robert B. Denhardt, Janet Vinzant Denhardt. The New Public Service: Serving Rather than Steering[J]. Public Administration Review, 2000,60 (6), 549-559.

② Anurat Anantanatorn, Samrit Yossomsakdi, Andy Fefta Wijaya, Siti Rochma. Public Service Management in Local Government, Thailand[J]. International Journal of Applied Sociology, 2015,5(1): 5-15.

bureaucracy	官僚机构
effectiveness	效用
equity	公平
equality	平等
formulation	制定
participate in	参与

👤 FURTHER READING

The New Public Service

Theorists of citizenship, community and civil society, organizational humanists, and postmodernist public administrationists have helped to establish a climate in which it makes sense today to talk about a New Public Service. Though we acknowledge that differences exist in these viewpoints, we suggest there are also similarities that distinguish the cluster of ideas we call the New Public Service from those associated with the New Public Management and the old public administration. Moreover, there are a number of practical lessons that the New Public Service suggests for those in public administration. These lessons are not mutually exclusive, rather they are mutually reinforcing. Among these, we find the following most compelling.

(1) Serve, rather than steer. An increasingly important role of the public servant is to help citizens articulate and meet their shared interests, rather than to attempt to control or steer society in new directions.

(2) The public interest is the aim, not the by-product. Public administrators must contribute to building a collective, shared notion of the public interest. The goal is not to find quick solutions driven by individual choices. Rather, it is the creation of shared interests and shared responsibility.

(3) Think strategically, act democratically. Policies and programs meeting public needs can be most effectively and responsibly achieved through collective efforts and collaborative processes.

(4) Serve citizens, not customers. The public interest results from a dialogue about shared values, rather than the aggregation of individual self-interests. Therefore, public servants do not merely respond to the demands of "customers," but focus on building relationships of trust and collaboration with and among citizens.

(5) Accountability isn't simple. Public servants should be attentive to more than the market; they should also attend to statutory and constitutional law, community values, political norms, professional standards, and citizen interests.

(6) Value people, not just productivity. Public organizations and the networks in which they participate are more likely to succeed in the long run if they are operated through processes of collaboration and shared leadership based on respect for all people.

(7) Value citizenship and public service above entrepreneurship. The public interest is better advanced by public servants and citizens committed to making meaningful contributions to society rather than by entrepreneurial managers acting as if public money were their own.

Source: available at

Public Administration Review,2000,(6):549-559.

1.4
What is Public Service Management?

1.4.1 Definition of Public Service Management

Public service management is the guiding, organizing, directing, coordinating and controlling of public services by the government and other public organizations based on public demands and interests.

In China, there is a college major entitled Public Service Management which was first set in two universities—Northeastern University and Yunnan University in 1999, and now there are over 500 universities having this major.

1.4.2 Public Service Motivation

One key point in public service management is public service motivation (PSM). Although it is of recent vintage, the concept of public service motivation (PSM) represents a positive example of theoretical development in public administration. This theory has significant practical relevance, as it deals with the relationship between motivation and the public interest. The construct of the public interest is central to traditional public administration scholarship (Appleby 1945; Herring 1936). In recent years, this theoretical development has been gradually joined by empirical work as scholars have sought to operationalize what public interest means for employees, why they develop a strong sense of public service, and how that sense influences their behavior (e.g., Alonso and Lewis 2001; Brewer and Selden 1998; Brewer, Selden, and Facer 2000; Crewson 1997, Houston 2000; Perry 1996, 1997).

Perry and Wise provide the widely accepted definition of PSM: "An individual's predisposition to respond to motives grounded primarily or uniquely in public institutions and organizations." [1] PSM is important not only to motivation but also to productivity, improved management practices, accountability, and trust in government, making it one of the major topics of investigation in public administration today. The relevance of PSM, though particularly high for government, is not limited to this sector, as employees in the private and nonprofit sectors also exhibit PSM to varying degrees.[2] Therefore, PSM not only helps us understand the traditional differences among the public, nonprofit, and private sectors, but, given the increasingly blurry boundaries between sectors, it is useful in understanding public-regarding behaviors in organizations that are characterized by varying levels of publicness.[3]

✿ Vocabulary

Public Service Management	公共事业管理
empirical	经验的
predisposition	素质

☷ FURTHER READING

Ireland Unveils Three-year Public Service Reform Plan

Ireland on Tuesday published a new public service reform plan, setting out an ambitious new phase of reform measures in this sector in three years.

"The new reform plan will set the basis for a new public service, one that is focused on delivering better outcomes for citizens and business customers; one that is efficient and responsive; and one in which public servants are empowered to meet the challenges and opportunities of the future." said Public Expenditure and Reform Minister Brendan Howlin, while launching the plan.

Just over two years since Ireland's first public service reform plan was published, the new Public Service Reform Plan 2014-2016 builds on the progress made on implementing the first reform plan and sets out an ambitious new phase of reform.

There are four key themes running through the new reform plan: delivery of improved outcomes for service users; achieving and utilizing the "reform dividend"; greater digitalization

---

[1] James L. Perry, Lois R. Wise. The Motivational Bases of Public Service[J]. Public Administration Review, 1990, 50(3):368.

[2] Dennis Wittmer. Serving the People or Serving for Pay: Reward Preferences among Government, Hybrid Sector, and Business Managers[J]. Public Productivity and Management Review, 1991,14(4):369-383.

[3] Barry Bozeman. All Organizations Are Public: Bridging Public and Private Organizational Theories. Jossey-Bass: San Francisco, 1991, 286.

and use of open data; and more openness, transparency and accountability.

While maintaining the necessary emphasis on efficiency and cost reduction, Howlin said the next phase of reform would focus on achieving the best outcomes for people, the economy and society as a whole.

He said savings would be reinvested in improved resources and reform dividends would underpin and sustain the agenda of reform.

He added a rationalization of state agencies would be completed by the end of the year.

At the launch, Brian Hayes, minister of state for public service reform, acknowledged the progress made, and also the need to maintain the focus on delivery.

"While we have made considerable progress in terms of public service reform, we still have further work to do. We must continue to drive the implementation of the reform program with energy and commitment." he said.

The reform plan advocates increased digital delivery of services and better sharing of data across the public service.

Under the plan, Ireland will introduce a data sharing and governance bill to address data protection issues that may arise. The rollout of the public services card will be accelerated and possibly extended to other transactions. Postcodes will be introduced by the summer of 2015.

There is to be further amalgamation of functions such as payroll and pensions in shared services initiatives.

The plan also advocates further outsourcing. Among the functions that may be considered for outsourcing are debt management and medical assessments.

It also outlines deadlines for the government's legislative reform program and initiatives in individual sectors.

By the end of this year, all post-primary schools will have access to broadband.

In health sector, there will be a review of the fair deal nursing home scheme with a view to providing more financial support for home care.

There are also measures to facilitate the transition to universal health insurance. A free general practitioner service will be provided to the entire population by early 2016. A Patient Safety Agency is to be established on an administrative basis in 2014, initially within the Health Service Executive (HSE) structures.

Since 2008, Ireland has cut public expenditure by 13.5 percent, and the public sector pay bill by 17 percent. Staff numbers have fallen from 320,000 to 288,500 at present. Ireland is aiming to get staff numbers down to 287,000 by the end of this year and reach 282,500 by 2015.

However, the demand for public services has risen dramatically over the same period. Social welfare payments are up over 18 percent since 2008. Another 600,000 people are now eligible for medical cards, bringing the national total to 1.8 million or 40 percent of the population. The number of children in schools is up to 49,000, while the number of pensioners has risen by 13 percent.

Source: available at

http://news.xinhuanet.com/english/world/2014-01/15/c_126004807.htm

1.5

Control of Public Service Quality

Control of public service quality is a recent trend in the context of public administration. Most services in the public sector were originally conceived in response to the failure of the commercial or private sector to deliver adequate quality in key areas for the wellbeing of society as a whole. Since then, quality in the public sector domain has traditionally been a response to failure. The attention to public sector organizations has more recently been concerned with ensuring that their services are not merely responsive, but are as consistent and fair as possible in meeting public needs.[1]

For more than a decade, there has been significant public sector reform at all levels of government. Such reform has been stimulated by increasing difficulties in public sector financing, coupled with pressure caused by the globalization of most aspects of social and economic life. Most public sector organizations have a variety of customers paying directly or indirectly for services. Other customers make little or no financial contribution towards the provision of services, and yet another type of customer might pay for a particular public service, but not experience its benefits through direct use.[2]

Although there was an assumption in the past that reaching people and delivering services constituted "effectiveness", in times of limited resources there is an increasing demand on public agencies to demonstrate their value to society.[3] There is also an increasing demand for customer service initiatives, and these often have to be funded on a shoestring budget, or

---

[1] M. Donnelly. Making the Differences: Quality Strategy in the Public Sector[J]. Managing Service Quality, 1999,(1): 47-52.

[2] M. Donnelly, M. Wisniewski, J. F. Dalrymple, A. C. Curry. Measuring Service Quality in Local Government: the SERVQUAL Approach[J]. International Journal of Public Sector Management, 1995,(7):15-20.

[3] K. Navaratnam, K. Harris. Quality Process Analysis: a Technique for Management in the Public Sector[J]. Management Service Quality, 1995,(3):23-28.

resources through budget reallocation away from other activities.[①] Modern communications, with the wide dissemination of information to the general public, also produce increasing expectations and demands. A natural response to all these factors has been the development of new methods for improving performance.[②]

At the heart of most public sector reform, initiatives have been the philosophy that value for money can best be achieved by a separation of roles between those who set the policy and those who deliver the service. This shift to a more contract-based system gives public service managers freedom to manage the operational delivery of services—within the policy and resources framework established by political authorities. Within this framework, however, managers should have incentives to use their freedom to improve the efficiency and effectiveness of their organization. In the private sector, this incentive is supplied by the competitive nature of the market (that is, low-quality organizations go out of business). Most public sector services, by contrast, do not operate in a competitive environment, and therefore do not experience this pressure to improve. A significant stimulus to improve performance has been the creation of alternative means of replicating the sort of competitive pressure that exists in the private sector. These alternative means have included a requirement by central government for local authorities to put certain activities out to competitive tender, and a requirement for all public services to consider areas of work that might be transferred to the private sector.[③] The underlying assumptions have been that the private sector is more efficient than the public sector, and that by applying commercial models of management and quality improvement, standards of services can be increased without any increase in public spending. Quality management has become one of the main methods of meeting the challenges posed by the increasing economic pressure on public expenditure. Quality initiatives have been linked to the commercialization of public services, and to the needs and demands of sovereign customers in the market place. The quality of outputs has become a focus of attention, rather than a mere examination of the value of inputs. Quality management has come to be viewed as the answer to the main criticisms of public services—inefficiency, wastefulness, and remoteness from those whom they serve.[④] Quality has come to

---

① M. Donnelly, M. Wisniewski, J.F. Dalrymple, A.C. Curry. Measuring Service Quality in Local Government: the SERVQUAL Approach[J]. International Journal of Public Sector Management, 1995,(7):15-20.

② A. Ancarani, G. Capaldo. Management of Standardised Public Services: a Comprehensive Approach to Quality Assessment[J]. Managing Service Quality: An International Journal, 2001,(5):331.

③ J. Cowper, M. Samuels. Performance Benchmarking in the Public Sector: the UK Experience[A]. Benchmarking, Evaluation and Strategic Management in the Public Sector, PUMA Work on Performance Management, OECD, Paris, 1997.

④ A. Erridge, R. Fee, J. McIlroy. Public Sector Quality: Political Project or Legitimate Goal?[J]. International Journal of Public Sector Management, 1998,(5):341-353.

be defined in terms of fixed standards (representing fitness for use) and now allows for external models of evaluation (such as quality audits). This approach has ensured that clear standards have been set up, and that resources have been used as efficiently as possible to meet these standards.[①]

During the 1990s, public service quality initiatives have been launched in numerous countries at various levels of government.

These initiatives have involved:

- Professional standard setting;
- Service excellence based on users' perception of quality;
- Government-granted rights and choice for consumers;
- Involvement of consumer movements.

The continuous need for improving both efficiency and effectiveness in a situation of scarce resources and rising public expectations in the public sector (that is, civil services, health management, and so on) is one of the major challenges faced by managers in the public sector all over the world. Public managers need to update their role by redesigning objectives and work positions, and by taking into account legal constraints and innovations. In such a modified situation, it is not sufficient to reengineer established operative systems. It is also necessary to assign a key role to quality management.[②]

Many pressures on the public sector now make quality management appear much more attractive. However, such quality management can be perceived merely as a fashionable management practice, unless distinctive systems for quality management in public services are developed, avoiding uncritical adoption of private sector practices.[③]

⚙ Vocabulary

conceive	获得
wellbeing	幸福
domain	领域
stimulate	促进
globalization	全球化
demonstrate	证明
shoestring	用钱极少的

---

① I. Kirkpatrick, M. Lucio. The Politics of Quality in the Public Sector[M]. London: Routledge, 1995:279.

② A. Ancarani, G. Capaldo. Management of Standardised Public Services: a Comprehensive Approach to Quality Assessment[J]. Managing Service Quality: An International Journal, 2001,(5):332-333.

③ T. Redman, B. Mathews, A. Wilkinson, E. Snape. Quality Management in Services: Is the Public Sector Keeping Pace?[J]. International Journal of Public Sector Management, 1995,(7):21-34.

performance	绩效
tender	投标
remoteness	远离

💁 FURTHER READING

The Implementation of the Main Programs to Achieve Quality in Public Service Provision at São Paulo State Government

On December 12th, 1995, the Permanent Program of Quality and Productivity (PPQP) was created, at São Paulo State Government, aiming to ensure for the citizens an effective service for their needs, by the continuous and permanent improvements of the services provided, with reductions in the costs and gains in the productivity.

In this way, the program's actions aim essentially, to achieve the following objectives:

To improve the quality of the public service provision;

To develop and to value the people that work in the several agencies;

To obtain the commitment and the involvement of the civil servants from all the positions and functions;

To finish with the wastes and mistakes;

To improve technology and incorporate it into the services.

It is important to emphasize that this program does not intend to present a "closed" model or methodology. Each agency can choose between different approaches and managerial tools, such as Total Quality Management (TQM), ISO 9000 or the Brazilian Quality National Award 34, since they follow the basic principles and guidelines from Decree n. 40.536/95.

The introduction to PPQP has produced significant changes in the citizens life:

At the Public Attorney Office, the long waiting line that was there everyday, ended.

At the Commercial Board of The State of São Paulo (Jucesp) the firms used to take 90 days long to get the business inscription number, nowadays they take 48 hours.

In order to intensify the relationship between the government and society, the government has created the Integrated Communication System, which broadcasts public document information, in addition to extending the services of the Diário Oficial, on the Internet home page. (www.imprensaoficial.com.br)

Source: available at

http://www.gwu.edu/~ibi/minerva/Fall2000/Ernesto.Jeger.pdf

Chapter 2
Public Service Provision in China

2.1
Public Service Units in China

2.1.1 What Is Public Service Unit?

The "Public Service Unit" (PSU), or public institutions, or shiye danwei(Chinese: 事业单位), is one of the four categories[1] of public sector institutions or danwei in China. Most shiye danwei are created to be public service providers. A State Council decree in 1998 defines a PSU as a "social service organization established by the state for the purpose of social public benefit", it is created "by a state organ or other organization with state-owned assets" and carries out activities in education, science and technology, culture, health, or in other areas.[2]

China has 1.11 million PSUs with a total employment of nearly 31.53 million in 2014. PSU performance is therefore crucial for improving service delivery in the public sector to a level commensurate with China's stated goals of a "well-off" society and "people-centered" development.

2.1.2 How the PSUs Operate?

A majority of the institutions receive funding from governments while also make money of their own. As a byproduct of a planned economy, public institutions are viewed as suffering from low efficiency, rigid operation and unprofessional management. Past reform efforts, aiming to "push PSUs into the market," have achieved much. Some institutions, such as media and publishing houses, are encouraged to be restructured into stand-alone companies that may

---

① The other three are Communist Party or government departments (dangzheng jiguan), state-owned enterprises (SOEs) (including state-owned financial institutions), and state-sponsored social organizations(shetuan).

② The World Bank. China—Deepening Public Service Unit Reform to Improve Service Delivery[R]. Document of the World Bank, 2005.1.

also collect funds from stock markets. So far, national news websites, like Xinhuanet.com, Peopledaily.com and CNTV.cn, have undergone the initial stages of reform. But, at the same time the reform also introduced undesirable incentives in services delivery. Nearly half of PSUs' funding is raised through charging fees, which not only often cross-subsidize the public service delivery of the unit, but also allow for bonuses and welfare for staff on top of formal salaries. This gave a strong incentive for PSUs and their supervisory departments to distort the market in which PSUs are operating. With the rise in income inequality, reliance on user charges for financing service delivery is increasingly becoming a barrier to access for the poor. The efficiency of PSUs also suffered from overstaffing. In recent years the government has made very large additional injections of funds.

Government departments, PSUs and SOEs are often intertwined, making the boundary between PSUs and other public sector institutions blurred. In particular, it is common for PSUs to have their own business entities, which may include listed companies controlled by universities and research institutes, as well as other less visible business operations. The boundary between the government and PSUs is fluid as well.

PSUs are run by the government. They are affiliated with, and supervised by, authorities at any of the following six levels: ①the State Council; ②a central ministry; ③a provincial (or municipal) government; ④a prefecture (or municipal) government; ⑤a county (or municipal, or district) government; ⑥a township government. The affiliation and supervisory relationship is determined when they are created. Organs of the Communist Party of China (CPC) are involved directly in supervision of some PSUs, such as those of the mass media. According to the State Council Decree 252 in 1998, when a PSU is created at a particular level of the government, one department of the government, the "approving authority", will approve the establishment of the PSU, which will then get itself registered with the Offices for Posts and Establishments of the appropriate level of government, and one department of the government will act as the PSU's "supervisory department (zhuguan bumen)." The latter often holds the power to appoint the management of the PSU, review and approve its budgetary, financial and staffing plans, and evaluate its performance.[①]

Vocabulary

State Council	国务院
decree	法令，规定

---

① The World Bank. China—Deepening Public Service Unit Reform to Improve Service Delivery[R]. Document of the World Bank, 2005.2.

state-owned	国有的
people-centered	以人为本的
well-off society	小康社会
publishing house	出版社
restructure	重构，重组
SOE(state-owned enterprise)	国有企业

👤≡ FURTHER READING

China Reforms Public Institution Leadership Recruitment

China has adopted new measures to select management of public institutions, such as allowing headhunters to participate in the process.

Reforms of the personnel system are key to reforming non-profit non-governmental organizations, a process that has been under way for years, said Prof. Wang Yukai of the Chinese Academy of Governance.

Wang has been studying public institution reforms for years and is a government consultant on public administration.

According to a regulation issued on Tuesday by the general office of the Communist Party of China Central Committee, a more competitive selection process will be introduced, including entrusting "relevant agencies" to select leaders. According to Wang, such agencies may include headhunters.

The regulation will help implement reforms of public institutions and make them provide better service to the public, Wang said.

China has more than one million public institutions founded using state assets. They mainly engage in education, technological, cultural, and health services.

However, their close relations with government have hindered their development and burdened public finance. Authorities have said that they will not approve new public institutions.

Reforms of public institutions are expected to make their management more like that of for-profit companies in order to adapt to market competition.

Wang said an appointment system for public institution management teams should be promoted, as stipulated by the regulation, in order to rid them of reliance on "iron rice bowl" positions—secure and lifelong jobs that have been highly sought after.

The regulation also ordered implementation of a tenure system for members of management teams, stating that a person may not hold a post for more than ten years in a public institution.

The regulation stresses that candidates must have both integrity and ability to act as part of the management team, and they should possess both political integrity and professional competence.

Source: available at

http://news.xinhuanet.com/english/2015-06/03/c_134294167.htm

2.2

Public Service Provision in China—Science and Technology Services

2.2.1　The Basic Regulation on Science and Technology Services

According to *The Law of the People*'s *Republic of China on Science and Technology Progress*, The State practices a basic guideline of basing economic construction and social development on science and technology and orienting science and technology undertakings to economic construction and social development.

The State protects the freedom of scientific research and encourages scientific exploration and technological innovation so as to raise its science and technology to an advanced level in the world.

The State and the whole society shall respect knowledge, esteem talent, value the creative work of scientific and technological personnel, and protect intellectual property rights.

The State, in compliance with the demands of scientific and technological progress and the socialist market economy, shall restructure and improve science and technology system, and establish a mechanism capable of effectively integrating science and technology with economy.

The State shall encourage scientific research and technology development, popularize and apply the achievements made in science and technology, transform traditional industries, develop high-tech industries, and enhance activities employing science and technology to serve economic construction and social development.

The State shall disseminate scientific and technological knowledge to raise the scientific and cultural level of all the citizens.

The State shall encourage government, organs, enterprises, institutions, social organizations and citizens to participate in and support activities aimed at science and technology progress.

The State Council shall formulate science and technology development programmes, determine major science and technology projects and other major projects closely related to science and technology, and secure the coordination of science and technology progress with economic construction and social development.

Opinions from scientific and technological workers shall be fully solicited in the course of formulating science and technology development programmes and important policies and determining major science and technology projects and major projects closely related to science and technology, and a principle of scientific decision-making process shall be followed.

The administrative department in charge of science and technology under the State Council shall be responsible for the macroscopic management and overall coordination of the nation-wide science and technology work. Other administrative departments concerned under the State Council shall be responsible for the relevant science and technology progress work within the scope of their functions and responsibilities as prescribed by the State Council.

Local people's governments at various levels shall adopt effective measures to promote science and technology progress.

The State shall render assistance to minority nationality regions and remote and poor areas to accelerate the development of science and technology.

The Government of the people's Republic of China shall actively promote science and technology cooperation and exchanges with foreign governments and international organizations, encourage research and development agencies, institutions of higher learning, social organizations and scientific and technical workers to establish cooperative relations of various forms with foreign science and technology circles.

The State shall encourage research and development of new technologies, new products, new materials and new techniques, and promote activities of advancing rationalization proposals, and enhancing technological innovation and technical collaboration so as to steadily improve product quality, labor productivity and economic returns, and develop thereby social productive forces.

2.2.2 Development of Science and Technology Services in China

In recent decades science and technology have developed rapidly in China. The Chinese government has placed emphasis through funding, reform, and societal status on science and technology as a fundamental part of the socio-economic development of the country as well as for national prestige. China has made rapid advances in areas such as infrastructure, high-tech manufacturing, academic publishing, patents, and commercial applications and is now in some areas and by some measures a world leader. China is now increasingly targeting indigenous innovation and aims to reform remaining weaknesses.

The State Council of the People's Republic of China in 1995 issued the "Decision on Accelerating S&T Development" which described planned Science & Technology development for the coming decades. It described S&T as the chief productive force affecting economic development, social progress, national strength, and living standards. S&T should become closely associated with market needs. Not only Soviet style institutes should do research but also universities and private industries. State institutions should form joint ventures with Chinese or foreign venture capital in order for S&T developments to reach the industry. S&T personal should become more occupationally mobile, pay should be linked to economic results, and age and seniority should become less important for personal decisions. Intellectual property rights should be respected. Information exchange should improve and there should be competition and open bidding on projects. The environment should be protected. Chinese indigenous S&T in certain key areas should be especially promoted. Public officials should improve their understanding of S&T and incorporate S&T in decision making. Society, including Communist Party youth organizations, labor unions and the mass media, should actively promote respect for knowledge and human talents.

During the last 30 years China concentrated on building physical infrastructure such as roads and ports. One policy during the last decade has been asked for technology transfer in order for foreign companies to gain access to the Chinese market. China is now increasingly targeting indigenous innovation.

⚙ Vocabulary

economic construction	经济建设
scientific research	科学研究
scientific exploration	科学发现
technological innovation	技术创新
personnel	人员
intellectual property rights	知识产权
the socialist market economy system	社会主义市场经济体制
high-tech	高技术
disseminate	传播

macroscopic	宏观的
render	给予
minority nationality regions	少数民族地区
national strength	国力
labor union	工会
indigenous innovation	自主创新

👤 FURTHER READING

Public Institution Reform on Course

Experts said the reform of public institutions was underway in China and praised the government's pledge to deepen reform, in an effort to transform government functioning, after a reform road map was recently unveiled by the Communist Party of China (CPC) Central Committee.

The detailed plan to comprehensively deepen reform in China was released on Friday after it was approved at the key Third Plenary Session of the 18th CPC Central Committee last week.

Wang Feng, deputy director of the State Commission Office for Public Sector Reform, said on Sunday that the reform was underway as per plan, with the classification of those institutions affiliated to the State Council, mostly complete.

According to Wang, the reform aims to offer better public services. The government will pay for more public services while encouraging public service units to separate from the government and become enterprises and social organizations.

Similar to government departments but contrary to private businesses, public institutions in China are financed by the national budget and do not have their own earnings. They cover sectors such as education, science, culture, health, agriculture, forestry, water conservation and the media.

The State Council had issued a guideline in 2012 in which it outlined that an efficient, clearly-defined and regulated mechanism for public institutions by 2020 should be established.

The State Council set 2015 as the deadline for completion of the classification of public institutions, by when institutions with administrative roles should be merged into government bodies and those with business operations gradually transformed into enterprises.

Those providing social services would retain their status as public institutions with further strengthening of their welfare roles.

The reform of public institutions such as schools, research facilities and hospitals would not impact social welfare benefits enjoyed by staffers, experts said.

Zhu Lijia, director of Public Administration Studies at the Chinese Academy of Governance, told the Global Times, why the reform was favored.

"The administrative ranks in those institutions are a product of the planned economy and have acquired power-oriented issues. When staff in those institutions begin to pursue official positions, their work efficiency suffers." Zhu said.

Modern management systems, such as having a board of directors, should be introduced, he added.

Zhu's opinion was echoed by Nie Gaomin, director of Economic Structure and Management Institute with the National Development and Reform Commission, who told the Global Times on Monday that China should also work to remove official-oriented ideas in peoples' minds.

Source: available at

http://www.globaltimes.cn/content/825881.shtml

2.3
Public Service Provision in China—Education Services

2.3.1 Basic Regulation on Education Services

According to *The Education Law of the People's Republic of China*, with education being the foundation for construction of socialist modernization, the state shall give priority to the development of educational undertakings. The whole society shall pay attention and render support to the educational undertakings. The whole society shall respect teachers. Education activities shall be in the benefit of public interests of the state and the society. The state shall separate education from religion. Any organization or individual may not employ religion to obstruct activities of the state education system. Citizens of the People's Republic of China shall have the right and duty to be educated. Citizens shall enjoy equal opportunity of education regardless of their ethnic community, race, sex, occupation, property or religious belief etc.

The State Council and all local People's government at different levels shall supervise and manage the educational work according to the principle of management by different levels and division of labour with individual responsibility.

Secondary and lower education shall be managed by the local People's government under the leadership of the State Council.

Higher education shall be managed by the State Council and the People's government of province, autonomous region or municipality directly under the central government.

The department of the State Council in charge of educational administration shall be responsible for the educational works of the whole country, make overall plans and coordinate the management of educational undertakings of the whole country.

The departments in charge of educational administration under the local People's government at and above the county level shall be responsible for the educational works within the jurisdiction of the respective administrative region.

Other relevant departments of the People's government at and above the county level shall be responsible for relevant educational work within their terms of reference.

The State Council and the local People's government at and above the county level shall report to the People's congress at the respective level or its standing committee on educational works, budgets and financial accounts of educational expenditures and submit to their supervision.

2.3.2   Development of Education Services in China

The Chinese government has placed priority on developing education, putting forward the strategy of revitalizing the country through science and education, making constant efforts to deepen the reform of educational system, and implementing the nine-year compulsory education. Governments at all levels are increasing investment in education and encourage people to run education through different channels and in different forms.

China's school education includes pre-school, primary school, secondary school, high school, university and college, as well as graduate school education.

(1) Pre-school education is for 3-5 year olds and takes place in kindergartens.

(2) Primary education is from 6-11. Primary schools are usually run by local educational authorities and over free tuition, although there are some private schools owned by enterprises and individuals.

(3) Secondary schooling is for children from 12-17 years of age. Education of this kind is run by local governments and various business authorities. State-run secondary schools include junior middle schools and senior middle schools, both with three grades or years. The first three years of secondary school are compulsory and tuition is free. Senior middle school is not compulsory and students must pay minimal tuition fees. Private secondary schools often offer specialized education and have a more vocational bent, but the qualifications they offer are considered to be on the same level as those of state-run middle schools. However, graduates

from secondary professional schools are seen to have achieved a higher level in some ways akin to a university education. Students graduating from junior middle schools usually go on to senior middle schools, although some move to vocational high schools or secondary professional schools for 3-5 years of study.

(4) For higher education there are vocational courses as well as undergraduate, postgraduate, and doctoral degrees. Higher education is offered in universities, colleges, institutes, and vocational colleges. These institutions conduct academic and scientific research and provide social services as well as courses to students. To enter a university or college, students have to take the national entrance examination, which takes place every June and is now open to people of all ages. Selection is based on each student's marks in this exam. And due to the number of people sitting the exam, getting into university is highly competitive.[①]

Since the implementation of reform and opening up, the reform and development of higher education have made significant achievements. A higher education system with various forms, which encompasses basically all branches of learning, combines both degree-education and non-degree education and integrates college education, undergraduate education and graduate education, has taken shape. Higher education in China has played an important role in the economic construction, science progress and social development by bringing up large scale of advanced talents and experts for the construction of socialist modernization.

Chinese economic system used to be very highly centralized. To adapt to that, the former higher education system was also centralized, with education provided by the central and local governments respectively and directly under their administration. The disadvantages of this system were that the state undertook too many responsibilities and the schools lacked the flexibility and autonomy to provide education according to the needs of the society, and with central departments and local governments providing education separately, the structure of education was irrational and segmented. There were too many single disciplinary higher education institutions (HEIs) and professional HEIs. With the establishment of disciplines over-lapped, the efficiency of some HEIs fell very low which in return hampered the improvement of education quality. Therefore, the structural reform of higher education has become a key for other higher education reforms. The reforms of higher education consist of five parts: reforms of education provision, management, investment, recruitment and job-placement, and the inner-institute management, among which management reform is of most importance and difficulty. The overall objectives of higher education reform are to smooth the relationship among government,

---

① Chinese Service Center for Scholarly Exchange. China's Education System[EB/OL]. www.china.org.cn/english/LivinginChina/185292.htm.2006-10-20.

society and HEIs, setting up and perfecting a new system in which the state is responsible for the overall planning and macro management while the HEIs follow the laws and enjoy the autonomy to provide education according to needs of the society.

After several years' endeavor, the structural reform of higher education has gained heartening achievements. In the field of education provision reform, the old system in which the state undertook the establishment of all HEIs has been broken, and a new system in which the government take main responsibility with the active participation of society and individuals has been taking shape. The development of HEIs run by social forces are fully encouraged and supported.

Regarding management system reform, the relationship among universities, government and society has been gradually smoothed out by various ways such as joint establishment, adjustment, cooperation and merger. A two-level education provision system has taken shape in which the central and local government will take different responsibilities to provide education with the former responsible for the overall planning and management. As a result, the overlapping of education was overcome. At the same time, the government streamlines their administration and delegate more power to the HEIs, expanding their autonomy of providing education for the society according to the laws.

With regard to the financing system, the old system in which the funding of higher education depended on the governments only has been changed and a new system capable of pooling resources from diverse channels with the main responsibilities on government has been gradually established and perfected.

With regard to the reform of system of recruitment, fees charging and graduates job-placing, on the basis that all citizens should enjoy the legally equal right of receiving higher education, which should be consistently stick to, in the light of local economic development, a new system in which all students should pay reasonable contribution to their own higher education has taken shape. Simultaneously, a scholarship system for excellent student both academically and morally and a loan, stipend and taking part-time jobs system for students with family economic difficulties has been brought into common practice, ensuring that none students will drop out of school because of economic reasons. After their graduation, the students will mainly select their own jobs under the guidance of the state policy. In addition, the Ministry of Education (MOE) is undertaking the reform of examination and recruitment of HEIs which will help HEIs to select talents and expand the autonomy of schooling, thus laying the foundation of training creative talents, and also help the secondary schools to implement comprehensive quality oriented education.

With regard to the reform of internal administration mechanism, the key lies in the personnel system and the allotment system reforms. On the basis of reasonable organization structure delimitation, all the teaching staff carries out the post responsibility system and appointment system and working achievements are emphasized concerning the personal income allotment, which strengthens the encouragement mechanism in allotment and mobilized the enthusiasm of the teaching.[1]

⚙ Vocabulary

socialist modernization	社会主义现代化
undertakings	事业
supervise	监督
the People's congress	人民代表大会
compulsory education	义务教育
tuition	学费
vocational courses	职业课程
undergraduate	本科
encompass	包含，涉及
degree-education	学位教育
non-degree education	非学位教育
higher education institutions (HEIs)	高等院校
recruitment	招录
job-placement	就业
inner-institute management	单位内部管理
simultaneously	同时
the Ministry of Education	教育部
allotment	分配
delimitation	定界

👤 FURTHER READING

9.42 Million Students Sit National College Entrance Exam in 2015

About 9.42 million Chinese high school graduates, slightly less than the population of Sweden, will sit for the national college entrance examination, known as Gaokao, which kicks

---

[1] Ministry of Education of the People's Republic of China. China's Higher Education[EB/OL]. http://www.china.org.cn/english/LivinginChina/185284.htm, 2006-10-20.

off on Sunday.

The number has marked a tiny increase from that in 2014, which stood at 9.39 million, according to statistics from the Ministry of Education.

The Chinese government has motivated staff nationwide to escort the exam. Police were sent to roads and exam sites for students' security and drivers have been told not to whistle while passing schools and should give way to cars transporting examinee or test papers.

Despite the huge army of high school seniors pursuing higher education, Chinese universities face a growing survival crisis after decades of explosive expansion.

The number of students taking what is generally considered the single most important test any Chinese person can take, has fallen for five straight years since 2009. It peaked at 10.5 million in 2008.

The amount of examinees stopped declining in 2014, but the modest recovery has not brought relief to the looming survival crisis, according to a 2015 report on Chinese university admissions released by China Education online on Tuesday.

Source: available at

http://www.chinadaily.com.cn/china/2015-06/07/content_20929526.htm

2.4
Public Service Provision in China—Public Cultural Services

2.4.1 Definition and Contents of Public Cultural Services

Public Cultural Services are all cultural products and services offered to the people freely or non-profitably in order to improve the social scientific, cultural and moral accomplishment.

The contents of public cultural services include:

(1) Cultural services as public welfare: libraries, cultural centers, art galleries, science and technology museums.

(2) Cultural products and services needed for spreading and carrying forward socialist ideology and values.

(3) All grass-roots cultural activities, according to China's situation for enriching the people's leisure life.

(4) Some high cultures.

2.4.2　Managing Organs of Public Cultural Services in China

Most of China's public cultural services are managed by the Chinese government on five different levels.

Top level: central departments, including Ministry of Culture and State Administration of Press, Publication, Radio, Film and Television.

The Ministry of Culture is the national administrative organ for cultural and art undertakings. According to the plan approved by the State Council in March 1989, its main powers and responsibilities are: to administer art undertakings, mass cultural undertakings, libraries, cultural undertakings in minority nationality areas and the cultural work of juveniles and children; to administer training and education of cultural and art personnel, scientific research on art, and scientific and technological work on culture and the arts; to administer art markets and cultural and art exchange with Taiwan, and cultural and art exchange and liaison with foreign countries; to administer the State Cultural Relics Bureau.

Second level: province, autonomous region and municipality directly under the central government. Corresponding organs are set up in the governments of provinces, autonomous regions and municipalities of Beijing, Tianjin, Shanghai and Chongqing, including a provincial or municipal cultural bureau, bureau of press, publication, radio, film and television.

Third level: city and prefecture. For the most part only cultural bureaus are set up in governments at this level.

Fourth level: county. Only cultural bureaus.

Fifth level: township and town. Each township (town) government appoints a cadre in charge of cultural undertakings.

2.4.3　Development of Public Cultural Services in China

In recent years, Party committees, governments and cultural departments at various levels, in light of the decisions and arrangements by the central leadership, took as the objective a modern public cultural service system that covers the whole society and guarantees the people's basic cultural rights. As a result, overall progress has been made with breakthroughs in key sectors, investment in public culture has continued to increase, a public cultural service network that reaches all urban and rural areas has taken shape, major cultural programs benefiting the people have been proceeding steadily, innovative approaches have been developed and implemented, the level of equality in public cultural service has been significantly raised, and public cultural service has become more institutionalized and standardized.

According to statistics, spending on culture reached 140 billion RMB yuan nationwide in the first three years of the 12th Five-Year Plan period, exceeding the total of the 11th Five-Year Plan period which registered 122 billion RMB yuan. Since the policy of free access to public cultural facilities was launched in 2008, the central government has earmarked nearly 20 billion RMB yuan as support. As a result, public libraries and cultural centers have been setup in every county and comprehensive cultural stations in every township. Over the past few years, a number of major cultural programs have been initiated to benefit the general public, such as the nationwide project for sharing of cultural information resources, the project for the promotion of digital libraries, the project for the construction of public E-reading rooms, the project for mobile stage vehicles, and the project for the training of cultural professionals at the grassroots level. About 50,000 museums, art museums, libraries and cultural stations nationwide have been opened to public for free. The construction of national pilot zones on the public cultural service system has been kicked off, with an aim to gather experience and seek feasible approaches. The Spring Rain Project, an initiative that cultural volunteers serve frontier areas, facilitated coastal and inland areas' cultural aid to and cultural exchange with frontier provinces. Various measures have been adopted to guarantee cultural rights of peasant workers, the senior, children and the handicapped. Official documents have been formulated to regulate the land use, construction and service of public libraries and cultural centers. Legislation process for the Law on Guaranteeing Public Cultural Service and the Law on Public Libraries is proceeding well.

Despite some achievements have been made, efforts to establish a modern public cultural service system have yet to come up with the objective to build a well-off society, the current economic and social development level, and the general public's ever-increasing cultural and spiritual needs. Cultural development still lags behind the development of education, public health and science and technology. It is generally the practice that the government's responsibility is often off the place, absent from the place, or in the wrong place, the participation of the general public is far from sufficient, investment and construction are given much more emphasis than output and management and the equality of public cultural service remains at a quite low level.

The Third Plenary Session of the18th CPC Central Committee explicitly proposed the objective to build a modern public cultural service system. In order to implement this decision, the Ministry of Culture will make further efforts in the following key sectors: first, improving the coordination mechanism for the construction of the public cultural service system and facilitating the integrated development of cultural resources sharing and culture-to-benefit-the-people projects at the grassroots level; second, speeding up standardization of public cultural service based on the general public's needs; third, advancing the equalization of basic pubic cultural service and offering more policy and fiscal support to rural, poverty-stricken areas and special groups; fourth, deepening reform in cultural system and seeking effective ways to separate administration and operation; and fifth, developing diverse players of socialized service and establishing the mechanism to purchase service from the society.[1]

⚙ Vocabulary

accomplishment	素养
public welfare	公共福利
socialist ideology	社会主义意识形态
high culture	高雅文化
grass-roots cultural activities	基层文化活动
Ministry of Culture	文化部
State Administration of Press, Publication, Radio, Film and Television	新闻出版广电总局
juveniles	未成年人
autonomous region	自治区
municipality	直辖市
cadre	干部
breakthrough	突破
peasant worker	农民工
the handicapped	残疾人
well-off society	小康社会
ever-increasing	不断增长的
culture-to-benefit-the-people project	文化惠民工程

👤 FURTHER READING

More Cultural Public Services to Outsourced

China's government is trying to involve the private sector in more public services related to culture by offering government procurement contracts.

---

① Cai Wu. Public Cultural Service System Well Underway[J]. China & The World Cultural Exchange, 2014,(8): 8.

The State Council, China's cabinet, on Monday issued an instruction to expand government procurement of cultural services such as sporting events, museums and libraries, as well as a list of 38 different cultural services that are open to private contractors.

The policy is an effort to supplement the limited funds and resources the government spends on public cultural services.

About 117.27 billion yuan (19 billion US dollars) in government funding was spent on public cultural services in 2013, according to the Ministry of Culture.

Although the figure had almost doubled from that of 2010, it did not meet the actual demand and a large part of the fund went to operational use other than improvement of the services, the ministry said in a statement.

The new policy encourages local governments to outsource activities such as non-profit sport events, film screening events and book clubs, protecting traditional cultural heritage and running museums, libraries and public theaters.

The private parties should be legally registered and qualified. They need to obtain the government procurement contracts through set procedures but local governments are allowed to design the procedures according to local situations, the State Council document said.

Wu Zhinan, a research fellow with the Shanghai Academy of Social Sciences, told Xinhua that the new policy was to break the monopoly of government-sponsored cultural institutions in public cultural services.

If properly designed and implemented, the policy would bring constructive competition and improve the quality of public cultural services, Wu said.

However, the procedure for bidding for such contracts should be tightly supervised and open to the public so as to prevent backdoor activities, he said.

Source: available at

http://news.xinhuanet.com/english/2015-05/11/c_134229828.htm

2.5
Public Service Provision in China—Public Health Services

2.5.1 Basic Public Health Service in China

Basic public health service is an important part of China's work to equalize basic health services and continue medical and health system reforms. It deals with major health issues for urban and rural people, with the focus on children, pregnant women, the elderly and people with chronic diseases, and provides free basic service from the government to benefit all.

The basic public health service covers widely, as shown in figure 2.1.

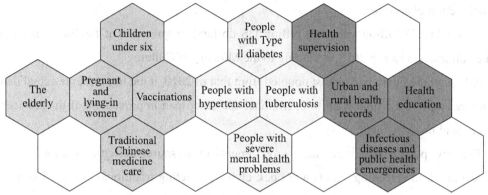

Figure 2.1　The basic public health service

With the basic public health service, the people will get the benefits including:

(1) Improved health awareness and independent health management information;

(2) Improved health quality with the focus on special groups;

(3) Better dietary approaches and help in changing a bad lifestyle;

(4) Prevention and control of infectious and chronic diseases.[①]

2.5.2　The Development of Public Health Service in China

China pays great attention to protecting and improving its people's health. As the Constitution stipulates, "The state develops medical and health services, promotes modern medicine and traditional Chinese medicine..., all for the protection of the people's health." Based on this constitutional stipulation, China has put in place a complete system of laws and regulations concerning medical and health services.

Over the years, China has worked hard to develop its medical and health services with Chinese characteristics in accordance with the policy of "making rural areas the focus of our work, putting disease prevention first, supporting both traditional Chinese medicine and Western medicine, relying on science, technology and education, and mobilizing the whole of society to join the efforts, improving the people's health and serving socialist modernization". Thanks to unremitting efforts that have been made, medical and healthcare systems covering both urban and rural residents have taken shape, the capabilities of disease prevention and control have been enhanced, the coverage of medical insurance has expanded, continuous progress has been made

---

① Feng Hui, Chen Lu. China's public health service[EB/OL]. http://www.en.nhfpc.gov.cn, 2015-03-30.

in medical science and technology, and the people's health has been remarkably improved.

To put into place basic medical and healthcare systems covering both urban and rural residents, and ensure that every resident has access to safe, effective, convenient and affordable basic medical and health services, China has kept advancing the reform of its medical and healthcare system, and made important achievements in the current stage.

The people's health has been improved. Judging from important indicators that give expression to national health, the health of the Chinese people is now among the top in developing countries. In 2010, the life expectancy was 74.8 years-72.4 years for males and 77.4 years for females; the maternal mortality rate went down from 51.3 per 100,000 in 2002 to 26.1 per 100,000 in 2011; the infant mortality rate and the mortality rate of children under the age of five have kept dropping, with the former going down from 29.2 per thousand in 2002 to 12.1 per thousand in 2011, and the latter, from 34.9 per thousand to 15.6 per thousand, attaining ahead of schedule the UN Millennium Development Goal in this regard.

Medical and healthcare systems covering both urban and rural residents have been put in place. Of these systems, the first is the public health service system, which covers disease prevention and control, health education, maternity and child care, mental health, health emergency response, blood collection and supply, health supervision, family planning and some other specialized public health services, and a medical and healthcare system based on community-level healthcare networks that provides public health services. The second is the medical care system. In the rural areas, it refers to a three-level medical service network that comprises the county hospital, the township hospitals and village clinics, with the county hospital performing the leading role, and township hospitals and village clinics service at the base. And in the cities and towns, it refers to a new type of urban medical health service system that features division of responsibilities as well as cooperation among various types of hospitals at all levels and community healthcare centers. The third is the medical security system. This system comprises mainly the basic medical security, supported by many forms of supplementary medical insurance and commercial health insurance. The basic medical security system covers basic medical insurance for working urban residents, basic medical insurance for non-working urban residents, a new type of rural cooperative medical care and urban-rural medical aid, which cover, respectively, the employed urban population, unemployed urban population, rural population and people suffering from economic difficulties. And the fourth is the pharmaceutical supply system, which covers the production, circulation, price control, procurement, dispatching and use of pharmaceuticals. The recent work is focused on establishing a national system for basic drugs.

With years of effort, China has made remarkable achievements in the development of its healthcare undertakings, which, however, still fall far short of the public's demands for healthcare as well as the requirements of economic and social development. Especially when China turned from a planned economy to a market economy, the old medical care system has undergone great changes. So it became an issue of major importance for the Chinese government to provide better and more accessible medical and health services to the public. In the 1980s, the Chinese government initiated reform of the medical and healthcare systems, and speeded up the reform in 2003 after a success in the fight against the SARS. In March 2009, the Chinese government promulgated the "Opinions on Deepening Reform of the Medical and Health Care Systems", setting off a new round of reform in this regard. The basic goal of this reform was to provide the whole nation with basic medical and health services as a public product, and ensure that everyone, regardless of location, nationality, age, gender, occupation and income, enjoys equal access to basic medical and health services. And the basic principles to be followed in the reform were to ensure basic services, improving such services at the grass-roots level and establishing the effective mechanisms.

Medical reform is a social program that covers a wide range and involves difficult tasks. And it is a hard and complicated task to deepen this reform in China, a developing country with a large population, low per-capita income and a wide gap between urban and rural areas. For over three years, the Chinese government has worked hard to strike a balance between improving medical and health services on one hand and economic and social development on the other, trying to find a solution to this worldwide problem. Thanks to the persistent efforts made, China has made positive progress in this new round of medical reform.[1]

⚙ Vocabulary

pregnant women	孕期妇女
chronic disease	慢性病
health awareness	健康意识
dietary	膳食
infectious disease	传染病
the Constitution	宪法
Chinese characteristics	中国特色
unremitting	坚持不懈的
pharmaceutical	药物的

---

① Information Office of the State Council, PRC. Medical and Health Services in China[EB/OL]. http://www.scio.gov. cn, 2012-12-30.

procurement	采购
dispatching	调度
basic drug	基本药物

👤☰ FURTHER READING

China to Boost TCM Health Service

China is going to establish a Traditional Chinese Medicine (TCM) health service system by 2020, according to a plan recently issued by the General Office of State Council.

The Plan said the health service sector was expected to become an important force for promoting the change of economic society.

It has put forward four specific goals: significantly improving medical treatment service capabilities; constantly innovating technology used in health services; further improvement in health insurance services; and continual optimization of the development environment for health service industry.

To ensure the development goals can be successfully achieved, the plan stresses policies changes, including lowering market entrance, providing legitimate land resource, reinforcing guidance of investment and financing, taxation and price policy.

On the other hand, series of safeguard measures have been put forward, including strengthening government organization and implementation, promoting role of industry association, optimizing standards and regulations to construct a friendly environment.

Moreover, implementation of key construction projects includes three types: guiding social forces into implementation; implementing special channel within responsibilities of relevant departments and building public welfare infrastructure construction with central of local finance.

TCM health services refer to the activities that maintain and improve people's physical and psychological health by applying TCM theory, method and technology.

Rooted in Chinese culture, TCM has absorbed and incorporated advanced ideas and philosophy of natural and social sciences at different stages in the past thousands of years.

Source: available at

http://usa.chinadaily.com.cn/china/2015-05/22/content_20791956.htm

Chapter 3
The Essence of Classics in Public Service Management

3.1

History of Administrative Theories

Lorenz Von Stein, an 1855 German professor from Vienna, is considered to be the founder of the science of public administration in many parts of the world. In the time of Von Stein, public administration was considered to be a form of administrative law, but Von Stein believed this concept was too restrictive.

Von Stein taught:

- Public administration relies on many preestablished disciplines such as sociology, political science, administrative law and public finance. Further, public administration is an integrating science.

- Public administrators need to be concerned with both theory and practice. Practical considerations are at the forefront of the field, but theory is the basis of the best practices.

- Public administration is a science because knowledge is generated and evaluated according to the scientific method.

3.1.1　Initial Period (1887—1918)

In the United States of America, Woodrow Wilson is considered to be the father of public administration. He first formally recognized public administration in an 1887 article entitled "*The Study of Administration*".

The later president wrote that "it is the object of administrative study to discover, first, what government can properly and successfully do, and, secondly, how it can do these proper things with the utmost possible efficiency and at the least possible cost either of money or of energy".

Wilson was more influential to the science of public administration than Von Stein, primarily due to the article "*The Study of Administration*", in which he advocated four concepts:

- Separation of politics and administration.

- Comparative analysis of political and private organizations.

- Improving efficiency with business-like practices and attitudes toward daily operations.

- Improving the effectiveness of public service through management and by training civil servants, merit-based assessment.

Frank J. Goodnow is considered to be an important early scholar in the field of public administration and administrative law, as well as an expert in government. He was one of the principal founders of the American Political Science Association and became its first president in 1903. A focal point of controversy in political science has been the distinction Goodnow delineated in his classic treatise *Politics and Administration* (1900) between politics, as the sphere in which the will of the state is articulated, and administration, as the range of methods and techniques through which the state's purposes are carried out. This is also known as dichotomy of politics and administration. Goodnow argued for the centrality of law in public administration. (Other public administration theorists have argued that other non-legal values ought to guide civil servants.)

Frederick W. Taylor is regarded as the father of scientific management, and was one of the first management consultants and director of a famous firm. With respect to the principle of scientific decision making and techniques such as time study, standardization, goal setting, money as a motivator, scientific selection, and rest pauses, Taylor's views are fundamentally correct and have been generally accepted.

Henri Fayol's classic work *Industrial and General Administration*, was one of the first comprehensive statements of a general theory of management. He proposed that there were six primary functions of management and 14 principles of management. The six functions are:

- to forecast and plan.

- to organize.

- to command or direct.

- to coordinate.

- to develop output.

- to control (French: contrôler: in the sense that a manager must receive feedback about a process in order to make necessary adjustments and must analyze the deviations).

The 14 principles are:

- division of work.

- authority.

- discipline.

- unity of command.

- unity of direction.
- subordination of individual interests to the general interest.
- remuneration.
- centralization.
- scalar chain.
- order.
- equity.
- stability of tenure of personnel.
- initiative.
- esprit de corps.

3.1.2 Orthodox Period (1919—1945)

Max Weber, the German sociologist was widely considered as one of the founding architect of bureaucracy, his analysis emphasized that modern state institutions are increasingly based on rational-legal authority. He argued that bureaucracy constitutes the most efficient and rational way in which human activity can be organized, and that systematic processes and organized hierarchies were necessary to maintain order, maximize efficiency and eliminate favoritism.

Leonard Dupee White, as an important founder of public administration, studied administration in the context of grouped U.S. presidential periods. His book *Introduction to the Study of Public Administration* was considered as the first textbook of public administration.

In a 1937 staff paper written by Luther Gulick and Lyndall Urwick for the Brownlow Committee, POSDCORB first appeared and then was widely used in the field of public administration. The acronym stands for steps in the administrative process: Planning, Organizing, Staffing, Directing, Coordinating, Reporting and Budgeting, and this acronym reflects the classic view of administrative management.

Mary Parker Follett pioneered the understanding of lateral processes within hierarchical organizations, the importance of informal processes within organizations, and the idea of the "authority of expertise". She recognized the holistic nature of community and advanced the idea of "reciprocal relationships" in understanding the dynamic aspects of the individual in relationship to others.

3.1.3 Criticizing and Transforming Period (1946—1959)

Chester Irving Barnard's classic book *The Functions of the Executive* (1938) sets out a theory of organization and discusses the functions of executive in organizations from his conception of cooperative systems. He summarized the functions of the executive as follows:

- Establishing and maintaining a system of communication;
- Securing essential services from other members;
- Formulating organizational purposes and objectives.

Herbert A. Simon's classic book *Administrative Behavior* (1947) addresses a wide range of human behaviors, cognitive abilities, management techniques, personnel policies, training goals and procedures, specialized roles, criteria for evaluation of accuracy and efficiency, and all of the ramifications of communication processes. The centerpiece of this book is the behavioral and cognitive processes of making rational decisions. An operational administrative decision should be correct and efficient, and it must be practical to implement with a set of coordinated means.

Parkinson's law is the adage which states that "work expands so as to fill the time available for its completion". This was first articulated by Cyril Northcote Parkinson as part of the first sentence of a humorous essay published in *The Economist* in 1955, it was later reprinted together with other essays in the book *Parkinson's Law: The Pursuit of Progress* (1958). He derived the dictum from his extensive experience in the British Civil Service.

In the book *The Human Side of Enterprise*, Douglas Murray McGregor identified an approach of creating an environment within which employees are motivated via authoritative, direction and control or integration and self-control, which he called theory X and theory Y, respectively.

Charles Edward Lindblom is one of the early developers and advocates of the theory of Incrementalism in policy and decision-making. This view (also called Gradualism) takes a "baby-steps", "Muddling Through" or "Echternach Theory" approach to decision-making processes. In it, policy change is, under most circumstances, evolutionary rather than revolutionary. He came to this view through his extensive studies of welfare policies and Trade Unions throughout the industrialized world. These views were set out in two articles, separated by 20 years: "The Science Of 'Muddling Through'" (1959) and "Still Muddling, Not yet through" (1979), both published in Public Administration Review.

3.1.4 Period of Application and Development (1960s—1970s)

Yehezkel Dror is a founder of policy science. In his article *"Policy Analysts: A New Professional Role in Government Service"* (1967), he referred some of the important weaknesses of systems analysis from the point of view of the public. Then he said that: "The aim of policy analysis is to permit improvements in decision-making and policy-making by permitting fuller consideration of a broader set of alternatives, within a wider context, with the help of more systematic tools."

Laurence Johnston Peter formulated Peter Principle in his classic book *The Peter Principle*. The principle holds that in a hierarchy, members are promoted so long as they work competently. Eventually they are promoted to a position at which they are no longer competent (their "level of incompetence"), and there they remain, being unable to earn further promotions. Peter's corollary states that "in time, every post tends to be occupied by an employee who is incompetent to carry out its duties"[1] and adds that "work is accomplished by those employees who have not yet reached their level of incompetence". "Managing upward" is the concept of a subordinate finding ways to subtly manipulate his or her superiors in order to prevent them from interfering with the subordinate's productive activity or to generally limit the damage done by the superiors' incompetence. This principle can be modeled and has theoretical validity for simulations.

3.1.5 Challenging and Creative Period (1970s—1980s)

In 1968 Frederickson came up with "a theory of social equity and put it forward as the 'third pillar' of public administration". Frederickson thought that: "Public administration works to seek the changes which would enhance its objectives-good management, efficiency, economy, and social equity." "New Public Administration, in its search for changeable structures, tends to experiment with or advocate modified bureaucratic-organizational forms. Decentralization, devolution, projects, contracts, sensitivity training, organization development, responsibility expansion, confrontation, and client involvement are all essentially counter-bureaucratic notions that characterize new Public Administration."[2]

Fred Edward Fiedler introduced the contingency modeling of leadership in 1967, with the now-famous Fiedler contingency model. Fred Fiedler's contingency model focused on a contingency model of leadership in organizations. This model contains the relationship between leadership style and the favorableness of the situation. Situational favorableness was described by Fiedler in terms of three empirically derived dimensions.

---

① L. J. Peter, R. Hull. The Peter Principle: Why Things Always Go Wrong. New York: William Morrow and Company,1969.8.

② H. George Frederickson. Toward a New Public Administration[A]. In Frank Marini, ed. Toward a New Public Administration: The Minnowbrook Perspective[M]. New York: Chandler, 1971:386.

- The leader-member relationship, which is the most important variable in determining the situation's favorableness.
- The degree of task structure, which is the second most important input into the favorableness of the situation.
- The leader's position power obtained through formal authority, which is the third most important dimension of the situation.

Peter Drucker coined the term "management by objectives (MBO)" in his 1954 book *The Practice of Management.* Management by objectives, also known as management by results (MBR), is a process of defining objectives within an organization so that management and employees agree to the objectives and understand what they need to do in the organization in order to achieve them. The essence of MBO is participative goal setting, choosing course of actions and decision making. An important part of the MBO is the measurement and the comparison of the employee's actual performance with the standards set. Ideally, when employees themselves have been involved with the goal setting and choosing the course of action to be followed by them, they are more likely to fulfill their responsibilities.

3.1.6 Summarizing and Probing Period (1980s—)

James McGill Buchanan received the Nobel Memorial Prize in Economic Science in 1986 because of his work on public choice theory. Buchanan's work initiated research on how politicians' self-interest and non-economic forces affect government economic policy. Public choice theory has been described as "the use of economic tools to deal with traditional problems of political science". Its content includes the study of political behavior. In political science, it is the subset of positive political theory that models voters, politicians, and bureaucrats as mainly self-interested. In particular, it studies such agents and their interactions in the social system either as such or under alternative constitutional rules. These can be represented in a number of ways, including standard constrained utility maximization, game theory, or decision theory. Public choice analysis has roots in positive analysis ("what is") but is often used for normative purposes ("what ought to be"), to identify a problem or suggest how a system could be improved by changes in constitutional rules, the subject of constitutional economics.

David H. Rosenbloom is best known for coming up with three approaches that define the American foundation of public administration: the managerial, political, and legal.

- Managerial—The Managerial foundation is used to manage the performance of organizations so that they can be successful. Key areas include administrative decision-making, managerial techniques, leaders, and employee contributions. By these elements working together, organizations are able to operate successfully.

- Political—The Political approach discusses how the political officials oversee the different administrative decisions. Politicians have the final say on the laws that public administrators are tasked with executing.

- Legal—The Legal approach was, according to Rosenbloom, the most crucial. The Rule of Law involves orderliness, comprehension, and spells out when and how tasks will be completed. Rosenbloom argues that in order to carry out their tasks, public administrators must be competent in their legal and constitutional obligations and restrictions.

David Osborne and Ted Gaebler's book *Reinventing Government: How the Entrepreneurial Spirit is Transforming the Public Sector* (1992), describes how decentralization and entrepreneurship can revitalize government and outlines ten principles guiding an entrepreneurial public organization.

⚙ Vocabulary

administrative law	行政法
restrictive	限制的，限定的
preestablished	预设的
public finance	公共财政
integrating science	一体化的科学
efficiency	效率
comparative analysis	比较分析
business-like	事务性的
effectiveness	效用
civil servant	公务员
merit-based	以优秀业绩为基础的
focal point	焦点
delineate	描述
dichotomy	二分法
centrality	向心性，集中度
scientific management	科学管理
consultant	顾问
standardization	标准化
coordinate	协调
feedback	反馈

bureaucracy	官僚制
eliminate	消除
favoritism	徇私，偏袒
context	语境
acronym	首字母缩略词
lateral	横向的
hierarchical	等级(制度)的
reciprocal	互相的，互惠的
dynamic	动态的
formulate	构想，规划，阐述，制定
cognitive	认知的，认识的
specialized	专业的
evaluation	评估
ramification	结果，后果
rational	理性的
operational	操作的
implement	执行，工具
adage	谚语
articulate	用言语表达
derive	得出，导出
dictum	宣言，格言
approach	路径，方法
incrementalism	渐进主义
decision-making	决策
evolutionary	进化的
revolutionary	革命性的
welfare	福利
Trade Unions	工会
industrialized	工业化的
policy analysts	政策分析师
system	体系，系统，制度
systematic	系统的
Peter Principle	彼得原理
competent	胜任的

incompetent	不胜任的
promotion	提升
corollary	推论
accomplish	完成
subordinate	附属的，下级
subtly	隐约地，微妙地
manipulate	操作，处理
theoretical	理论的，假设的
validity	效力，正确性
simulation	模仿，模拟
social equity	社会公平
pillar	支柱
enhance	提高
New Public Administration	新公共行政
advocate	提倡，拥护
modified	改进的，修正的
decentralization	分散，去中心化
devolution	转移，授权
sensitivity training	敏感性训练
confrontation	对抗，对峙
involvement	参与
Fiedler contingency model	菲德勒权变模型
empirically	以经验为主地
dimension	维度
formal authority	正式权威
management by objectives (MBO)	目标管理
participative	参与的
performance	绩效
public choice theory	公共选择理论
subset	子集
constitutional rules	宪法规则
utility maximization	效用最大化
game theory	博弈论
positive analysis	实证分析

normative analysis	规范分析
constitutional economics	宪政经济学
contribution	贡献
element	要素，原理
oversee	监督
the final say	最终决定权
legal	法律的，合法的
orderliness	规律，秩序井然
comprehension	理解，内涵
obligation	义务，责任
restriction	限制，管制
reinventing government	重塑政府
entrepreneurial spirit	企业家精神
revitalize	使复兴

☷ FURTHER READING

The American Society for Public Administration

The American Society for Public Administration is the largest and most prominent professional association for public administration. It is dedicated to advancing the art, science, teaching and practice of public and non-profit administration. ASPA's four core values are Accountability and Performance, Professionalism, Ethics and Social Equity.

Professionalism is promoted through chapters and sections. Members have an opportunity to advance their careers by becoming involved in their local public administration community. Additionally, members gain exposure to major public service issues by joining ASPA's 21 sections. These sections focus on finance, budgeting, human resources, health and human services, ethics and more. Sections provide additional networking opportunities through conferences and other professional development activities. They also have a variety of award and scholarship opportunities.

ASPA's Center for Accountability and Performance (CAP) addresses the requirement for all levels of government to move to performance-based, results-driven management, through education, training, advocacy, technical assistance, resource sharing and research.

Additionally, ASPA provides three publications for its members. The PA TIMES is a monthly newspaper that focuses on issues in public management and the best practices in the field of public administration. The Bridge is ASPA's biweekly newsletter that details the organization's latest news as well as current news in the public service field. The Public Administration Review (PAR) is ASPA's premier publication. It is a bimonthly scholarly journal that links theory and public management practice together.

ASPA promotes ethics and integrity in public service and governance worldwide. ASPA has a Code of Ethics in which it implores its members to adhere to while working in the field of public service. Also, through membership in ASPA's Section on Ethics, members can access a variety of resources including the leading ethics journal in the field, Public Integrity, and Ethics Today, an award-winning electronic newsletter.

ASPA promotes dialogue on social equity issues in all areas of public service such as public budgeting, government hiring practices, diversity in academia and others. Additionally, each year at the national conference, ASPA hosts the Gloria Hobson Nordin Social Equity Award Luncheon where it honors a public administrator who has distinguished him or herself in achieving fairness, justice and equity in government.

Source: website of ASPA available at

http://www.aspanet.org/public/ASPA/About_ASPA/ASPA/About_ASPA/About_ASPA. aspx?hkey=98af1db8-67b2-4ac6-9731-953b52f982db

3.2
The Essence of Classics in Public Service Management

3.2.1 The Study of Administration[①]

The author of *The Study of Administration* is Thomas Woodrow Wilson, as shown in Figure 3.1.

Figure 3.1   Thomas Woodrow Wilson (1856-1924)

---

① Woodrow Wilson. The Study of Administration[J]. Political Science Quarterly,1941, 56(3): 494 (originally published in 1887).

Wilson was a political science professor and president of Princeton University who subsequently was elected governor of New Jersey and president of the United States.[①] Woodrow Wilson's 1887 article, *"The Study of Administration"*, is widely regarded as the essay that signaled the beginning of the field of public administration.

The followings are the essences of this article.

1. Necessity 必要性

I suppose that no practical science is ever studied where there is no need to know it.

我认为绝没有任何一门实用科学，当还没有了解它的必要时，会有人对它进行研究。

Administration is the most obvious part of government; it is government in action; it is the executive, the operative, the most visible side of government, and is of course as old as government itself.

行政是政府最明显的部分，它是行动中的政府；它是政府的执行者，政府的操作者，政府中最显著的方面，当然，它的历史也和政府一样悠久。

No one wrote systematically of administration as a branch of the science of government until the present century had passed its first youth and had begun to put forth its characteristic flower of systematic knowledge.

在本世纪度过它最初的青春年华，并开始吐放它在系统知识方面独特的花朵之前，谁也没有从作为政府科学的一个分支的角度来系统地拟定过行政学著作。

The functions of government are every day becoming more complex and difficult.

The idea of the state and the consequent ideal of its duty are undergoing noteworthy change; and "the idea of the state is the conscience of administration".

Seeing every day new things which the state ought to do, the next thing is to see clearly how it ought to do them.

政府的职能变得日益复杂且难以执行。

关于国家以及随之而来的关于国家职责的观念正在发生引人注目的变化，而"关于国家的观念正是行政管理的灵魂"。

当你了解国家每天应该做的新事情之后，紧接着就应该清楚了解国家应该如何去做这些事情。

The question was always: who shall make law, and what shall that law be?

The other question, how law should be administered with enlightenment, with equity, with speed, and without friction, was put aside as "practical detail" which clerks could arrange after doctors had agreed upon principles.

---

① Robert D. Miewald. Woodrow Wilson[A].In Jay M. Shafritz (Ed.), International Encyclopedia of Public Policy and Administration[M]. Boulder : Westview Press,1998.2410.

It is getting to be harder to run a constitution than to frame one.

人们常问：由谁制定法律以及制定什么法律？

另一个问题是：如何抱着启蒙的理想，公平迅速而又不受阻碍地实施法律。这一问题被看做"实际工作中的细节问题"，在专家学者们就理论原则取得一致意见后由办事人员进行处理。

与制定宪法相比较，"贯彻"宪法变得愈加困难了。

This is why there should be a science of administration which shall seek to straighten the paths of government, to make its business less unbusinesslike, to strengthen and purify its organization, and to crown its dutifulness. This is one reason why there is such a science.

这就是为什么应该有行政科学的原因，它旨在使政府不走弯路，专心处理公务减少闲杂事务，加强和纯洁政府的组织机构，为政府带来尽职尽责美誉。这就是为什么会有这门学科的原因之一。

2. Object & tasks 目标与任务

It is the object of administrative study to discover, first, what government can properly and successfully do, and, secondly, how it can do these proper things with the utmost possible efficiency and at the least possible cost either of money or of energy.

On both these points there is obviously much need of light among us; and only careful study can supply that light.

行政学研究的目标，首先要弄清楚政府能够恰如其分地完成什么任务，其次要弄清楚政府怎样才能事半功倍地完成这些专门的任务。

在这两个问题上，我们显然需要更多的启示；并且只有通过仔细的研究才能得到答案。

3. Relationship with politics 与政治的关系

The science of administration is the latest fruit of that study of the science of politics which was begun some twenty-two hundred years ago. It is a birth of our century, almost of our own generation.

行政科学是政治科学的最新研究成果。政治科学大约在两千二百年前就开始了。行政科学起源于本世纪，并且几乎是我们这一代的产物。

Administrative questions are not political questions. Although politics sets the tasks for administration, it should not be suffered to manipulate its offices.

行政管理的问题不是政治问题，虽然政治确定了行政管理的任务，但却无须费心管理其机构。

Politics is state activity, in things great and universal. Administration is the activity of the state in individual and small things. Politics is thus the special province of the statesman, administration of the technical official. "Policy does nothing without the aid of administration", but administration is not therefore politics.

政治是"在重大而且带普遍性的事项"方面的国家活动，而行政管理是国家在个别和细微事项方面的活动。因此，政治是政治家的特殊活动范围，而行政管理则是技术性职员的事情。"政策如果没有行政管理的帮助就将一事无成"，但行政管理并不因此等同于政治。

The field of administration is a field of business. It is removed from the hurry and strife of politics; it at most points stands apart even from the debatable ground of constitutional study.

It is a part of political life only as the methods of the counting house are a part of the life of society; only as machinery is part of the manufactured product.

行政管理的领域是事务性领域。它避免了政治领域的那种混乱和冲突。在大多数问题上，它甚至与宪法研究方面具有争议性的基础也迥然不同。

行政管理作为政治生活的一个组成部分，这如同企业办公室所采用的工作方法是社会生活的一部分，机器是制造品的一部分是一样的，但仅止于此。

4. Methodology 方法论

To determine just what are the best methods by which to develop it. Why should we not use such parts of foreign contrivances as we want, if they be in any way serviceable?

要确定什么是发展这一研究工作的最佳方法。如果有我们可以以某种方式利用的外国的发明创造，那我们为什么不加以利用呢？

We are in no danger of using them in a foreign way. We borrowed rice, but we do not eat it with chopsticks. We borrowed our whole political language from England, but we leave the words "king" and "lords" out of it.

我们以一种外来的方式应用它们是不会有危险的。我们引进了大米，但我们却不用筷子吃饭。我们的全部政治词汇都是从英国引进的，但我们却从中淘汰了"国王"和"贵族"。

5. Personnel administration 人事行政

The question for us is, how shall our series of governments within governments be so administered that it shall always be to the interest of the public officer to serve, not his superior alone but the community also, with the best efforts of his talents and the soberest service of his conscience.

我们的问题是，如何使我们的政府更具行政能力，使政府官员能够殚精竭虑，公正无私，以为民服务为己任，而不仅仅是为了取悦领导。

How shall such service be made to his commonest interest by contributing abundantly to his sustenance to his dearest interest by furthering his ambition, and to his highest interest by advancing his honor and establishing his character?

如何通过优渥的待遇，光明的前程，提高荣誉感，以及培养其品质的方式，使为人民服务成为他(行政官员)最普通的责任，最珍贵的义务，以及最崇高的理想。

The ideal for us is a civil service cultured and self-sufficient enough to act with sense and vigor, and yet so intimately connected with the popular thought, by means of elections and constant public counsel, as to find arbitrariness of class spirit quite out of the question.

我们理想中的文官是这样的。他们受过良好教育，充满自信，行动理智果敢，但是通过选择和定期的公众咨询，他们依然密切关注人民的心声，决不武断专行。

6. Supervision 监督

What part shall public opinion take in the conduct of administration?

The right answer seems to be, that public opinion shall play the part of authoritative critic.

在行政管理活动当中，群众舆论将起什么作用？

准确的答案似乎是：公共舆论将起权威性评判家的作用。

But as superintending the greater forces of formative policy alike in politics and administration, public criticism is altogether safe and beneficent altogether indispensable.

但是无论是在政治还是在行政方面，为了对制定基本政策的这一重大权力进行监督，公众的批评是完全安全有益，不可缺少的。

Let administrative study find the best means for giving public criticism this control and for shutting it out from all other interference.

行政学研究应该找到一些最佳方法，这些方法能够给予公众舆论这种控制监督的权力，同时使之避免其他一切干扰。

3.2.2 Politics and Administration[①]

The author of *Politics and Administration* is Frank Johnson Goodnow, as shown in Figure 3.2.

Figure 3.2 Frank Johnson Goodnow (1859-1939)

---

① Frank J. Goodnow. Politics and Administration: A Study in Government[M]. New York: The MacMillan Company, 1900.

Frank Johnson Goodnow is the first president of the American Political Science Association in 1903. During the years 1913-1914 he served as a legal adviser to the Yuan Shikai government in China, helping draft the new constitution. In 1914 he became the third president of Johns Hopkins University. He is considered to be an important early scholar in the field of public administration and administrative law, as well as an expert in government.[1]

The followings are the essences of his book.

There are two functions of the government. These two functions of government may for purposes of convenience be designed respectively as Politics and Administration. Politics has to do with policies or expressions of the state will. Administration has to do with the execution of these policies.

为了方便起见，政府的两种职能可以分别称作"政治"与"行政"。政治与政策或国家意志的表达相关，行政则与这些政策的执行相关。

There are, then, in all governmental systems two primary or ultimate functions of government, viz (namely), the expression of the will of the state and the execution of that will.

因此，在所有的政府体制中都存在着两种主要的或基本的政府职能，即国家意志的表达职能和国家意志的执行职能。

There are also in all states separate organs, each of which is mainly busied with the discharge of one of these functions. These functions are, respectively, Politics and Administration.

在所有的国家中也都存在着分立的机关，每个分立的机关大部分时间内忙于两种职能中的一种。这两种职能分别就是：政治与行政。

3.2.3   The Principles of Scientific Management[2]

The author of *The Principles of Scientific Management* is Frederick Winslow Taylor, as shown in Figure 3.3.

Figure 3.3   Frederick Winslow Taylor (1856-1915)

---

① http://en.wikipedia.org/wiki/Frank_Johnson_Goodnow

② Frederick W. Taylor. The Principles of Scientific Management[M]. New York, USA and London, UK: Harper &Brothers, 1911.

Frederick Winslow Taylor was born in 1856 in a wealthy family. He was a mechanical engineer who sought to improve industrial efficiency. Taylor is regarded as the father of scientific management, and was one of the first management consultants, in Peter Drucker's description.[①]

The followings are the essences of his book.

1. Introduction 前言

President Roosevelt in his address to the Governors at the White House, prophetically remarked that "The conservation of our national resources is only preliminary to the larger question of national efficiency."

罗斯福总统在白宫向各州长讲话时曾预言："保护我们国家的资源，只是提高全国性效率这一重大问题的前奏。"

The whole country at once recognized the importance of conserving our material resources and a large movement has been started which will be effective in accomplishing this object. As yet, however, we have but vaguely appreciated the importance of "the larger question of increasing our national efficiency."

整个美国很快认识到保护物质资源的重要意义，并开展了有效实现这一目标的大规模运动。但直到现在，美国人对"提高全国性效率这一重大问题"重要性的认识，依然模糊不清。

We can see our forests vanishing, our water-powers going to waste, our soil being carried by floods into the sea; and the end of our coal and our iron is in sight. But our larger wastes of human effort, which go on every day through such of our acts as are blundering, ill-directed, or inefficient, and which Mr. Roosevelt refers to as a lack of "national efficiency", are less visible, less tangible, and are but vaguely appreciated.

我们可以看到，我们的森林在消失，我们的水力资源在浪费掉，我们的土壤在被洪水冲刷到大海里去，我们的煤和铁在日渐枯竭。但是，由于我们的重大失误、指挥不当或工作效率低下造成的日复一日的人力资源上的更大浪费，不正是罗斯福总统所指的"全国性效率"不足吗？人们对这方面的浪费却视而不见，或即使看见了也模糊不清。

This paper has been written:

First. To point out, through a series of simple illustrations, the great loss which the whole country is suffering through inefficiency in almost all of our daily acts.

撰写本文有以下目的：

第一，通过一系列简明的例证，指出几乎在所有日常行为中，由于我们的效率低下而使全美国遭受到的巨大损失。

Second. To try to convince the reader that the remedy for this inefficiency lies in systematic

---

① http://en.wikipedia.org/wiki/Frederick_Winslow_Taylor

management, rather than in searching for some unusual or extraordinary man.

第二，试图说明根治效率低下的良药在于系统化的管理，而不在于收罗某些独特的或不同寻常的人物。

Third. To prove that the best management is a true science, resting upon clearly defined laws, rules, and principles, as a foundation. And further to show that the fundamental principles of scientific management are applicable to all kinds of human activities, from our simplest individual acts to the work of our great corporations, which call for the most elaborate cooperation. And, briefly, through a series of illustrations, to convince the reader that whenever these principles are correctly applied, results must follow which are truly astounding.

第三，证明最先进的管理是真正的科学，说明其理论基础是明确定义的规律、准则和原则，并进一步表明可把科学管理原理应用于几乎所有人类的活动中去。从最简单的个人行为到我们那些需要紧密合作的大型公司的活动，都可以找到其应用。简而言之，通过一系列实例，让读者相信，无论何时，只要正确地运用这些原理，就能立竿见影，其成效着实令人震惊。

This paper was originally prepared for presentation to The American Society of Mechanical Engineers. The illustrations chosen are such as, it is believed, will especially appeal to engineers and to managers of industrial and manufacturing establishments, and also quite as much to all of the men who are working in these establishments. It is hoped, however, that it will be clear to other readers that the same principles can be applied with equal force to all social activities: to the management of our homes; the management of our farms; the management of the business of our tradesmen, large and small; of our churches, our philanthropic institutions, our universities, and our governmental departments.

本文原本是作为向美国机械工程师协会提交的报告。我坚信，这里所选择的实例能够引起工业和制造业的工程师、管理者和这些企业所有人的极大兴趣。当然，也希望读者明白，同样的原理能以同样的效力运用到所有社会活动中，这些活动包括家庭管理、农场管理、大小商人的商业管理、教堂管理、慈善机构管理、大学管理以及政府各部门的管理，等等。

2. Chapter 1: Fundamentals of Scientific Management 第一章 科学管理的基础

The principal object of management should be to secure the maximum prosperity for the employer, coupled with the maximum prosperity for each employee.

管理的主要目标应该是使雇主的财富最大化，同时也使每一位雇员的财富最大化。

No one can be found who will deny that in the case of any single individual the greatest prosperity can exist only when that individual has reached his highest state of efficiency; that is, when he is turning out his largest daily output.

没人会否认，在单个人工作的情况下，只有其劳动生产率达到最高，即只有在其实现了日产出最大时，才可实现其财富最大化。

The truth of this fact is also perfectly clear in the case of two men working together. To illustrate: if you and your workman have become so skilful that you and he together are making two pairs of shoes in a day, while your competitor and his workman are making only one pair, it is clear that after selling your two pairs of shoes you can pay your workman much higher wages than your competitor who produces only one pair of shoes is able to pay his man, and that there will still be enough money left over for you to have a larger profit than your competitor.

对于两个人一起工作的情况，上述事实也十分清楚。为说明这一道理，假设你和你的帮手工作技能熟练到每天可制作两双鞋，而你的竞争者和他的帮手每天却只能生产一双鞋。显然，与每天只能制作一双鞋的竞争对手相比，在卖掉两双鞋以后，你可以支付给你的帮手更多的工资，而且你可以比你的竞争对手赢得更多的利润。

These principles appear to be so self-evident that many men may think it almost childish to state them. Let us, however, turn to the facts, as they actually exist in this country and in England. The English and American peoples are the greatest sportsmen in the world. Whenever an American workman plays baseball, or an English workman plays cricket, it is safe to say that he strains every nerve to secure victory for his side. He does his very best to make the largest possible number of runs. The universal sentiment is so strong that any man who fails to give out all there is in him in sport is branded as a "quitter", and treated with contempt by those who are around him.

这些原理看来显而易见，以致不少人可能认为再拿来论述几乎是幼稚的。可是，让我们看看那些确确实实存在于美国和英国的事实吧。英国人和美国人是世界上最伟大的运动员。无论什么时候，美国工人参加棒球比赛或者英国工人参加板球比赛，可以有把握地说，他总会竭尽全力以使自己所在的球队赢得胜利，他将全力以赴争取得到最高的得分。在比赛中，群情激奋，任何没有使出浑身解数的队员都将被打上"懦夫"的烙印，而受到大家的鄙视。

When the same workman returns to work on the following day, instead of using every effort to turn out the largest possible amount of work, in a majority of the cases this man deliberately plans to do as little as he safely can—to turn out far less work than he is well able to do—in many instances to do not more than one-third to one-half of a proper day's work. And in fact if he were to do his best to turn out his largest possible day's work, he would be abused by his fellow-workers for so doing, even more than if he had proved himself a "quitter" in sport. Under working, that is, deliberately working slowly so as to avoid doing a full day's work, "soldiering", as it is called in this country, "hanging it out", as it is called in England, "ca canae", as it is called in Scotland, is almost universal in industrial establishments, and prevails also to a large extent in the building trades; and the writer asserts without fear of contradiction that this constitutes the greatest evil with which the working-people of both England and America are now afflicted.

可是，当这同一位工人第二天回到工作岗位时，他便不再尽其所能以完成更多的任务，更多的情况却是，他在思考着如何才能少干活。结果是完成的工作远比其所能完成的要少。通常情况下，他只完成不到正常水平三分之一或一半的工作量。事实是，如果他竭尽全力以便每天完成尽可能多的工作任务，那么他会遭受同事的辱骂，其所遭到的伤害甚至比在赛场得到了"懦夫"的称号还要严重。少干活就是偷懒，以避免每天完成更多的工作任务，在美国称为"磨洋工"，在英国称为"怠工"。这种磨洋工现象在工业企业界几乎是普遍的，在建筑业也有一定程度的流行。我声明在作以上阐述时并不惧怕反驳，因为这些现象确实构成了当今最大的时弊，英国和美国的劳动人民正为此而深感苦恼。

There are three causes for this condition, which may be briefly summarized as:

First. The fallacy, which has, from time immemorial been almost universal among workmen, that a material increase in the output of each man or each machine in the trade would result in the end in throwing a large number of men out of work.

造成这种情况的主要原因有以下三条：

第一，甚至从史前时期以来就在工人中广为流传一种谬论：在商业中，如果每个人或每台机器的产出增加了，那么最终将导致大量工人的失业。

Second. The defective systems of management which are in common use, and which make it necessary for each workman to soldier, or work slowly, in order that he may protect his own best interests.

第二，通常实行的不完善的管理制度，使得每个工人为了保护其最大利益而必然要"磨洋工"。

Third. The inefficient rule-of-thumb methods, which are still almost universal in all trades and in practicing which our workmen waste a large part of their effort.

第三，单凭经验行事的生产率低下的方法，这种方法在各行各业仍十分普遍，导致我们的工人浪费了大量的劳动。

This paper will attempt to show the enormous gains which would result from the substitution by our workmen of scientific for rule-of-thumb methods.

本文将尝试阐明：工人们摈弃单凭经验行事的方法，采用科学的工作方法以取而代之，将取得巨大收益。

3. Chapter 2: The Principles of Scientific Management 第二章　科学管理原理

These new duties are grouped under four heads:

First. they develop a science for each element of a man's work, which replaces the old rule-of-thumb method.

这些新的任务归纳为以下四个方面：

第一，提出工人操作的每一动作的科学方法，以代替过去单凭经验从事的方法。

Second. They scientifically select and then train, teach, and develop the workman, whereas in the past he chose his own work and trained himself as best he could.

第二，科学地挑选工人，并进行培训和教育，使之成长成才，而不是像过去那样由工人选择各自的工作，并各尽其能地进行自我培训。

Third. They heartily cooperate with the men so as to insure all of the work being done in accordance with the principles of the science which has been developed.

第三，与工人密切合作，以确保所有工作都按照所制定的科学原则行事。

Fourth. There is an almost equal division of the work and the responsibility between the management and the workmen. The management take over all work for which they are better fitted than the workmen, while in the past almost all of the work and the greater part of the responsibility were thrown upon the men.

第四，管理者与工人的工作和职责几乎是均分的。管理者应该承担起那些自身比工人更胜任的工作，而在过去，管理者把几乎所有的工作和大部分职责都推给了工人。

It is this combination of the initiative of the workmen, coupled with the new types of work done by the management, that makes scientific management so much more efficient than the old plan.

也正是工人"积极性"的组合，加上管理者所承担的新工作，才使科学管理比过去的管理制度更加有效。

To summarize: Under the management of "initiative and incentive" practically the whole problem is "up to the workman", while under scientific management fully one-half of the problem is "up to the management".

归纳起来，在"积极性加激励"的管理制度下，实际上全部问题由"工人决定"，而在科学管理制度下，一半的问题由"管理者决定"。

Those who are afraid that a large increase in the productivity of each workman will throw other men out of work, should realize that the one element more than any other which differentiates civilized from uncivilized countries—prosperous from poverty-stricken peoples—is that the average man in the one is five or six times as productive as the other. It is also a fact that the chief cause for the large percentage of the unemployed in England (perhaps the most virile nation in the world), is that the workmen of England, more than in any other civilized country, are deliberately restricting their output because they are possessed by the fallacy that it is against their best interest for each man to work as hard as he can.

有些人担心每个人劳动生产率的大幅提高将导致其他人失业。这些人应该认识到，正是劳动生产率上的差异导致了文明与不开化、富裕与贫穷之间的区别。在这个地区，一般人的劳动生产率可能是另一个地区的五六倍。事实是，造成英国(也许是世界上最朝气蓬勃的国家)大量失业的主要原因是，比起在别的国家来，英国人的劳动生产率受到了更多的、有意的限制。他们深受这一谬论的影响：竭尽全力工作不符合工人自身的利益。

The general adoption of scientific management would readily in the future double the productivity of the average man engaged in industrial work. Think of what this means to the whole country. Think of the increase, both in the necessities and luxuries of life, which becomes available for the whole country, of the possibility of shortening the hours of labor when this is desirable, and of the increased opportunities for education, culture, and recreation which this implies. But while the whole world would profit by this increase in production, the manufacturer and the workman will be far more interested in the especial local gain that comes to them and to the people immediately around them. Scientific management will mean, for the employers and the workmen who adopt it—and particularly for those who adopt it first—the elimination of almost all causes for dispute and disagreement between them. What constitutes a fair day's work will be a question for scientific investigation, instead of a subject to be bargained and haggled over. Soldiering will cease because the object for soldiering will no longer exist. The great increase in wages which accompanies this type of management will largely eliminate the wage question as a source of dispute. But more than all other causes, the close, intimate cooperation, the constant personal contact between the two sides, will tend to diminish friction and discontent. It is difficult for two people whose interests are the same, and who work side by side in accomplishing the same object, all day long, to keep up a quarrel.

通过实行科学管理，从事工业生产的工人很容易成倍地提高其劳动生产率。想想看，这对整个国家意味着什么？工作时间缩短了，而人们所需要的生活必需品和奢侈品都实现了增长，教育、文化和娱乐的机会大大增加了，所有这些又意味着什么？当整个世界由于这种增长而受益时，厂商和工人更关心的却是他们本身及其周围与他们直接有关的人们所能得到的个别利益。对采用这一科学，特别是最先采用这一科学的人们来说，科学管理就意味着消除了管理者和工人之间的一切分歧和矛盾。什么是合理的工作日，这属于科学研究要解决的问题，而不再是谈判和讨价还价的主题。"磨洋工"不存在了，因为"磨洋工"的目标已不复存在。实施这种管理模式，带来了工资的大幅增长，这就从根本上排除了因工资而引起的纠纷。更为突出的是，劳资双方的亲密协作和稳定的个人关系，使得双方的摩擦和不满减少了。利益一致、为完成共同目标而整天并肩工作的劳资双方就不再发生争吵。

The low cost of production which accompanies a doubling of the output will enable the companies who adopt this management, particularly those who adopt it first, to compete far better than they were able to before, and this will so enlarge their markets that their men will have almost constant work even in dull times, and that they will earn larger profits at all times.

This means increase in prosperity and diminution in poverty, not only for their men but for the whole community immediately around them.

产量的成倍增长，带来了生产成本的下降。这就使采用这一管理模式的公司(特别是那些首先采用的公司)比起以前，更具竞争力。其市场得以扩大，即使在淡季，也有稳定的工作，公司总能挣到更多的钱。

这意味着增加财富，减少贫穷。受益者不仅仅是这些工人，而且还有与他们近邻的整个社区。

3.2.4　14 Principles of Management[①]

The author of *14 Principles of Management* is Henri Fayol, as shown in Figure 3.4.

Figure 3.4　Henri Fayol(1841-1925)

Henri Fayol was a French mining engineer and director of mines who developed a general theory of business administration. He was one of the most influential contributors to modern concepts of management, having proposed that there are five primary functions of management: ① planning, ② organizing, ③ commanding, ④ coordinating, and ⑤ controlling.

Fayol believed management theories could be developed, then taught.

His theories were published in a monograph titled General and Industrial Management (1916).

This is an extraordinary little book that offers the first theory of general management and statement of management principles.

According to Claude George (1968), a primary difference between Fayol and Taylor was that Taylor viewed management processes from the bottom up, while Fayol viewed it from the

---

① Henri Fayol. General and Industrial Management[M]. Translated by C. Storrs. London: Sir Isaac Pitman & Sons,1949.

top down.[①]

The followings are the essences of his book.

Division of Work. Specialization allows the individual to build up experience, and to continuously improve his skills. Thereby he can be more productive.

工作分工(Division of Work)。专业化允许个人积累经验,持续不断地提高技能,从而更富有生产力。

Authority and Responsibilities. The right to issue commands, along with which must go the balanced responsibility for its function.

权威与责任(Authority and Responsibilities)。发布命令的权力,必须与相应的责任相匹配。

Discipline. Employees must obey, but this is two-sided: employees will only obey orders if management play their part by providing good leadership.

纪律(Discipline)。员工必须遵守纪律,但这一点具有两面性:只有当管理者自身具有高超的领导力、恪尽职守,员工才会遵守纪律。

Unity of Command. Each worker should have only one boss with no other conflicting lines of command.

统一指挥(Unity of Command)。每个员工都只能有一个上级,以确保他所执行的命令不会相互冲突。

Unity of Direction. People engaged in the same kind of activities must have the same objectives in a single plan. This is essential to ensure unity and coordination in the enterprise. Unity of command does not exist without unity of direction but does not necessarily flows from it.

统一方向(Unity of Direction)。在一项单独的行动计划中,每一名参与者的目标都必须相同。这一点对于组织的团结和协调非常重要。尽管统一的方向不一定产生统一的指挥,但是如果没有统一的方向,就绝不可能有统一的指挥。

Subordination of individual interest (to the general interest). Management must see that the goals of the firms are always paramount.

个体利益服从整体利益(Subordination of Individual Interest to the General Interest)。管理者必须意识到企业目标永远是至高无上的。

Remuneration. Payment is an important motivator although by analyzing a number of possibilities, Fayol points out that there is no such thing as a perfect system.

人事报酬(Remuneration)。尽管通过分析各种可能性,法约尔指出没有一个完美的组织系统,但是他还是认为人事报酬是这个系统中的一个非常重要的促进因素。

---

① http://en.wikipedia.org/wiki/Henri_Fayol

Centralization (or Decentralization). This is a matter of degree depending on the condition of the business and the quality of its personnel.

中心化或去中心化(Centralization or Decentralization)。这是一个度的问题，取决于企业的环境条件和人员条件。

Scalar Chain (Line of Authority). A hierarchy is necessary for unity of direction. But lateral communication is also fundamental, as long as superiors know that such communication is taking place. Scalar chain refers to the number of levels in the hierarchy from the ultimate authority to the lowest level in the organization. It should not be over-stretched and consist of too-many levels.

层次链/权威线(Scalar Chain/Line of Authority)。为了方向统一，一定的层级是需要的。但是最高领导者明白平级沟通常常发生，所以横向联系也是组织沟通的基本方式。层次链指的是从高层权威到基层人员的组织层级，它不应该过长，不能包含过多层级。

Order. Both material order and social order are necessary. The former minimizes lost time and useless handling of materials. The latter is achieved through organization and selection.

秩序(Order)。对于组织管理来说，物质秩序和社会秩序都是必要的，物质秩序使得损失和浪费最小化，而社会秩序则来源于组织与选举。

Equity. In running a business a "combination of kindliness and justice" is needed. Treating employees well is important to achieve equity.

平等(Equity)。对于企业经营者来说，必须做到"友好和公正"的完美组合，善待员工对实现平等非常重要。

Stability of Tenure of Personnel. Employees work better if job security and career progress are assured to them. An insecure tenure and a high rate of employee turnover will affect the organization adversely.

人员任期稳定性(Stability of Tenure of Personnel)。在工作职位稳定和职业前景看好的情况下，员工的工作绩效会更好。人员的不当任用以及离职率过高对企业都会有负面影响。

Initiative. Allowing all personnel to show their initiative in some way is a source of strength for the organization. Even though it may well involve a sacrifice of "personal vanity" on the part of many managers.

主动性(Initiative)。通过一些适当的方式调动全体人员的主动性，是一个增强组织实力的有效方法。这一点做得好，也许会让一些管理人员感到"空虚"。

Esprit de Corps. Management must foster the morale of its employees. He further suggests that: "real talent is needed to coordinate effort, encourage keenness, use each person's abilities, and reward each one's merit without arousing possible jealousies and disturbing harmonious relations."

团队精神(Esprit de Corps)。管理人员必须不断鼓舞雇员士气。法约尔进一步建议：

"真正优秀的团队需要协调努力、互相鼓励、调用每个人的聪明才智，并不偏不倚地对每个人的优点给以回报。"

3.2.5　The Science of Muddling Through[①]

The author of *The Science of Muddling Through* is Charles Edward Lindblom, as shown in Figure 3.5.

Figure 3.5　Charles Edward Lindblom

Charles Edward Lindblom is a Sterling Professor Emeritus of Political Science and Economics at Yale University. He is a former president of the American Political Science Association and the Association for Comparative Economic Studies and also a former director of Yale's Institution for Social and Policy Studies.[②]

The followings are the essences of his article.

Suppose an administrator is given responsibility for formulating policy with respect to inflation. He might start by trying to list all related values in order of importance, e.g., full employment, reasonable business profit, protection of small savings, prevention of stock market crash. Then all possible policy outcomes could be rated as more or less efficient in attaining a maximum of these values. This would of course require a prodigious inquiry into values held by members of society and an equally prodigious set of calculations on how much of each value is equal to how much of each other value. He could then proceed to outline all possible policy alternatives. In the third step, he would undertake systematic comparison of his multitude of alternatives to determine which attains the greatest amount of values.

假定一个行政官员负责针对通货膨胀制定政策。开始时，他可能会根据其重要程度列出所有相关的价值，比如说，完全就业，合理商业利润，保护小额存款，防止股市崩盘等

---

①　Charles E. Lindblom. The Science of Muddling Through[J]. Public Administration Review, 1959,(2):79-88.

②　https://en.wikipedia.org/wiki/Charles_E._Lindblom

等。接下来，在达到这些价值最大化的过程中，政策所有可能的后果会根据效果的多寡加以估价。当然，这种估价需要对社会成员拥有的价值观做大量的调查，也需要大量能计算一种价值在多大程度与另一种价值等同的估算方法。第二步，他会列出所有可能的替代政策。第三步，他会在大量的替代政策中做系统的比较以决定使价值最大化的那种政策。

In comparing policies, he would take advantage of any theory available that generalized about classes of policies. In considering inflation, for example, he would compare all policies in the light of the theory of prices.

Since no alternatives are beyond his investigation, he would consider strict central control and the abolition of all prices and markets on the one hand and elimination of all public controls with reliance completely on the free market on the other, both in the light of whatever theoretical generalizations he could find on such hypothetical economies. Finally, he would try to make the choice that would in fact maximize his values.

在比较政策过程中，他会利用任何可以利用的从各种政策总结出来的理论。例如，针对通货膨胀，他会比较所有相关的价格理论。由于替代政策没有超出他的调查，所以一方面，他会考虑实行严格的中央控制以及取消所有价格和市场；另一方面，他会考虑取消所有完全依赖自由市场的公共管理。根据任何一般化的理论，他都会发现以上这样的经济假设。事实上，最后他会尽量做出能使他的各种价值最大化的选择。

He would find that the policy alternatives combined objectives or values in different ways. For example, one policy might offer price level stability at the cost of some risk of unemployment; another might offer less price stability but also less risk of unemployment. Hence, the next step in his approach—the final selection—would combine into one the choice among values and the choice among instruments for reaching values.

他会找到以不同方式把目标和价值结合在一起的替代政策。例如，一项政策可能以失业风险为代价保持价格的稳定水平；另一种政策可能以较不稳定价格水平换来较少的失业风险。因此，在此方法的下一步，他会把价值选择与达到价值的手段选择结合在一起做出最后选择。

I propose in this paper to clarify and formalize the second method, much neglected in the literature. This might be described as the method of successive limited comparisons. I will contrast it with the first approach, which might be called the rational comprehensive method. More impressionistically and briefly—and therefore generally used in this article—they could be characterized as the branch method and root method, the former continually building out from the current situation, step-by-step and by small degrees; the latter starting from fundamentals anew each time, building on the past only as experience is embodied in a theory, and always prepared to start completely from the ground up.

在这篇论文中我提出明确第二种方法，使其公式化。这种方法在典籍中被大大忽视了。我把它描述为有限连续方法。我还会把它与可称为理性—综合的第一种方法加以对照比较。在这篇文章中一般使用令人印象深刻和简单明了的枝方法和根方法。前者不断地从当前位置逐步地、小幅度地建立起来；后者每次都是从基础重新开始，把过去的经验在理论中具体化，常常准备完全从头开始。

Rational-Comprehensive (Root)

la. Clarification of values or objectives distinct from and usually prerequisite to empirical analysis of alternative policies.

2a. Policy-formulation is therefore approached through means-end analysis: First the ends are isolated, then the means to achieve them are sought.

3a. The test of a "good" policy is that it can be shown to be the most appropriate means to desired ends.

4a. Analysis is comprehensive; every important relevant factor is taken into account.

5a. Theory is often heavily relied upon.

理性综合法(根方法)

1a. 明确区分目标与行动，将目标当作政策分析的前提。

2a. 在目标与手段的分析中，先确立目标，再寻找手段。

3a. 认为"好"的政策是实现目标的最佳手段。

4a. 主张综合全面的分析。

5a. 过分强调理论的作用。

Successive Limited Comparisons (Branch)

1b. Selection of value goals and empirical analysis of the needed action are not distinct from one another but are closely intertwined.

2b. Since means and ends are not distinct, means-end analysis is often inappropriate or limited.

3b. The test of a "good" policy is typically that various analysts find themselves directly agreeing on a policy (without their agreeing that it is the most appropriate means to an agreed objective).

4b. Analysis is drastically limited:

i) Important possible outcomes are neglected.

ii) Important alternative potential policies are neglected.

iii) Important affected values are neglected.

5b. A succession of comparisons greatly reduces or eliminates reliance on theory.

连续有限比较法(枝方法)(渐进调适)

1b. 不区分目标与行动，它们是联系着的。

2b. 不区分目标与手段，认为这种区分是不适当的且有限的。

3b. 认为"好"的政策是由"共识"所产生的。

4b. 它主张有限分析：忽略了重要的后果、可行方案和价值标准。

5b. 主张通过连续比较来减少对理论的信赖。

3.2.6 Reinventing Government: How the Entrepreneurial Spirit is Transforming the Public Sector①

The authors of *Reinventing Government: How the Entrepreneurial Spirit is Transforming the Public Sector* are David Osborne and Ted Gaebler. David Osborne is the author of *Laboratories of Democracy*, is a frequent contributor to the Washington Post, Governing, and other publications. He is also a consultant to state and local governments. David Dsborne is shown in Figure 3.6.

Figure 3.6　David Osborne

Ted Gaebler is a former city manager of Visalia, California, and Vandalia, Ohio, and is the president of the Gaebler Group, a division of MRC, a public-sector management-consulting firm, in San Rafael, California. Ted Gaebler is shown in Figure 3.7.

Figure 3.7　Ted Gaebler

The followings are the essences of *Reinventing Government: How the Entrepreneurial Spirit*

---

① David Osborne, Ted Gaebler. Reinventing Government: How the Entrepreneurial Spirit Is Transforming the Public Sector[M]. Boston: Addison-Wesley Publishing Company, 1992.

is Transforming the Public Sector.

1. Contents 目录

Catalytic Government:Steering Rather Than Rowing

起催化作用的政府：掌舵而不是划桨

Community-Owned Government:Empowering Rather Than Serving

社区拥有的政府：授权而不是服务

Competitive Government:Injecting Competition into Service Delivery

竞争性政府：把竞争机制注入服务提供中去

Mission-Driven Government:Transforming Rule-Driven Organizations

有使命感的政府：改变照章办事的组织

Results-Oriented Government:Funding Outcomes, Not Inputs

讲究效果的政府：按效果而不是按投入拨款

Customer-Driven Government:Meeting the Needs of the Customer, Not the Bureaucracy

受顾客驱使的政府：满足顾客的需要，不是官僚政治的需要

Enterprising Government:Earning Rather Than Spending

有事业心的政府：有收益而不浪费

Anticipatory Government:Prevention Rather Than Cure

有预见的政府：预防而不是治疗

Decentralized Government:From Hierarchy to Participation and Teamwork

分权的政府：从等级制到参与和协作

Market-Oriented Government:Leveraging Change Through the Market

以市场为导向的政府：通过市场力量进行变革

2. Preface 前言

We feel a responsibility to make explicit the underlying beliefs that have driven us to write this book—and that have no doubt animated its conclusions.

First, we believe deeply in government. We do not look at government as a necessary evil. All civilized societies have some form of government.

Government is the mechanism we use to make communal decisions: where to build a highway, what to do about homeless people, what kind of education to provide for our children.

我们感到有责任阐明促使我们撰写此书的一些基本信念，这些信念毫无疑问地推动我们做出了书中的结论。

第一，我们对政府充满信心。我们并没有把政府视作一种不得不忍受的邪恶。一切文明社会都有某种形式的政府。政府是我们用来做出公共决策的一种机制，我们要决定在哪

里造公路，怎样处理无家可归的人，给我们的孩子提供什么样的教育。

It is the way we provide services that benefit all our people: national defense, environmental protection, police protection, highways, dams, water systems.

It is the way we solve collective problems. Think of the problems facing American society today: drug use; crime; poverty; homelessness; illiteracy; toxic waste; the specter of global warming; the exploding cost of medical care.

How will we solve these problems? By acting collectively. How do we act collectively? Through government.

政府是我们向大家提供有益服务的方式，这些服务包括国防、环境保护、警察保护、公路、水坝、供排水系统。

政府是我们解决共同问题的方式。想一想美国社会今天面临的种种问题，如吸毒、犯罪、贫困、流浪汉、文盲、有毒废物、全球气温升高的阴影、医疗保健成倍剧增的费用。

我们怎么解决这些问题呢？靠集体行动。我们怎样集体行动呢？通过政府采取行动。

Second, we believe that civilized society cannot function effectively without effective government—something that is all too rare today.

We believe that industrial-era governments, with their large, centralized bureaucracies and standardized, "one-size—fits-all" services, are not up to the challenges of a rapidly changing information society and knowledge-based economy.

第二，我们认为没有一个有效的政府，文明社会就不能有效地运作，不过今天有效的政府实属凤毛麟角。

我们认为，工业时代的政府官僚机构既庞大又集权化，提供标准化的服务千篇一律不看对象，因而不足以迎接迅速变化的信息社会和知识经济的挑战。

Third, We believe that the people who work in government are not the problem; the system in which they work are the problem.

第三，我们认为问题不在于政府中工作的人，问题在于他们工作所在的体制。

Fourth, we believe that neither traditional liberalism nor traditional conservatism has much relevance to the problems our governments face today.

We will not solve our problems by spending more or spending less, by creating new public bureaucracies or by "privatizing" existing bureaucracies.

At some times and in some places, we do need to spend more or spend less, create new programs or privatize public functions.

But to make our governments effective again we must reinvent them.

第四，我们认为，无论是传统的自由主义还是传统的保守主义都不是解决我们各级政府今天所面临问题的有效之道。

我们解决我们的问题，既不靠大把花钱增加政府的开支，也不靠节制支出缩小预算；既不靠新建一批政府官僚机构，也不用对现有的官僚机构实行"私有化"。

在某些时候某些地方，我们确实需要多花钱或者少花钱，需要制订一些新的计划或者把一些政府功能私有化。

但是，为了使我们的政府重新变得有效，我们一定要改革政府。

Finally, we believe deeply in equity—in equal opportunity for all Americans.

We believe there are ways to use choice and competition to increase the equity in our school system.

最后，我们对平等抱有坚定的信念，所有的美国人都应有平等的机会。

我们认为有办法通过选择和竞争来提高我们教育体系的平等程度。

We use the phrase entrepreneurial government to describe the new model we see emerging across America.

This phrase may surprise many readers, who think of entrepreneurs solely as business men and women.

But the true meaning of the word entrepreneur is far broader.

It was coined by the French economist J. B. Say, around the year 1800.

"The entrepreneur" Say wrote, "shifts economic resources out of an area of lower and into an area of higher productivity and greater yield."

An entrepreneur, in other words, uses resources in new ways to maximize productivity and effectiveness.

我们使用"企业家政府"一词来指在美国各地出现的新模式。

这个词也许会使许多读者感到意外，读者们认为企业家就是男、女生意人。

但是，"企业家"一词的真正含义要广泛得多。

1800年法国经济学家J. B. 萨伊创造了这个词。

萨伊写道，"企业家把经济资源从生产率较低的地方转移到较高的地方得到更大的产出。"换言之，企业家运用新的方法最大化生产效率和效益。

Say's definition applies equally to the private sector, to the public sector, and to the voluntary, or third, sector.

When we talk about the entrepreneurial model, we mean public sector institutions that habitually act this way—that constantly use their resources in new ways to heighten both their efficiency and their effectiveness.

萨伊所下的定义，既适用于私营部门，也同样适用于公共部门和志愿者参加的第三部门。

我们说到企业家式的模式时，指的是习惯性地这般行事的公共部门机构，不断地以新的方式运用其资源来提高其效率和效能。

3. Introduction: an American Perestroika 绪论：美国改革

As the 1980s drew to a close, *Time* magazine asked on its cover: "Is Government Dead?"

As the 1990s unfold, the answer—to many Americans—appears to be yes.

Our public schools are the worst in the developed world. Our health care system is out of control. Our courts and prisons are so overcrowded that convicted felons walk free. And many of our proudest cities and states are virtually bankrupt.

当20世纪80年代接近尾声的时候，《时代》周刊在其封面上提出了一个问题："政府已死？"

当20世纪90年代开始的时候，对于许多美国人来说，答案似乎是肯定的。

我们的公立学校是发达国家中最差的，我们的卫生医疗系统已经失控。我们的法院和监狱已是人满为患，已经判了刑的犯人只好释放。许多我们最引以自豪的城市和州已经破产。

Confidence in government has fallen to record lows. By the late 1980s, only 5 percent of Americans surveyed said they would choose government service as their preferred career. Only 13 percent of top federal employees said they would recommend career in public service. Nearly three out of four Americans said they believed Washington delivered less value for the dollar than it had 10 years earlier.

对政府的信任一再降到创纪录的最低点。20世纪80年代后期，接受民意测验的人中只有5%的人说，他们将把在政府里工作选为理想的职业。联邦高级雇员中只有13%的人说，他们愿意推荐别人在公共部门工作。将近四分之三的美国人说，他们认为华盛顿政府现在给他们的东西在价值上还不如10年前多。

The Rule Book

Throughout the Defense, people buy by the book.

For example, there is a simple steam trap which costs $ 100. When it leaks, it leaks $ 50 a week worth of steam. The lesson is, when it leaks, replace it quick. But it takes us a year to replace it, because we have a system that wants to make sure we get the very best buy on this $ 100 itcm, and maybe by waiting a year we can buy the item for $ 2 less. In the meantime, we've lost $3,000 worth of steam."

规则手册

整个国防部的人都是按规则手册行事的。一个价值100美元的普通蒸汽阀门，一旦漏汽，一周要损失50美元的蒸汽。由此我们可以懂得，一漏汽就要马上更换。但是，我们要花一年的时间来更换它，因为我们的体制规定采购这类价值100美元以上的东西要买最合算的，所以，也许等一年便可以买到便宜2美元的阀门。在这段时间里我们要损失价值3000美元的蒸汽。

Why government can't be "run like a business"?

为何政府不能"像企业那样来运作"？

Many people, who believe government should simply be "run like a business," may assume this is what we mean. It is not.

Government and business are fundamentally different institutions.

Business leaders are driven by the profit motive; government leaders are driven by the desire to get reelected.

Businesses get most of their money from their customers; governments get most of their money from taxpayers.

Businesses are usually driven by competition; governments usually use monopolies.

许多人认为政府可以简单地"像企业那样来运作"，他们也许会以为我们的意思也是如此。那就弄错了。

政府和企业是两种根本不同的机构组织。企业领导者的行为动机是获取利润，政府领导者的行为动机是再次连任。企业的大部分收入来自其顾客，而政府的大部分收入则来自纳税人。企业的动力通常来自竞争，政府则来自种种垄断。

The fact that government cannot be run just like a business does not mean it cannot become more entrepreneurial, of course.

Any institution, public or private, can be entrepreneurial, just as any institution, public or private, can be bureaucratic. Few Americans would really want government to act just like a business—making quick decisions behind closed doors for private profit.

If it did, democracy would be the first casualty, but most Americans would like government to be less bureaucratic. There is a vast continuum between bureaucratic behavior and entrepreneurial behavior, and government can surely shift its position on that spectrum.

政府不可能像企业那样运作，当然这一事实并不意味着它不可能有较强的企业家精神。任何机构，无论公营私营，都可以有企业家的精神，正像任何公私机构，都会出现官僚主义。很少美国人真的要求政府像一个企业那样行事——因为私人利润而关起门来迅速作出决策。如果它真的这么干，民主将首先受到损害。但是大多数美国人要求政府减少官僚主义。在官僚主义行为和企业家行为之间是一个巨大的连续体，政府肯定可以在这个区域内调整自己的位置。

4. A Third Choice 第三种选择

Our fundamental problem today is not too much government or too little government. We have debated that issue endlessly since the tax revolt of 1978, and it has not solved our problems.

Our fundamental problem is that we have the wrong kind of government. We do not need more government or less government, we need better government. To be more precise, we need better governance.

今天我们面临的根本问题不是政府的大小。自从1978年的抗税运动以来，我们已经无数次地辩论过这个问题，但这依然没有解决我们的问题。我们的根本问题在于政府的类型错了。我们不需要什么大政府或者小政府，我们需要一个更好的政府。说得更精确一些，我们需要更好的政府治理。

Governance is the process by which we collectively solve our problems and meet our society's needs. Government is the instrument we use. The instrument is outdated, and the process of reinvention has begun. We do not need another New Deal, nor another Reagan Revolution. We need an American perestroika.

政府治理指的是我们共同解决自己的问题和满足我们社会需要的过程。政府是我们使用的一种工具。一旦这个工具过时了，重新发明的过程就开始了。我们不需要再来一次新政，也不需要再来一次里根革命。我们需要的是一种美国式的改革。

5. Many Arrows in the Quiver 箭袋里的许多箭(政府工具)

Traditional	传统类
1. Creating Legal Rules and Sanctions	1. 建立法律规章和制裁手段
2. Regulation or Deregulation	2. 管制或者放松管制
3. Monitoring and Investigation	3. 进行监督和调查
4. Licensing	4. 颁发许可证
5. Tax Policy	5. 税收政策
6. Grants	6. 拨款
7. Subsidies	7. 补助
8. Loans	8. 贷款
9. Loan Guarantees	9. 贷款担保
10. Contracting	10. 合同承包
Innovative	创新类
11. Franchising	11. 特许经营
12. Public-Private Partnerships	12. 公私伙伴关系
13. Public-Public Partnerships	13. 公共部门之间的伙伴关系
14. Quasi-public corporations	14. 半公半私的公司
15. Public enterprise	15. 公营企业
16. Procurement	16. 采购
17. Insurance	17. 保险
18. Rewards	18. 奖励
19. Changing public investment policy	19. 改变公共投资政策

20. Technical Assistance	20. 技术支持
21. Information	21. 信息
22. Referral	22. 介绍推荐
23. Volunteers	23. 志愿服务者
24. Vouchers	24. 有价证券
25. Impact Fees	25. 后果费
26. Catalyzing Nongovernmental Efforts	26. 催化非政府行动
27. Convening Nongovernmental Leaders	27. 召集非政府领导人开会
28. Jawboning	28. 政府施加压力
Avant-Garde	先锋派类
29.Seed Money	29. 种子资金
30. Equity investments	30. 股权投资
31. Voluntary associations	31. 志愿者协会
32. Coproduction or self-help	32. 共同生产或自力更生
33. Quid pro quos	33. 回报性安排
34. Demand management	34. 需求管理
35. Sale, exchange, or use of property	35. 财产的出售、交换与使用
36. Restructuring the market	36. 重新构造市场

Tasks best suited to each sector are shown in Table 3.1.

Table 3.1　Tasks Best Suited to Eash Sector

(E=effective, I=ineffective, D=depends on context)

	Category	Public	Private	Third
Best suited to public sector	Policy management	E	I	D
	Regulation	E	I	D
	Enforcement of equity	E	I	E
	Prevention of discrimination	E	D	D
	Prevention of exploitation	E	I	E
	Promotion of social cohesion	E	I	E
Best suited to private sector	Economic tasks	I	E	D
	Investment tasks	I	E	D
	Profit generation	I	E	I
	Promotion of self-sufficiency	I	E	D
Best suited to third sector	Social tasks	D	I	E
	Tasks that require volunteer labor	D	I	E
	Tasks that generate little profit	D	I	E
	Promotion of individual responsibility	I	D	E
	Promotion of community	D	I	E
	Promotion of commitment to welfare of others	D	I	E

3.2.7　The New Pubic Service: Serving Rather than Steering[①]

The authors of *The New Public Service: Serving Rather than Steering* are Robert B. Denhardt and Janet V. Denhardt. Robert B. Denhardt is a Professor in the School of Public Affairs at Arizona State University. He was born in Kentucky and received Ph.D. in Public Administration from the University of Kentucky in 1968. Denhardt is best known for his work in public administration theory and organizational behavior, especially leadership and organizational change. In *The New Public Service: Serving, not Steering*, he developed a new model of governance that stresses the need to engage citizens in governance of their communities. Robert B. Denhardt is shown in Figure 3.8.

Figure 3.8　Robert B. Denhardt

Janet V. Denhardt is a professor in the School of Public Affairs at Arizona State University and member of the American Society for Public Administration. Her teaching and research interests lie primarily in organization theory and organizational behavior. Janet V. Denhardt is shown in Figure 3.9.

Figure 3.9　Janet V. Denhardt

The followings are the essences of this article.

Public management has undergone a revolution. Rather than focusing on controlling bureaucracies and delivering services, public administrators are responding to admonishments

---

① Robert B. Denhardt, Janet Vinzant Denhardt. The New Public Service: Serving Rather than Steering[J]. Public Administration Review, 2000,60 (6), 549-559.

to "steer rather than row", and to be the entrepreneurs of a new, leaner, and increasingly privatized government.

公共管理已经经历了一切改革。公共行政官员不再关注控制官僚机构和提供服务，而是正在对"掌舵而非划桨"的告诫做出反应，试图成为新型的、有偏向且日益私人化的政府企业家。

Accordingly, public administrators should focus on their responsibility to serve and empower citizens as they manage public organizations and implement public policy. In other words, with citizens at the forefront, the emphasis should not be placed on either steering or rowing the governmental boat, but rather on building public institutions marked by integrity and responsiveness.

因此，行政官员在管理公共组织和执行公共政策时，应当强调他们服务于公民和授权予公民的职责。换言之，将公民置于第一位时，重点不应当放在驾驶或划动政府这条船，而应当放在构建具有完整性和回应性的公共机构之上。

Like the New Public Management and the old public administration, the New Public Service consists of many diverse elements, and many different scholars and practitioners have contributed, often in disagreement with one another. Yet certain general ideas seem to characterize this approach as a normative model and to distinguish it from others.

如同新公共管理和传统公共行政一样，新公共服务也包含许多不同的构成要素，许多学者和实践家都有所贡献，他们通常也相互争论。然而，其中一些普遍性观点似乎可以把新公共服务途径概括为标准模式，并将其与其他研究途径区别开来。

While the New Public Service has emerged both in theory and in the innovative and advanced practices of many exemplary public managers (Denhardt 1993; Denhardt and Denhardt 1999), in this section we will examine the conceptual foundations of New Public Service. Certainly the New Public Service can lay claim to an impressive intellectual heritage, including, in public administration, the work of Dwight Waldo (1948), and in political theory, the work of Sheldon Wolin (1960). However, here we will focus on more contemporary precursors of the New Public Service, including (1) theories of democratic citizenship; (2) models of community and civil society; (3) organizational humanism and discourse theory.

当前，新公共服务已经在理论上、在诸多优秀公共管理者创新性的先进实践中初露端倪。本部分中，我们将考察新公共服务的概念基础。当然，新公共服务可以追溯到我们仍旧记忆犹新的思想遗产，包括公共行政领域内德怀特·沃尔多(Dwight Waldo)的著作(1948)和政治理论方面的谢登·沃林(Sheldon Wolin)的著作(1960)。但是，我们在这里将更加关注新公共服务的当代先驱理论，包括：(1)民主社会的公民权理论；(2)社区和市民社会的模型；(3)组织人本主义和组织对话理论。

Serve, rather than steer. An increasingly important role of the public servant is to help citizens articulate and meet their shared interests, rather than to attempt to control or steer society in new directions.

服务而非掌舵。公务员越来越重要的作用就在于帮助公民表达和实现他们的共同利益，而非试图在新的方向上控制或驾驭社会。

While in the past, government played a central role in what has been called the "steering of society" (Nelissen et.al. 1999), the complexity of modern life sometimes makes such a role not only inappropriate, but impossible.

在过去，政府在所谓的"掌控社会"的过程中发挥了重要作用，但现代生活的复杂性有时却使得这样的作用不仅不合时宜，而且是不太可能。

In this new world, the primary role of government is not merely to direct the actions of the public through regulation and decree (though that may sometimes be appropriate), nor is it to simply establish a set of rules and incentives (sticks or carrots) through which people will be guided in the "proper" direction.

在这种新的现实条件下，政府的首要作用不仅仅是通过管制和命令来指挥公众的行动(尽管这样做有时可能是合适的)，也不是简单地建立一套惩戒规则和激励措施(胡萝卜或大棒)，将人们引导到"合适的"方向上来。

Rather, government becomes another player, albeit an important player in the process of moving society in one direction or another. Government acts, in concert with private and nonprofit groups and organizations, to seek solutions to the problems that communities face.

相反，尽管政府在推动社会朝某个方向发展的过程中是重要的参与者，但它事实上已经成为另一种意义上的参与者。政府与私人的或非营利的团体和组织协同行动以寻求社区所面临问题的解决方案。

In this process, the role of government is transformed from one of controlling to one of agenda setting, bringing the proper players to the table and facilitating, negotiating, or brokering solutions to public problems (often through coalitions of public, private, and non-profit agencies).

在此过程中，政府的作用从控制转变为议程设定，把合适的参与者集中到谈判桌前进行磋商和谈判，或者作为中间人促成公共问题的解决方案(通常是通过公共机构、私人机构和非营利机构结成联盟的形式进行)。

The public interest is the aim, not the byproduct. Public administrators must contribute to building a collective, shared notion of the public interest. The goal is not to find quick solutions driven by individual choices. Rather, it is the creation of shared interests and shared responsibility.

公共利益是目标而非副产品。公共行政官员必须致力于建立集体的、共享的公共利益观念，这个目标不是要在个人选择的驱使下找到快速解决问题的方案，而是要创造共享利益和共同责任。

The New Public Service demands that the process of establishing a vision for society is not something merely left to elected political leaders or appointed public administrators. Instead, the activity of establishing a vision or direction is something in which widespread public dialogue and deliberation are central.

新公共服务提出，建立社会远景目标的过程并不能只委托给民选的政治领袖或被任命的公共行政官员。事实上，在确立社会远景目标或发展方向的行为当中，广泛的公众对话和协商是非常重要的。

The role of government will increasingly be to bring people together in settings that allow for unconstrained and authentic discourse concerning the direction society should take. Based on these deliberations, a broad-based vision for the community, the state, or the nation can be established and provide a guiding set of ideas (or ideals) for the future.

政府的作用将更多地体现在把人们聚集到能无拘无束、真诚地进行对话的环境中，共商社会应该选择的发展方向。以这些协商为基础，才能建立具有广泛基础的社区、国家或民族的远景目标，才能为未来提出指导性的理想。

It is less important for this process to result in a single set of goals than it is for it to engage administrators, politicians, and citizens in a process of thinking about a desired future for their community and their nation.

相比之下，通过这种协商过程来形成一系列简单的目标并不重要；重要的是通过该过程，促使行政官员、政治家和公民处于思考社区和国家预期发展前景的过程之中。

Think strategically, act democratically. Policies and programs meeting public needs can be most effectively and responsibly achieved through collective efforts and collaborative processes.

战略地思考，民主地行动。符合公共需要的政策和计划，通过集体努力和协作的过程，能够最有效地、最负责任地得到贯彻执行。

To realize a collective vision, the next step is establishing roles and responsibilities and developing specific action steps to move toward the desired goals.

为了实现集体的远景目标，下一步就是要确定角色和职责，并拟定具体的行动步骤，迈向预期的理想目标。

Again, the idea is not merely to establish a vision and then leave the implementation to those in government；rather, it is to join all parties together in the process of carrying out programs that will move in the desired direction.

同样，这种思想并不只是确立远景目标。然后交给政府工作人员去实施；相反，它意味着将各方力量集中到实施计划的过程中，而这些计划将通向理想的目的地。

Through involvement in programs of civic education and by developing abroad range of civic leaders, government can stimulate a renewed sense of civic pride and civic responsibility.

通过参与和推动公民教育计划、培养更多的公民领袖，政府就可以激发公民自豪感和社会责任感的回归。

We expect such a sense of pride and responsibility to evolve into a greater willingness to be involved at many levels, as all parties work together to create opportunities for participation, collaboration, and community.

我们希望这样的自豪感和责任感能够演变成在多个层次上都得到体现的强烈愿望，因为所有各方都共同致力于创造参与、合作、达成一致的机会。

Serve citizens, not customers. The public interest results from a dialogue about shared values, rather than the aggregation of individual self-interests. Therefore, public servants do not merely respond to the demands of "customers", but focus on building relationships of trust and collaboration with and among citizens.

服务于公民而不是顾客。公共利益源于对共同价值准则的对话协商，而不是个体自我利益的简单相加。因此，公务员不仅仅要回应"顾客"的需求，而且更要关注建设政府与公民之间、公民与公民之间的信任与合作关系。

The New Public Service recognizes that the relationship between government and its citizens is not the same as that between a business and its customers. In the public sector, it is problematic to even determine who the customer is, because government serves more than just the immediate client.

新公共服务理论认为，政府与公民之间的关系不同于工商企业与其顾客之间的关系。在公共部门中，即使是确定谁是顾客都很困难，因为政府的服务对象远不止直接的顾客。

Government also serves those who maybe waiting for service, those who may need the service even though they arc not actively seeking it, future generations of service recipients, relatives and friends of the immediate recipient, and on and on. There may even be customers who don't want to be customers—such as those receiving a speeding ticket.

政府也服务于这样一些人：等待服务的人，没有积极地寻求服务但可能需要服务的人，服务受益者的后辈，直接受益者的亲友等。甚至也有一些不想成为顾客的顾客，比如那些因超速行驶收到罚单的人。

Accountability isn't simple. Public servants should be attentive to more than the market; they should also attend to statutory and constitutional law, community values, political norms, professional standards, and citizen interests.

责任并不是单一的。公务员不应当仅仅关注市场，他们也应该关注宪法和法令，关注社会价值观、政治行为准则、职业标准和公民利益。

The matter of accountability is extremely complex. Yet both the old public administration and the New Public Management tend to oversimplify the issue. For instance, in the classic version of the old public administration, public administrators were simply and directly responsible to political officials.

责任问题极其复杂。但传统公共行政和新公共管理都倾向于高度简化这个问题。例如，按照传统公共行政的经典解释，公共行政官员只是直接地对政治官员负责。

As Wilson wrote, "Policy will have no taint of officialism about it. It will not be the creation of permanent officials, but of statesmen whose responsibility to public opinion will be direct and inevitable."

正如威尔逊(Wilson)写道的那样，"政策将不再受官僚主义的玷污。它不会产生终身制的官员，而将产生政治家。政治家将不可避免地直接对公众舆论负责。"

Beyond this, accountability was not really an issue; politicians were expected to make decisions while bureaucrats carried them out. Obviously, over time, public administrators assumed great capacities for influencing the policy process.

除此之外，责任事实上并不成为问题；人们希望让政治家制定政策，让官僚们执行政策。很明显，公共行政官员将越来越具有影响政策过程的能力。

So, at the other end of the spectrum, in the vernacular of the New Public Management, the focus is on giving administrators great latitude to act as entrepreneurs. In their entrepreneurial role, the new public managers are called to account primarily in terms of efficiency, cost effectiveness, and responsiveness to market forces.

所以，用位于光谱另一端的新公共管理术语来解释，焦点在于赋予行政官员较大的空间，让他们按企业家的方式行事。在企业家角色中，新的公共管理者将主要在效率、成本有效性和回应性等方面被要求诉诸市场力量。

Value people, not just productivity. Public organizations and the networks in which they participate are more likely to succeed in the long run if they are operated through processes of collaboration and shared leadership based on respect for all people.

重视人而不只是生产率。公共组织及其所参与的网络，如果能在尊重所有人的基础上通过合作和共同领导的过程来运作，它们最终就更有可能获得成功。

In its approach to management and organization, the New Public Service emphasizes the importance of "managing through people". Systems of productivity improvement, process reengineering, and performance measurement are seen as important tools in designing management systems.

在管理和组织的方法方面，新公共服务理论强调"依靠人来管理"的重要性。生产率改进、过程再造和绩效测量等体系都被视为设计管理制度的重要工具。

But the New Public Service suggests that such rational attempts to control human behavior are likely to fail in the long term if, at the same time, insufficient attention is paid to the values and interests of individual members of an organization. Moreover, while these approaches may get results, they do not build responsible, engaged, and civic-minded employees or citizens.

但新公共服务理论认为，如果不能同时充分地关注组织个体成员的价值观和利益的话，那种控制人们行为的理性企图最终将会失败。况且，即使这些管理和组织方法能够取得成效，它们也不会培养出负责任的、活跃的和热心公益的雇员或公民。

Value citizenship and public service above entrepreneurship. The public interest is better advanced by public servants and citizens committed to making meaningful contributions to society rather than by entrepreneurial managers acting as if public money were their own.

超越企业家身份，重视公民权和公共服务。与企业家式的管理者视公共资金为已所有的行事方式相比，如果公务员和公民都致力于为社会做出有意义的贡献，那么公共利益就会得到更好的实现。

The New Public Management encourages public administrators to act and think as entrepreneurs of a business enterprise. This creates a rather narrow view of the objectives to be sought—to maximize productivity and satisfy customers, and to accept risks and to take advantage of opportunities as they arise.

新公共管理鼓励公共行政官员像工商业企业家一样去思考和行事，这导致了相当狭隘地看待所追求的目标——使生产率最大化、满足顾客需求、接受风险和充分利用风险带来的机会。

In the New Public Service, there is an explicit recognition that public administrators are not the business owners of their agencies and programs. Again, as King and Stivers (1998) remind us, government is owned by the citizens.

新公共服务理论明确提出，公共行政官员并不是其机构和项目的业务所有者。金和斯迪沃斯(1998)再次提醒我们，政府为公民所有。

✿ Vocabulary

initiative	主动
incentive	激励
ingenuity	灵活性

spasmodically	间断地
practical science	实用科学
systematically	系统地
characteristic	独特的
complex	复杂的
constitution	宪法
strife	冲突
contrivances	发明
soberest	冷静的
sustenance	生计
arbitrariness	任意，霸道，恣意
beneficent	善行的，有益的
rule-of-thumb	经验法则
flows from	从……产生
remuneration	报酬
morale	士气
keenness	敏锐
animated	鼓舞
communal	公共的
specter	幽灵
liberalism	自由主义
conservatism	保守主义
perestroika	改革
casualty	伤亡
continuum	连续统一体
spectrum	范围
governance	治理
admonishment	告诫
empower	授权
integrity	完整
responsiveness	回应性
deliberation	考虑
officialism	官僚主义

👤 FURTHER READING

Governance

Origin of the word

The word governance derives from the Greek verb κυβερνάω [kubernáo] which means to steer and was used for the first time in a metaphorical sense by Plato. It then passed on to Latin and then on to many languages.

Processes and governance

As a process, governance may operate in an organization of any size: from a single human being to all of humanity; and it may function for any purpose, good or evil, for profit or not. A reasonable or rational purpose of governance might aim to assure (sometimes on behalf of others) that an organization produces a worthwhile pattern of good results while avoiding an undesirable pattern of bad circumstances.

Perhaps the moral and natural purpose of governance consists of assuring, on behalf of those governed, a worthy pattern of good while avoiding an undesirable pattern of bad. The ideal purpose, obviously, would assure a perfect pattern of good with no bad. A government comprises a set of inter-related positions that govern and that use or exercise power, particularly coercive power.

A good government, following this line of thought, could consist of a set of inter-related positions exercising coercive power that assures, on behalf of those governed, a worthwhile pattern of good results while avoiding an undesirable pattern of bad circumstances, by making decisions that define expectations, grant power, and verify performance.

Politics provides a means by which the governance process operates. For example, people may choose expectations by way of political activity; they may grant power through political action, and they may judge performance through political behavior.

Conceiving of governance in this way, one can apply the concept to states, to corporations, to non-profits, to NGOs, to partnerships and other associations, to project, and to any number of humans engaged in some purposeful activity.

Different definitions

The World Bank defines governance as: The manner in which power is exercised in the management of a country's economic and social resources for development.

The Worldwide Governance Indicators project of the World Bank defines governance as: The traditions and institutions by which authority in a country is exercised.

This considers the process by which governments are selected, monitored and replaced;

the capacity of the government to effectively formulate and implement sound policies and the respect of citizens and the state of the institutions that govern economic and social interactions among them.

An alternate definition sees governance as: The use of institutions, structures of authority and even collaboration to allocate resources and coordinate or control activity in society or the economy.

According to the United Nations Development Program's Regional Project on Local Governance for Latin America, Governance has been defined as the rules of the political system to solve conflicts between actors and adopt decision (legality). It has also been used to describe the "proper functioning of institutions and their acceptance by the public" (legitimacy). And it has been used to invoke the efficacy of government and the achievement of consensus by democratic means (participation).

According to the Governance Analytical Framework (GAF), governance can be defined in broader terms. It refers to the "processes of interactions and decision-making among the actors involved in a collective problem, that lead to the creation, reinforcement or reproduction of social norms and institutions". Governance processes are found in any society, and they can be analyzed from a non-normative perspective, the GAF. The proposed method is based on five analytical tools: problems, actors, social norms, processes and nodal points. The GAF was developed in the context of the research program NCCR North-South, and on the basis of a critique of existing approaches to governance.

Source: WIKIPEDIA available at: http://en.wikipedia.org/wiki/Governance

Chapter 4
Political Party and State Organ

4.1
Political Party

4.1.1 An Overview of Political Party

1. Definition of Political Party

A political party is a political organization that typically seeks to influence government policy, usually by nominating their own candidates and trying to seat them in political office.[①] Parties participate in electoral campaigns and educational outreach or protest actions. Parties often espouse an expressed ideology or vision bolstered by a written platform with specific goals, forming a coalition among disparate interests.

2. Partisan Style

Partisan style varies from government to government, depending on how many parties there are, and how much influence each individual party has.

(1) Nonpartisan

In a nonpartisan system, no official political parties exist, sometimes reflecting legal restrictions on political parties. In nonpartisan elections, each candidate is eligible for office on his or her own merits. In nonpartisan legislatures, there are no typically formal party alignments within the legislature. The administration of George Washington and the first few sessions of the United States Congress were nonpartisan. Washington also warned against political parties during his Farewell Address.

(2) Single Dominant Party

In single-party systems, one political party is legally allowed to hold effective power.

---

① Neil A. McDonald. The Study of Political Parties: Short Stories in Political Science [M]. Montana: Literary Licensing LLC, 2012.

Although minor parties may sometimes be allowed, they are legally required to accept the leadership of the dominant party. This party may not always be identical to the government, although sometimes positions within the party may in fact be more important than positions within the government. North Korea is an example.

In dominant-party systems, opposition parties are allowed, and there may be even a deeply established democratic tradition, but other parties are widely considered to have no real chance of gaining power. Examples of dominant party systems include the People's Action Party in Singapore, the African National Congress in South Africa, the Human Rights Protection Party in Samoa, and the Democratic Party of Socialists of Montenegro in Montenegro.

(3) Two Political Parties

In two-party systems, there are two political parties dominant to such an extent that electoral success under the banner of any other party is almost impossible. One right wing coalition party and one left wing coalition party is the most common ideological breakdown in such a system but in two-party states political parties are traditionally catch-all parties which are ideologically broad and inclusive.

The United States is widely considered a two-party system. Since the birth of the republic a conservative (such as the Republican Party) and a liberal (such as the Democratic Party) party, they have usually been the status quo within American politics, with some exceptions. Third parties often receive little support and are not often the victors in many races.

(4) Multiple Political Parties

Multi-party systems are systems in which more than two parties are represented and elected to public office.

Australia, Canada, Pakistan, India, Ireland, United Kingdom and Norway are examples with two strong parties and additional smaller parties that have also obtained representation. The smaller or "third" parties may form a part of a coalition government together with one of the larger parties or act independently from the other dominant parties.

More commonly, in cases where there are three or more parties, no single party is likely to gain power alone, and parties work with each other to form a coalition government. This has been an emerging trend in the politics of the Republic of Ireland since the 1980s and is almost always the case in Germany on national and state level.

| political party | 政党 |
| nominate | 提名 |

candidate	候选人
electoral campaign	选举运动
platform	纲领
legislature	立法，立法机关
congress	国会，代表大会
coalition	联盟
the Republican Party	共和党
the Democratic Party	民主党
single-party system	一党制
two-party system	两党制
multi-party system	多党制

👤 FURTHER READING

American Party System

To the outside observer, the American party system can be very difficult to understand. Parties appear to be coalitions of many interests. They are organizationally weak and in a constant state of crisis. In contrast, most European political parties have quite vivid public images based on class, regional, religious, linguistic, ethnic or ideological divisions.

While this is an oversimplified characterization of the two types of party system, it remains broadly true that American parties cover a narrower band of the ideological spectrum than do their European counterparts. Historically they have also been much less programmatic, offering their supporters very general and diffuse policy options rather than the more structured and specific policy programmes associated with European parties-although there are signs of some convergence in the two types of party systems in recent years. What is true of almost all party systems is that they are constantly developing and adapting to rapid social and economic changes—a fact which leads so many commentators to attach the label "crisis" to the most recent development or electoral event. The remarkable thing about the American system is that it has always had just two major parties—although not always the same two parties—competing for major offices at any one time. Moreover, these parties have been largely non-ideological and inclusive in style and policy substance, and this in a country constantly being buffeted by the very major social changes that immigration, industrialization and urbanization have brought. So a defining characteristic of both the Democrats and the Republicans is that they have constantly sought to appeal to as wide a spectrum of voters as possible. As such they have been obliged to promise general rather than specific benefits to voters. People's expectations of what government can do have therefore been raised. Once in office, however, party politicians have been obliged to focus on the provision of specific benefits.

Discussion:

➢ What are the differences between American party system and their counterparts in European countries?

➢ Why are the two dominant political parties in U.S. called the catch all parties?

Source: The Changing Role of Political Parties, available at http://www.blackwellpublishing. com/mckay/pdfs/chapter5.pdf.

4.1.2　The Ruling Political Party of People's Republic of China

The People's Republic of China (PRC) is formally a multi-party state under the leadership of the Communist Party of China (CPC) in a United Front similar to the popular fronts of former Communist-era Eastern European countries such as the National Front of Democratic Germany.

Under the one country, two systems scheme, the Special Administrative Regions of Hong Kong and Macau, which were previously colonies of European powers, operate under a different political system to the rest of the PRC. Currently, both Hong Kong and Macau possess multi-party systems.[①]

The central organizations of the CPC are shown in Figure 4.1.

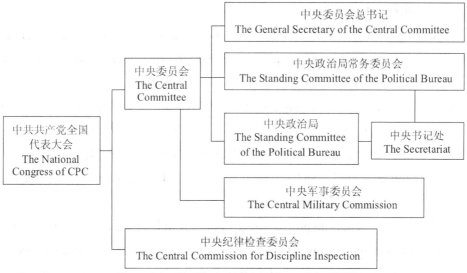

Figure 4.1　The Central organizations of the CPC

---

①　Roger Buckley. Hong Kong: The Road to 1997 [M]. Cambridge: Cambridge University Press, 1997.

1. History of the CPC

The Communist Party of China (CPC), also known as the Chinese Communist Party (CCP), is the founding and the ruling political party of the People's Republic of China (PRC). It is the world's largest political party. The legal power of the Communist Party is enshrined in the PRC constitution and its position as the supreme political authority in the PRC is realized through its control of all state and legislative processes.

The CPC was founded in July 1921. From 1921 to 1949, the CPC led the Chinese people in their arduous armed struggle and finally succeeded in overthrowing the rule of imperialism, feudalism and bureaucrat-capitalism and establishing the PRC. After the founding of the PRC, the CPC led the Chinese people of all ethnic groups in defending the independence and security of the country, successfully completing the transition from new democratic revolution to socialist revolution, carrying out systematic large-scale socialist construction, and achieving economic and cultural progress unparalleled in Chinese history.

After the Third Plenary Session of the Eleventh Party Central Committee at the end of 1978, the country embarked on the biggest change in the history of New China. From 1979, the CPC began to carry out the reform and opening-up policy initiated by Deng Xiaoping. In more than two decades since the initiation of the reform and opening-up, China's economic and social development has been crowned with remarkable success and the country has taken on a new look. This has been the best period since the founding of the PRC in which the Chinese people have reaped the most material benefits.[1]

2. The Nature of the CPC

The CPC is the vanguard of the Chinese working class, the faithful representative of the interests of the Chinese people of all ethnic groups and the core of leadership over the socialist cause of China.

CPC's maximum program of long objective is to realize the Communist social system and the minimum program at present is to build socialism with Chinese characteristics.

The CPC takes Marxism-Leninism, Mao Zedong Thought, Deng Xiaoping Theory, Jiang Zemin's "Three Represents", and Scientific Outlook on Development as the guidance of its actions.

The CPC's basic line for the primary stage of socialism is to unite with and lead the people of all ethnic groups in the endeavor to build China into a prosperous, strong, democratic and highly civilized modern socialist state by taking economic development as the central task,

---

① Xinhuanet.[EB/OL].[2012-03-08].www.xinhuanet.com.

adhering to the Four Cardinal Principles (adherence to the socialist road, the people's democratic dictatorship, the leadership of the Communist Party, and Marxism-Leninism and Mao Zedong Thought), persisting in reform and opening up, developing the spirit of self-reliance and pioneering enterprises with painstaking efforts.[①]

3. Central Organizations of the CPC

(1) The National Party Congress and the Central Committee

The central leading organ of the Party is the National Party Congress and the Central Committee it elects. The Central Committee is accountable to and reports its work to the National Congress.

The National Party Congress, held once every five years, is convened by the Central Committee. If the Central Committee deems it necessary, or over one-third of the provincial-level organizations express a demand, the congress may be held ahead of schedule; and if there is no special situation, its convening shall not be postponed.

The number of delegates to the National Party Congress and the method of election are decided by the Central Committee.

The Central Committee is elected for a term of five years. If the National Congress is held ahead of schedule or deferred, its term of office shall be changed accordingly.

When the National Congress is not in session, the Central Committee implements the resolutions of the National Congress, leads all the work of the Party, and represents the CPC outside the Party.

Members and alternate members of the Central Committee must have a Party standing of at least five years.

The number of members and alternate members of the Central Committee is decided by the National Congress. If posts of members of the Central Committee fall vacant, the vacancies shall be filled in proper order by alternate members in accordance with the number of votes they gain.

A plenary session of the Central Committee is held at least once a year by the Political Bureau of the Central Committee.

(2) The Political Bureau, its Standing Committee, the General Secretary, the Central Military Commission and the Secretariat

The leading organs of the Central Committee are the Political Bureau, its Standing Committee and general secretary of the Central Committee.

The Political Bureau of the Party Central Committee, the Standing Committee of the

---

① People's Daily Online. The Communist party Of China [EB/OL]. [2012-08-12]. http://english.people.com.cn/data/organs/cpc.html.

Political Bureau and the general secretary of the Central Committee are elected by the plenary session of the Central Committee.

The general secretary of the Central Committee must be elected from among members of the Standing Committee of the Political Bureau of the Central Committee.

When the plenum of the Central Committee is not in session, the Political Bureau of the Central Committee and its Standing Committee exercise the functions and powers of the Central Committee.

The general secretary of the Central Committee is responsible for calling sessions of both the Political Bureau of the Central Committee and its Standing Committee, and is in charge of the work of the Secretariat of the Central Committee.

The central military leading organ of the Party is the Central Military Commission.

Members of the Central Military Commission of the Party are decided on by the Central Committee.

The Secretariat of the Central Committee is the administrative body of the Political Bureau and its Standing Committee. Its members are nominated by the Standing Committee of the Political Bureau of the Central Committee and approved by the plenary session of the Central Committee.

Leading bodies and leaders of the Central Committee elected by each Central Committee shall continue to take charge of the day-to-day work of the Party while the next National Congress is in session, until a new central leading body and central leaders are elected by the next Central Committee.[1]

4. Party Members

Members of the CPC are vanguard fighters of the Chinese working class with communist consciousness.

Chinese workers, farmers, soldiers, intellectuals and other revolutionaries at 18 full years of age, who accept the Party Program and Party Constitution, are willing to participate in one Party organization and actively work in it, carry out Party resolutions and pay regular Party dues, may apply for membership in the CPC.

Party members must be admitted through a Party branch according to the principles of admitting members individually only, without exception.

Under special circumstances, the Party Central Committee, and provincial, autonomous regional and municipal Party committees can directly accept Party members.

---

[1] People's Daily Online. The Communist party Of China [EB/OL]. [2012-08-12]. http://english.people.com.cn/data/organs/cpc.html.

An applicant must fill in the form for Party membership and have two full Party members as sponsors. The applicant can become a full Party member only when his or her application has been passed by the Party branch meeting and approved by the Party organization at the next higher level, and only after assessment over a probationary period.

Each Party member, regardless of whether his or her post is high or low, must be entered into a Party branch, group or other specific organization, and must participate in the Party's regular organizational activities.[1]

5. Current Leadership

The incumbent members of the Politburo Standing Committee of the Communist Party of China are:

Xi Jinping: General Secretary of the Central Committee of the CPC, President of the PRC, Chairman of the Central Military Commission.

Li Keqiang: Premier of the State Council of the People's Republic of China

Zhang Dejiang: Chairman of the Standing Committee of the National People's Congress

Yu Zhengsheng: Chairman of the Chinese People's Political Consultative Conference

Liu Yunshan: Secretariat of the CPC Central Committee

Wang Qishan: Secretary of Central Commission for Discipline Inspection

Zhang Gaoli: Vice Premier of the State Council of the People's Republic of China

6. CPC's Leadership of the PRC

CPC's leadership over the country is mainly political, ideological and organizational, as reflected mainly in the following aspects:

First, organize and exercise leadership over the country's legislative and law enforcement activities.

Second, maintain leadership over the armed forces.

Third, provide leadership and manage the work of officials.

Fourth, organize and mobilize the society.

Fifth, give importance to ideological and political work.[2]

Vocabulary

| United Front | 统一战线 |
| one country, two systems | 一国两制 |

---

[1]　People's Daily Online. The Communist party Of China [EB/OL]. [2012-08-12]. http://english.people.com.cn/data/organs/cpc.html.

[2]　People's Daily Online. The Communist party Of China [EB/OL]. [2012-08-12]. http://english.people.com.cn/data/organs/cpc.html.

political system	政治体制
Communist Party of China	中国共产党
ruling political party	执政党
constitution	宪法
supreme political authority	最高政治权威
imperialism	帝国主义
feudalism	封建主义
bureaucrat-capitalism	官僚资本主义
socialist construction	社会主义建设
reform and opening-up	改革开放
socialist cause	社会主义事业
socialism with Chinese characteristics	有中国特色社会主义
Mao Zedong Thought	毛泽东思想
Deng Xiaoping Theory	邓小平理论
Four Cardinal Principles	四项基本原则
people's democratic dictatorship	人民民主专政
delegate	代表
alternate member	候补委员
plenary session	全体会议
General Secretary	总书记
secretariat	书记处
Party Constitution	党章
party member	党员
Party branch	党支部
incumbent	现任的

👥 FURTHER READING

Main Tasks of CPC's Discipline Inspection Commissions

The main tasks of the Party's commissions for discipline inspection at all levels are as follows: to uphold the Constitution and other statutes of the Party, to check up on the implementation of the line, principles, policies and resolutions of the Party and to assist the respective Party committees in improving the Party's style of work and in organizing and coordinating the work against corruption.

The commissions for discipline inspection at all levels shall frequently provide education for Party members on their duty to observe Party discipline and adopt decisions for the upholding of Party discipline, according to the Party Constitution amended and adopted in 2007.

They shall oversee Party members holding leading positions in exercising their power.

They shall examine and deal with relatively important or complicated cases of violation of the Constitution or other statutes of the Party by Party organizations or Party members and decide on or rescind disciplinary measures against Party members involved in such cases.

They shall deal with complaints and appeals made by Party members; and they shall guarantee the rights of Party members.

The commissions for discipline inspection at all levels shall report to the Party committees at the corresponding levels on the results of their handling of cases of special importance or complexity, as well as on the problems encountered. The local commissions for discipline inspection at all levels and primary commissions for discipline inspection shall also present such reports to the higher commissions.

Source: Available at http://www.chinadaily.com.cn/china/2012cpc/2012-11/13/content_15921867.htm

4.1.3   The Registered Minor Parties in People's Republic of China

1. Revolutionary Committee of the Kuomintang

The Revolutionary Committee of the Chinese Kuomintang is one of eight registered minor political parties (in addition to the Communist Party of China) in the People's Republic of China.

It was founded in 1948 by left-wing members who broke with the main Kuomintang (KMT) during the Chinese Civil War, especially those who were against Chiang Kai-shek's policies. The party claims to be the true heir of Sun Yat-sen's legacy. By the end of 2007, it had over 82,000 members.

Among the officially sanctioned political parties of the People's Republic of China, the Revolutionary Committee is seen as "second" in status to the Communist Party of China. Thus, the Revolutionary Committee is allotted the second highest number of seats in the People's Political Consultative Conference (30%).

2. China Democratic League

The China Democratic League was established in 1939 and took its present name in 1944.

In 1997, it adopted a constitution, which stipulated that its program was "to hold high the banner of patriotism and socialism, implement the basic line for the primary stage of socialism, safeguard stability in the society, strengthen services to national unity and strive for the promotion of socialist modernization, establishment and improvement of a market economy, enhancement of political restructuring and socialist spiritual civilization, emancipation and development of productive forces, consolidation and expansion of the united patriotic front and realization of the grand goals of socialism with Chinese characteristics."

The League is mainly made up by middle-level and senior intellectuals in the fields of culture, education, science and technology. As of the end of 2014, the party had a membership of more than 258,000. Of this total, 31.2% were from the field of compulsory education, 23.7% were in higher education, 9% were in science and technology, and 8.6% were in medicine.[1]

3. China Democratic National Construction Association

The China Democratic National Construction Association is one of the eight legally recognized political parties in the People's Republic of China that follow the direction of the Communist Party of China and is a member of the Chinese People's Political Consultative Conference. It was founded in Chongqing in 1945 by the Vocational Education Society, a former member of the China Democratic League.

Members are chiefly entrepreneurs from the manufacturing, financial, or commercial industries in both private and state sectors.

4. Chinese Peasants' and Workers' Democratic Party

The party was one of the founding parties of the China Democratic League. Currently it comprises a membership of 65,000, most of whom work in the fields of public health, culture and education, science and technology.

5. China Zhi Gong Party

The China Zhi Gong Party derives from the overseas Hung Society organization "Hung Society Zhigong Hall", based in San Francisco, USA. This organization was one of the key supporters of Sun Yat-sen in his revolutionary efforts to overthrow the Qing dynasty.

The party was founded in October 1925 in San Francisco. After the People's Republic of China was founded, at the invitation of the CPC, representatives of the CZGP attended the First

---

① 中国民主同盟网站. 中国民主同盟简介[EB/OL]. [2012-09-12]. http://www.dem-league.org.cn/mmgk/jianjie/11796.aspx.

Plenary Session of the CPPCC in 1949. They participated in drawing up the CPPCC Common Program and electing the Central People's Government. Since then, the CZGP has made an important contribution to implementing overseas Chinese policies and strengthening ties with Hong Kong and Macau compatriots as well as overseas Chinese for the reunification of the motherland.

In April 2007, Wan Gang, Deputy Chair of the Zhi Gong Party Central Committee, was appointed Technology Minister of the People's Republic of China. This was the first non-Communist Party ministerial appointment in China since the 1950s.

6. China Association for Promoting Democracy

The China Association for Promoting Democracy (CAPD) was founded in Shanghai on December 30th, 1945. The organization is mainly composed of middle-and high-ranking intellectuals who are engaged in educational and cultural work.

During the Anti-Japanese War (1937-1945), intellectuals in some academic circles became stranded in Shanghai. With the help of the Communist Party of China (CPC), they carried out an unyielding fight against Japanese intruders and the puppet government. After winning the war, they campaigned against civil war and dictatorship to pursue peace and democracy. The intellectuals then decided to establish a political party aimed at "carrying forward democratic spirit and promoting realization of democratic politics in China", forming the basic principles of CAPD.

The original political guidance and allegation of CAPD during the Democratic Revolution (1919-1949) included ending one party dictatorship, returning political power to the people, stopping civil war immediately and protecting people's free rights. After the founding of the PRC in 1949, the party took the Common Program as well as the general principles from the Articles of Association of the National Committee of the CPPCC as its guidelines. CAPD now conducts activities based on the Constitution of China and has helped to formulate the political route of accepting leadership within the CPC. CAPD branches at all levels actively participate in political events and make hard efforts to consolidate the people's political power, build socialism and promote cultural and educational development.[①]

7. Jiusan Society (Literally "September Third Society")

The party's name refers to the date of Chinese victory in the Sino-Japanese War (September 3, 1945).

When it was first established in May 1946, its political stand was to carry on the tradition of

---

① China .org .cn. China Association for Promoting [EB/OL]. [2012-11-08]. http://wiki.china.org.cn/wiki/index.php/China_Association_for_Promoting_Democracy.

democracy and science, oppose the civil war and practice democratic politics.

The party's mission statement is to "lead the nation to power and the people to prosperity", though this must be subordinate to the national interest. The party has a membership of over 68,000 members, mostly high-and medium-level intellectuals in the fields of science, technology, education, culture, and medicine.

8. Taiwan Democratic Self-Government League

The Taiwan Democratic Self-Government League (TSL for short) was founded in Hong Kong on November 12th, 1947. It is composed of public figures from Taiwan as a political alliance of socialist workers and patriots supporting socialism, a political party serving socialism and participating in the political life of the country in full cooperation with the Communist Party of China.

The program of TSL is: by taking the Constitution of the People's Republic of China as the supreme criteria for all of its activities and guided by Deng Xiaoping Theory, to firmly implement the basic line of the Communist Party of China for the initial stage of socialism. Its primary task is to hold high the banner of patriotism and socialism, unite with all of its members and the compatriots in Taiwan they keep in contact with and strive to help accelerate the pace of the reform and opening and socialist modernization, to maintain the political situation of stability and unity, further to perfect socialist democracy and legality and for the realization of "one state, two systems" and the peaceful reunification of the fatherland.[①]

4.1.4　Chinese People's Political Consultative Conference

1. An Overview of CPPCC

The Chinese People's Political Consultative Conference (CPPCC) is an organization of the patriotic United Front of the Chinese people. It is also an important organ for the development of multi-party cooperation and political consultation under the leadership of the CPC, and an important forum for promoting socialist democracy in the Chinese political system. The Communist Party of China, various democratic parties, democrats with no party affiliations, people's organizations and public figures from all walks of life jointly founded the CPPCC shortly before the birth of New China.[②]

2. Members

The present National Committee is composed of members of 34 units, i.e., the CPC, China

---

① China.org.cn. Taiwan Democratic Self-Government League [EB/OL]. [2013-11-08].http://wiki.china.org.cn/wiki/index.php/Taiwan_Democratic_Self-Government_League.

② China.org.cn. [EB/OL]. [2013-03-08]. http://www.china.org.cn/english/archiveen/27750.htm.

Revolutionary Committee of the Kuomintang, China Democratic League, China Democratic National Construction Association, China Association for the Promotion of Democracy, Chinese Peasants' and Workers' Democratic Party, China Zhi Gong Dang, Jiusan Society, Taiwan Democratic Self-government League, public personages without party affiliation, the Communist League of China, All-China Federation of Trade Unions, All-China Federation of Women, All-China Federation of Youth, All-China Federation of Industry and Commerce, China Association of Science and Technology, All-China Friendship Federation of Taiwan Compatriots, All-China Federation of Returned Overseas Chinese, representatives from the cultural and art circles, the fields of science, technology, social science, economics, agriculture, education, physical culture, journalism, publishing, medicine, social welfare, religion, and among ethnic minorities and the circle of friendship with foreign countries, specially invited people from Hong Kong, Macao and other specially invited personage. The present National Committee has 2,196 members, among whom 290 are members of the Standing Committee.

The eight non-Communist parties are those established before the founding of the People's Republic of China in 1949, which were then dedicated to the realization of a bourgeois republic in China and supported the CPC in the latter's effort of overthrowing the rule of the Kuomintang. They are independent in organization and enjoy political freedom, organizational independence and legal equality under the Constitution.[①]

3. Functions

The major function of the CPPCC is to conduct political consultation and exercise democratic supervision, organize its members from various non-Communist political parties, mass organizations and public personages from all walks of life to take part in the discussion and management of state affairs.[②]

4. Organizational Principles

All political parties and mass organizations who support the charter of the CPPCC may sit on the National Committee or local committees, upon agreement by the National Committee or local committees after deliberation. Individuals, invited by the National Committee or the standing committees of local committees, may also become members of the National Committee or local committees.

Local committees have the obligation to observe and carry out national decisions adopted by the National Committee and lower level committees have the obligation to observe and carry out regional decisions adopted by the higher level committees.

---

① China.org.cn. [EB/OL]. [2013-05-30]. http://www.china.org.cn/english/chuangye/55437.htm.

② China.org.cn. [EB/OL]. [2013-05-30]. http://www.china.org.cn/english/chuangye/55437.htm.

All units and individuals taking part in the CPPCC have the right to take part in political consultation, democratic supervision, discussion and management of state affairs, through the meetings, organization and activities of the CPPCC.

Decisions of the plenary session and Standing Committee of the National Committee and local committees will become effective only after the majority of the committee members have voted in their favor. All participating units and individuals have the obligation to observe and carry out the decisions. In case of different opinions, they may state their reservation on the precondition of firmly implementing them.

⚙ Vocabulary

left-wing member	左翼成员
Chinese Civil War	中国人民解放战争
seat	席位
stipulate	规定
patriotism	爱国主义
the primary stage of socialism	社会主义初级阶段
implement	执行、实施
socialist modernization	社会主义现代化
market economy	市场经济
socialist spiritual civilization	社会主义精神文明
emancipation	解放、释放
productive forces	生产力
entrepreneur	企业家
overthrow	推翻、倾覆
Qing dynasty	清朝
plenary session	全体会议
compatriot	同胞、同国人
draw up	草拟、起草
appointment	任命
intellectual	知识分子
dictatorship	专政、独裁
allegation	主张
formulate	制定
consolidate	巩固、加强

alliance	联盟、联合
one state, two systems	一国两制
political consultation	政治协商
affiliation	从属关系
bourgeois	资产阶级的
mass organization	群众组织

👤≡ FURTHER READING

Multi-party Cooperation and the Political Consultative System

Apart from the Communist Party of China (CPC), there are eight democratic parties in China. Multi-party cooperation and political consultation under the leadership of the CPC is the basic political system in China.

The multi-party cooperation system in China differs from the single-party system practiced in some socialist countries and also fundamentally varies from the multi-party or two-party system in some capitalist countries. It has its own prominent characteristics.

First, the CPC is the sole party exercising political leadership in this system of multi-party cooperation. Organizationally independent, the CPC and the democratic parties are totally equal under the Constitution, but politically, the latter are subject to the leadership of the former. The leading role of the CPC has been generally accepted by various parties and people across the country after decades of practice. The CPC's leadership over other parties features political leadership focusing on political principles, political orientation and major policy decisions.

Second, under the leadership of the CPC, the democratic parties maintain close cooperative ties with the CPC politically. Though a ruling party, the CPC does not arrogate political power to itself. In a general sense, the democratic parties exist neither as political opposition forces nor as parties out of office that pit their wits against the ruling party like those in multi-party countries. The relationship between these parties and the CPC is based on political cooperation rather than political competition aimed at assuming State power. In this cooperative political relationship, the CPC is at the helm of the State while the other parties jointly participate in the administration of State affairs.

Third, a consensus on socialism is the political foundation of the multi-party cooperation system. Since its founding, the CPC has consistently taken socialism (communism) as the objective it strives toward. Through years of struggle and practice, the other parties have gradually forsaken the old democratic republicanism and accepted the socialist economic system and the democratic republic. This consensus reached by both the CPC and these democratic parties has formed a solid political foundation for multi-party cooperation.

Fourth, the guiding principle of multi-party cooperation is long-term coexistence and mutual supervision, treating each other with full sincerity and sharing weal and woe. This is the ideological foundation of multi-party cooperation. It helps promote mutual supervision and political democracy, and also stabilizes and strengthens the multi-party political system.

Finally, forms of cooperation between the CPC and other parties are diverse. For instance, members of the democratic parties are selected and appointed to leading posts in the State power structure. Their representatives are invited to attend the CPC congress as non-voting delegates and their opinions are solicited through various symposiums and cordial discussions. The Chinese People's Political Consultative Conference (CPPCC) is the most important organization of all those serving as a channel and arena for cooperation between the CPC and other parties.

By the end of 2003, China's eight non-Communist parties had more than 600,000 members.

Statistics show more than 140,000 of those members had been elected as deputies to people's congresses at various levels. More than 8,000 of them held leading posts in governmental and judicial departments above county-level.

Discussion:

➤ Why does the multi-party cooperation system in China differ from the single-party system practiced in some socialist countries and also fundamentally vary from the multi-party or two-party system in some capitalist countries?

➤ What is the relationship between the democratic parties and the CPC based on?

➤ What is the political foundation of the multi-party cooperation system in China?

➤ What is the ideological foundation of multi-party cooperation in China?

Source: available at http://english.people.com.cn/92824/92845/92869/6441455.html.

State Organ

4.2.1 An Overview of State Organ

The organs of state include any of the four primary divisions of a state's sovereignty (namely, the executive, the legislature, the judiciary and the military). The Constitution of the People's Republic of China (PRC) stipulates that the country's central state organs comprise six components: the National People's Congress (NPC), the Presidency of the PRC, the State Council, the Central Military Commission, the Supreme People's Court and the Supreme People's Procuratorate (see Figure 4.2).

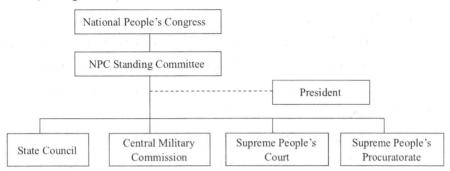

Figure 4.2   The central state organs of the People's Republic of China

The five organs—the Presidency of the PRC, the State Council, the Central Military Commission, the Supreme People's Court and the Supreme People's Procuratorate—are formed by the NPC, and are responsible to the NPC and its Standing Committee.

⚙ Vocabulary

organs of state	国家机关
presidency	总统职位
State Council	国务院
supreme	最高的，至高的
executive	行政的，执行的
legislature	立法机关
judiciary	司法机关
procuratorate	检察机关

4.2.2 Legislative Branch

1. National People's Congress

The people's congress system, which is practiced at every level, is China's fundamental political system. The Constitution of the PRC provides that state power belongs to the people. The National People's Congress (abbreviated NPC) and local people's congresses at all levels, formed through democratic elections, are organs representing the people in exercising state power.

The NPC is the highest organ of state power, with the First NPC in 1954 marking the establishment of the system. The NPC is held in the Great Hall of the People, Beijing, capital of the People's Republic of China. It is the largest parliament in the world. The NPC gathers each year along with the People's Political Consultative Conference (CPPCC) whose members represent various defined groups of society. NPC and CPPCC together are often called the Lianghui (Two Meetings), making important national level political decisions.

(1) Election and Membership

The NPC consists of deputies elected by 31 provinces, autonomous regions and municipalities directly under the Central Government, special administrative regions and the Chinese People's Liberation Army. Every ethnic minority has an appropriate number of representatives in the NPC.

The NPC consists of about 3,000 delegates. Delegates to the National People's Congress are elected for five-year terms via a multi-tiered representative electoral system. Delegates are elected by the provincial people's assemblies, who in turn are elected by lower level assemblies, and so on through a series of tiers to the local people's assemblies which are directly elected by the electorate.

There is a limit on the number of candidates in proportion to the number of seats available. At the national level, for example, a maximum of 110 candidates are allowed per 100 seats; at the provincial level, this ratio is 120 candidates per 100 seats. This ratio increases for each lower level of people's assemblies, until the lowest level, the village level, has no limit on the number of candidates for each seat. However, the Congress website says "In an indirect election, the number of candidates should exceed the number to be elected by 20% to 50%."

(2) Powers and Duties

The NPC exercises the legislative power of the state, including amending and supervising the enforcement of the Constitution and enacting and amending basic laws and laws governing other matters. It also enjoys the power to elect, decide on and remove leaders and members of the highest state organs, oversee the government, and examine and decide on major state issues in line with the Constitution and other state laws. The administrative, judicial, procuratorial, military and other organs of the state are created by the organ of state power, and are therefore supervised by and responsible to it.[①]

2. Standing Committee of the National People's Congress

The NPC Standing Committee is the permanent body of the NPC. It consists of Chairman, Vice Chairmen, the Secretary-General and other members. They are all elected by the NPC from

---

① 中华人民共和国外交部. [EB/OL]. [2013-04-12]. http://www.chinese-embassy.org.za/eng/zgjj/ssysz/spp/t244841. htm.

among its deputies for a term of five years, the same term as an NPC. The Standing Committee continues to function until a new Standing Committee is elected by the next NPC.

Nobody on the NPC Standing Committee shall hold office in any of the administrative, judicial or procuratorial organs of the state. The Chairman and Vice Chairmen of the Standing Committee shall serve no more than two consecutive terms. The following persons successively served as Chairman of the NPC Standing Committee since the establishment of the NPC: Liu Shaoqi, Zhu De, Ye Jianying, Peng Zhen, Wan Li, Qiao Shi and Li Peng. The Chairman of the Standing Committee of the 12th NPC is Zhang Dejiang.

The Chairman of the NPC Standing Committee directs the work of the Standing Committee. The Vice Chairmen and the Secretary-General assist the Chairman in his work. The Chairman, Vice Chairmen and Secretary-General constitute the Chairmen's Council, which handles the important day-to-day work of the Standing Committee.

The NPC Standing Committee normally meets once every two months. It may hold interim meetings when there is a special need. It is responsible to the NPC and reports to it on its work. The NPC has the power to alter or annul inappropriate decisions of its Standing Committee and to remove its members from office.[1]

⚙ Vocabulary

political system	政治制度
state power	国家权力
parliament	议会、国会
deputy	代表
autonomous region	自治区
municipality	自治市、直辖市
ethnic minority	少数民族
delegate	代表
electorate	选民、选区
candidate	候选人
indirect election	间接选举
legislative power	立法权
amend	修改、修正
administrative	行政的、管理的
judicial	司法的、法院的

---

① 中国人大网. [EB/OL]. [2012-05-17]. http://www.npc.gov.cn/englishnpc/Organization/node_2847.htm.

procuratorial	代理人的、代诉的
enforcement	执行、实施
enact	颁布、制定法律
Vice Chairman	副主席
Secretary-General	秘书长
consecutive terms	连任

👤 FURTHER READING

The United States Senate

The United States Senate is the upper house of the bicameral legislature of the United States, and together with the United States House of Representatives comprises the United States Congress. The composition and powers of the Senate are established in Article One of the U.S. Constitution.

Each U.S. state is represented by two senators, regardless of population. Senators serve staggered six-year terms. The chamber of the United States Senate is located in the north wing of the Capitol, in Washington, D.C., the national capital. The House of Representatives convenes in the south wing of the same building.

The Senate has several exclusive powers not granted to the House, including consenting to treaties as a precondition to their ratification and consenting or confirming appointments of Cabinet secretaries, federal judges, other federal executive officials, military officers, regulatory officials, ambassadors, and other federal uniformed officers, as well as trial of federal officials impeached by the House. The Senate is both a more deliberative and more prestigious body than the House of Representatives, due to its longer terms, smaller size, and statewide constituencies, which historically led to a more collegial and less partisan atmosphere. The Senate is sometimes called the "world's greatest deliberative body."

Discussion:

➤ How many senators is each U.S. state represented by?

➤ Does the size of population make a difference in the number of senators in each state?

➤ What exclusive powers does the Senate have?

Source: available at http://en.wikipedia.org/wiki/United_States_Senate.

4.2.3 The Presidency

The President of the People's Republic of China (formerly called Chairman of the People's Republic of China from 1954 to 1975), is the head of state of the PRC and the supreme representative of China both internally and externally. The presidency is an independent State apparatus and an important component of the State organs.

Citizens of the PRC who have the right to vote and stand for election and have reached the age of 45 are eligible for election as president of the PRC.

The president of the PRC is nominated by the Presidium of the NPC and elected by the NPC by voting based on a single candidate. The NPC has the power to remove from office the president of the PRC.

The president of the PRC is elected for a term of five years and shall serve no more than two consecutive terms.

In the event that the office of the president of the PRC falls vacant, the vice president succeeds to the office of the president. In the event that the office of the vice president of the PRC falls vacant, the NPC shall elect a new vice president to fill the vacancy. In the event that the offices of both the president and the vice president of the PRC fall vacant, the NPC shall elect a new president and a new vice president. Prior to such election, the chairman of the NPC Standing Committee shall temporarily act as the president of the PRC.[1]

In combination with the NPC Standing Committee, the president of the PRC exercises his or her functions and powers as the head of state. The president, in pursuance of decisions of the NPC or its Standing Committee, promulgates laws, appoints and removes members of the State Council, issues orders, receives foreign diplomatic representatives on behalf of the PRC, dispatches and recalls plenipotentiary representatives abroad, and ratifies and abrogates treaties and important agreements reached with foreign states.[2]

The term Zhuxi refers to the chairman in a committee, and was translated as such prior to the 1982 constitution (as in Chairman Mao Zedong, although Mao's title refers primarily to the position of Party Chairman which he held from 1943 until his death in 1976). The official translation switched to President after 1982 in conformity with Western terminology. However, Zhuxi stayed in Chinese, and in other contexts still corresponds to chairman in English. Meanwhile, the translation of English term President as the head of other states remained Zongtong, causing a bit of confusion with regard to usage.

 **Vocabulary**

| president | 总统，主席 |
| head of state | 国家元首 |

---

① 中华人民共和国外交部. [EB/OL]. [2012-08-12]. http://np.china-embassy.org/eng/ChinaABC/zz/t167465.htm.

② China .org .cn. [EB/OL]. [2013-07-20]. http://www.china.org.cn/english/features/38121.htm.

presidency	总统职位
eligible	合格的、有资格当选的
nominate	提名
presidium	主席团
vacant	空缺的
succeed to	继承、继任
in pursuance of	根据、按照
promulgate	颁布
diplomatic	外交的
dispatch	派遣、分派
plenipotentiary	全权代表、全权大使
ratify	批准、认可
abrogate	废除、废止
in conformity with	符合、遵照

👤≣ FURTHER READING

Thomas Jefferson

In the thick of party conflict in 1800, Thomas Jefferson wrote in a private letter, "I have sworn upon the altar of God eternal hostility against every form of tyranny over the mind of man."

This powerful advocate of liberty was born in 1743 in Albemarle County, Virginia, inheriting from his father, a planter and surveyor, some 5,000 acres of land, and from his mother, a Randolph, high social standing. He studied at the College of William and Mary, then read law. In 1772 he married Martha Wayles Skelton, a widow, and took her to live in his partly constructed mountaintop home, Monticello.

Freckled and sandy-haired, rather tall and awkward, Jefferson was eloquent as a correspondent, but he was no public speaker. In the Virginia House of Burgesses and the Continental Congress, he contributed his pen rather than his voice to the patriot cause. As the "silent member" of the Congress, Jefferson, at 33, drafted the Declaration of Independence. In years following he labored to make its words a reality in Virginia. Most notably, he wrote a bill establishing religious freedom, enacted in 1786.

Jefferson succeeded Benjamin Franklin as minister to France in 1785. His sympathy for the French Revolution led him into conflict with Alexander Hamilton when Jefferson was Secretary of State in President Washington's Cabinet. He resigned in 1793.

Sharp political conflict developed, and two separate parties, the Federalists and the Democratic-Republicans, began to form. Jefferson gradually assumed leadership of the Republicans, who sympathized with the revolutionary cause in France. Attacking Federalist policies, he opposed a strong centralized Government and championed the rights of states.

As a reluctant candidate for President in 1796, Jefferson came within three votes of election. Through a flaw in the Constitution, he became Vice President, although an opponent of President Adams. In 1800 the defect caused a more serious problem. Republican electors, attempting to name both a President and a Vice President from their own party, cast a tie vote between Jefferson and Aaron Burr. The House of Representatives settled the tie. Hamilton, disliking both Jefferson and Burr, nevertheless urged Jefferson's election.

When Jefferson assumed the Presidency, the crisis in France had passed. He slashed Army and Navy expenditures, cut the budget, eliminated the tax on whiskey so unpopular in the West, yet reduced the national debt by a third. He also sent a naval squadron to fight the Barbary pirates, who were harassing American commerce in the Mediterranean. Further, although the Constitution made no provision for the acquisition of new land, Jefferson suppressed his qualms over constitutionality when he had the opportunity to acquire the Louisiana Territory from Napoleon in 1803.

During Jefferson's second term, he was increasingly preoccupied with keeping the Nation from involvement in the Napoleonic wars, though both England and France interfered with the neutral rights of American merchantmen. Jefferson's attempted solution, an embargo upon American shipping, worked badly and was unpopular.

Jefferson retired to Monticello to ponder such projects as his grand designs for the University of Virginia. A French nobleman observed that he had placed his house and his mind "on an elevated situation, from which he might contemplate the universe."

He died on July 4th, 1826.

Discussion:

➢ When did Thomas Jefferson draft the Declaration of Independence?

➢ What led Thomas Jefferson into the conflict with Alexander Hamilton?

➢ What did Jefferson do after he assumed the Presidency?

Source: Michael Beschloss and Hugh Sidey (2009). The Presidents of the United States of America. The White House Historical Association. Available at http://www.whitehouse.gov/about/presidents/thomasjefferson.

4.2.4 Executive Branch

The executive branch of the People's Republic of China includes the central and local executive organs. The central executive organ refers to the Central Government, known as the State Council. Local executive organs are local people's governments at four levels: the provinces (autonomous regions and centrally administered municipalities), cities and prefectures, counties and townships.[①]

1. The State Council

The State Council of the People's Republic of China, namely the Central People's Government, is the highest executive organ of State power, as well as the highest organ of State administration. The State Council is composed of a premier, vice-premiers, State councilors, ministers in charge of ministries and commissions, the auditor-general and the secretary-general. The premier of the State Council is nominated by the president, reviewed by the NPC, and appointed and removed by the president. Other members of the State Council are nominated by the premier, reviewed by the NPC or its Standing Committee, and appointed and removed by the president. In the State Council, a single term of each office is five years, and incumbents cannot be reappointed after two successive terms.

The State Council follows the system of premier responsibility in work while various ministries and commissions under the State Council follow the system of ministerial responsibility. In dealing with foreign affairs, State councilors can conduct important activities on behalf of the premier after being entrusted by the premier of the State Council. The auditor-general is the head of the State Auditing Administration, in charge of auditing and supervising State finances. The secretary-general, under the premier, is responsible for the day-to-day work of the State Council and is in charge of the general office of the State Council.

The State Council is responsible for carrying out the principles and policies of the Communist Party of China as well as the regulations and laws adopted by the NPC, and dealing with such affairs as China's internal politics, diplomacy, national defense, finance, economy, culture and education.

Under the current Constitution, the State Council exercises the power of administrative legislation, the power to submit proposals, the power of administrative leadership, the power of economic management, the power of diplomatic administration, the power of social

---

① Wei, Yanming. The Relationship between Court, Congress and Government in China - From State Structure Perspective [EB/OL]. [2012-08-09]. http://www.stf.jus.br/repositorio/cms/portalStfInternacional/portalStfCooperacao_pt_br/anexo/Chinas_PresentationThe_Relationship_between.pdf.

administration, and other powers granted by the NPC and its Standing Committee.[①]

Each ministry supervises one sector. Commissions outrank ministries and set policies for and coordinate the related activities of different administrative organs. Offices deal with matters of ongoing concern. Bureaus and administrations rank below ministries.

1) Ministries and Commissions under the State Council

(1) Ministry of Foreign Affairs

The Ministry of Foreign Affairs (MOFA) of the People's Republic of China is an executive agency responsible for foreign relations between the People's Republic of China and other countries in the world. The agency is led by the Foreign Minister. The agency has its headquarters in Chaoyang District, Beijing. The agency is responsible for formulating foreign policies, decisions, foreign affairs documents, and statements in regards to the PRC. It also negotiates and signs bilateral and multilateral foreign treaties and agreements. The agency also dispatches foreign affairs representatives to other countries.

It represents P. R. China's interest in United Nations conferences, inter-governmental meetings, and the activities of international organizations. MOFA advises the central government in formulating diplomatic strategies, guidelines, and policies.

(2) Ministry of National Defense

The Ministry of National Defense (MND) was set up according to a decision adopted by the 1st Session of the 1st National People's Congress in 1954. In contrast to practice in other nations, the MND does not exercise command authority over the People's Liberation Army (PLA), which is instead subordinate to the Central Military Commission (CMC). Instead, the MND itself only serves as liaison body representing the CMC and PLA when dealing with foreign militaries in military exchange and cooperation.

Its official responsibilities had been to exercise unified administration over the development of the armed forces of the country such as recruitment, organization, equipment, training, scientific military research of the PLA and the ranking and remuneration of the officers and servicemen. However, in reality these responsibilities are carried out by the four General Headquarters of the PLA, which are under the control of the CMC.

(3) National Development and Reform Commission

The National Development and Reform Commission (NDRC) formerly State Planning Commission and State Development Planning Commission, is a macroeconomic management agency under the Chinese State Council, which has broad administrative and planning control

---

① The Chinese Government. [EB/OL]. [2012-12-09]. http://english.gov.cn/2005-08/05/content_20763.htm.

over the Chinese economy.

The NDRC's functions are to study and formulate policies for economic and social development, to maintain the balance of economic development, and to guide restructuring of China's economic system. The NDRC has twenty-six functional departments/bureaus/offices with an authorized staff size of 890 civil servants.

(4) Ministry of Education

The Ministry of Education of the People's Republic of China, formerly Ministry of Education, Central People's Government from 1949 to 1954, State Education Commission from 1985 to 1998, is headquartered in Beijing. After the restructure of the State Council in 1998, the State Education Commission became the Ministry of Education. It is the agency of the State Council which regulates all aspects of the educational system in mainland China. This includes compulsory basic education, vocational education and tertiary education.

The ministry certifies teachers, standardizes curriculum and textbooks, establishes standards and generally monitors the entire education system in an effort to "modernize China through education". It stresses technical education over more esoteric subjects.

(5) Ministry of Science and Technology

The Ministry of Science and Technology (MOST), formerly as State Science and Technology Commission, is a ministry of the government of the People's Republic of China which coordinates science and technology activities in the country.

MOST takes the lead in drawing up science and technology (S&T) development plans and policies, drafting related laws, regulations and department rules, and guaranteeing the implementation. It is responsible for drafting the National Basic Research Program, the National High-tech R&D Program and the S&T Enabling Program.[①]

(6) Ministry of Industry and Information Technology

The Ministry of Industry and Information Technology established in March 2008, is the state agency of the People's Republic of China responsible for regulation and development of the postal service, Internet, wireless, broadcasting, communications, production of electronic and information goods, software industry and the promotion of the national knowledge economy.[②]

The Ministry of Industry and Information Technology is not responsible for the regulation of content for the media industry. This is administered by the State Administration of Radio, Film and Television. The responsibility for regulating the non electronic communications industry in

---

① The Chinese Government. [EB/OL]. [2012-12-09]. http://www.most.gov.cn/eng/organization/Mission/index.htm.

② PRC Govt Website. The Chinese Government [EB/OL]. [2012-12-09]. http://www.gov.cn/english//2005-10/02/ content_74176.htm.

China falls on the General Administration of Press and Publication.

(7) State Ethnic Affairs Commission

The State Ethnic Affairs Commission is a commission under the State Council in charge of the work of all ethnic minorities of China. As one of the ministries at the central government administration level, it was initially set up after the foundation of the People's Republic of China in 1949.

The major functions of the State Ethnic Affairs Commission are as follow: to implement principles and policies of the CPC Central Committee and the State Council on ethnic issues; to organize studies on ethnic theories, ethnic policies and major issues in regard to ethnic initiatives; to promote the implementation of ethnic policies in fields pertaining to economic and social development, and to ensure coordination between such polices; to draft out laws, regulations, and policy decisions on ethnic issues, and to supervise their implementation; to safeguard the legal rights and interests of ethnic minority groups; to propose suggestions on the coordination of ethnic relations; to study and analyze issues regarding economic development and social programs among ethnic minority groups and areas, and offer suggestions for special policies, and so on.[1]

(8) Ministry of Public Security

The Ministry of Public Security (MPS) is the principal police and security authority of the mainland of the People's Republic of China and the government agency that exercises oversight over and is ultimately responsible for day-to-day law enforcement. It is headed by the Minister of Public Security. Prior to 1954, it was known as the Central Ministry of Public Security.

As the main domestic security agency in the People's Republic of China, the MPS is the equivalent of the National Police Agency in Japan or national police in other countries. It also controls and administers the People's Armed Police. Since the creation of the Ministry of State Security in 1983, the MPS has lost much authority and has not undertaken paramilitary functions, which are now within the province of the People's Armed Police, nor has it generally conduct domestic intelligence which since 1983 has been a primary responsibility of the Ministry of State Security.[2]

(9) Ministry of State Security

The Ministry of State Security (MSS) is the Chinese Government's intelligence arm, responsible for foreign intelligence and counterintelligence operations. Besides the MSS, the People's Liberation Army (PLA), General Staff Second and Third Departments also engage

---

① Sinoperi. [EB/OL]. [2012-12-09]. http://www.sinoperi.com/qiushi/Relatedreadings-Details.aspx?id=55.

② Creat account. Ministry of Public Security of the People's Republic of China [EB/OL]. [2012-09-09]. http://en.wikipedia.org/wiki/Ministry_of_Public_Security_of_the_People%27s_Republic_of_China.

in military intelligence and counterintelligence operations. The People's Republic of China's intelligence infrastructure is the third largest one after the United States and Russia. The MSS is responsible to the premier and state council.

In June 1983 the National People's Congress, perceiving a growing threat of subversion and sabotage, established the Ministry of State Security under the State Council. The new ministry was in charged of ensuring "the security of the state through effective measures against enemy agents, spies, and counterrevolutionary activities designed to sabotage or overthrow China's socialist system." At its inception, the ministry pledged to abide by the state constitution and the law and called upon the citizenry for their cooperation, reminding them of their constitutional obligations to "keep state secrets" and "safeguard the security" of the country.[①]

(10) Ministry of Supervision

The Ministry of Supervision is responsible for maintaining an efficient, disciplined, clean and honest government, and educating public servants about their duty and discipline.

The Ministry of Supervision was established as the People's Supervisory Commission in October 1949 after the founding of the People's Republic of China. It took on the present name Ministry of Supervision in September 1954. The ministry was abolished in April 1959 and was reestablished in July 1987 by the Sixth National People's Congress. This led to successive local supervisory authorities being created at the provincial and local levels. On May 9th, 1997, the Ministry of Supervision was legislated to enforce the Law of the People's Republic of China on Administration Supervision of the government agencies.[②]

(11) Ministry of Civil Affairs

The Ministry of Civil Affairs of the People's Republic of China is a ministry under the jurisdiction of the State Council of the People's Republic of China, responsible for social and administrative affairs. It was founded in May 1978. Its precedent was the Ministry of Internal Affairs of the People's Republic of China.

(12) Ministry of Justice

The Ministry of Justice is a ministry of the Chinese central government which is responsible for legal affairs. The range of responsibilities include judicial process, drafting legislation, developing legal framework, participating in national and international treaties, prosecution and sentencing. The ministry also ensures in the maintenance and improvement of China's system of law and justice and its national security.

The executive head of the ministry is the Justice Minister. This position is equivalent to

---

① Global Security org. [EB/OL]. [2013-10-09]. http://www.globalsecurity.org/intell/world/china/mss.htm.

② The Chinese Government. [EB/OL]. [2014-12-09]. http://english.gov.cn//2005-10/03/content_74320.htm.

Attorney General in other countries.①

(13) Ministry of Finance

The Ministry of Finance is the national executive agency of the Central People's Government which administers macroeconomic policies and the national annual budget. It also handles fiscal policy, economic regulations and government expenditure for the state.

The ministry also records and publishes annual macroeconomic data on China's economy. This includes information such as previous economic growth rates in China, central government debt and many other indicators regarding the Chinese economy.

The Ministry of Finance's remit is smaller than its counterparts in many other states. Macroeconomic management is primarily handled by the National Development and Reform Commission (NDRC). State-owned industries are the responsibility of the State-owned Assets Supervision and Administration Commission, and there are separate regulators for banking, insurance and securities. It either does not handle regulation of the money markets or interest rates. These, together with other aspects of monetary policy, are governed by the People's Bank of China (PBC), China's central bank. The Ministry, NDRC and PBC are equal in status, with their political heads all sitting on the State Council.②

(14) Ministry of Human Resources and Social Security

The Ministry of Human Resources and Social Security (MOHRSS) is a ministry under the State Council which is responsible for national labor policies, standards, regulations and managing the national social security. This includes labor force management, labor relationship readjustment, social insurance management and legal construction of labor.③

The ministry is created from the former Ministry of Personnel and Ministry of Labor and Social Security. The MOHRSS has responsibility for managing the employment market in mainland China. Due to the financial crisis of 2008, the ministry has recommended companies to prevent and control large staff reduction. It also required other government agencies to provide assistance to labor-intensive industries and enterprises to create more employment. MOHRSS stressed that priority be given to migrant workers, laid-off workers, poor people and graduates from universities and colleges in offering jobs.

(15) Ministry of Land and Resources

The Ministry of Land and Resources is a ministry under the jurisdiction of the State Council

---

① 法制网. [EB/OL]. [2013-08-09]. http://www.legalinfo.gov.cn/english/AboutMOJ/AboutMOJ.htm.

② Ministry of Finance of the People's Republic of China [EB/OL]. [2014-12-09]. http://en.wikipedia.org/wiki/Ministry_of_Finance_of_the_People%27s_Republic_of_China.

③ The Chinese Government. [EB/OL]. [2014-08-09]. http://english.gov.cn/2005-10/02/content_74185.htm.

of China. It is responsible for the regulation, management, preservation and exploitation of natural resources, such as land, mines and oceans.

The Ministry of Land and Resources was set up on April 8th, 1998 in the restructuring of the State Council. On the basis of the Scheme for the Organizational Reform of the State Council approved by the first meeting of the 9th NPC and the Notice of the Organizational Setup issued by the State Council, the former Ministry of Geology and Mineral Resources, State Land Administration, State Oceanic Administration and State Bureau of Surveying and Mapping merged to form the Ministry of Land and Resources. The State Administration of National Oceans and the State Bureau of Surveying and Mapping have remained existing as departments under the jurisdiction of the newly formed Ministry.[①]

(16) Ministry of Environmental Protection

The Ministry of Environmental Protection, formerly State Environmental Protection Administration (SEPA), is a cabinet-level ministry in the executive branch of the Chinese Government. It replaced the SEPA during the March 2008 National People's Congress sessions in Beijing.

The Ministry is the nation's environmental protection department in charge of protecting China's air, water, and land from pollution and contamination. Directly under the State Council, it is empowered and required by law to implement environmental policies and enforce environmental laws and regulations. Complementing its regulatory role, it funds and organizes research and development. In addition, it also serves as China's nuclear safety agency.[②]

(17) Ministry of Housing and Urban-Rural Development

The Ministry of Housing and Urban-Rural Development is a Central Government agency under the State Council, responsible for drafting policies, laws, and development plans related to city, village, and town planning and construction, the building industry, and municipal jobs.

It was created from the older Ministry of Construction in the 2007-2008 round of reorganization of the State Council.

(18) Ministry of Transport

The Ministry of Transport is the government agency responsible for road, air and water transportation regulations. However, it is not in charge of the conventional railway transportation, which is administrated by the Ministry of Railways.

---

① www.gov.cn. The Establishment of the Ministry of Land and Resources [EB/OL]. [2013-10-09]. http://www.mlr. gov.cn/mlrenglish/about/history/.

② 中华人民共和国环境保护部. [EB/OL]. [2014-08-13]. http://english.mep.gov.cn/# http://en.wikipedia.org/wiki/ Ministry_of_Environmental_Protection_of_the_People%27s_Republic_of_China.

In early March 2008, the National People's Congress announced the creation of the super ministry for road, air and water transport. The Ministry of Communications, Civil Aviation Administration and the State Postal Bureau are merged into the new Ministry of Transport.

The Ministry of Transport has several agencies reporting to it. They are the Civil Aviation Administration of China, State Post Bureau which is synonymous with China Post, China Maritime Safety Administration (a Coast Guard type agency).

(19) Ministry of Water Resources

The Ministry of Water Resources is a branch of the State Council in charge of the administration of water. The ministry has such tasks as to formulate policies, regulations, development strategies, long and medium-term plans of water conservation, draft related laws, regulations and supervise their implementation, and exercise unified management of water resources.[1]

There are several authorities responsible for water management in China. Water pollution is the responsibility of the environmental authorities, but the water itself is managed by the Ministry of Water Resources. Sewage is administered by the Ministry of Housing and Urban-Rural Development, but groundwater falls within the realm of the Ministry of Land and Resources.[2]

(20) Ministry of Agriculture

The Ministry of Agriculture is an executive state agency within the government of the People's Republic of China. It is in charge of rural areas and rural economic development.

Its major responsibilities are to study and formulate development strategies, long- and medium-term development plans for agriculture and rural economy and organize the implementation of such strategies and plans, study and draw up industrial policies for agriculture, take care of the drafting of various agricultural laws and regulations, study and propose opinions on deepening economic restructuring of the rural economy; represent the state to exercise the rights of inspection, administration of the fishery industry and the supervision and management of fishing harbors, draft laws and regulations on animal and plant disease prevention and inspection, organize and supervise disease prevention and inspection of animals and plants in the country, conduct inter-governmental matters concerning agriculture, organize international economic and technological exchange and cooperation, and undertake the routine work of the State Council's

---

① 　China.org.cn. Ministry of Water Resources [EB/OL]. [2013-09-13]. http://wiki.china.org.cn/wiki/index.php/Ministry_of_Water_Resources.

② 　Xiangcong Ma. China's Environmental Governance. [EB/OL]. [2013-10-23]. http://www.chinadialogue.net/article/show/single/en/789-China-s-environmental-governance.

Leading Group for Poverty Relief and Development.①

(21) Ministry of Commerce

The Ministry of Commerce, formerly Ministry of Foreign Trade and Economic Co-operation, is an executive agency of the State Council of China.

In charge of domestic and international trade and international economic cooperation, the Ministry of Commerce has such major responsibilities as to study and formulate policies and regulations for standardizing market operation and circulation order, promote the establishment and improvement of the market system, deepen the reform of the circulation system, monitor and analyze market operation and the situation of commodity supply and demand, conduct international economic operation, coordinate anti-dumping, anti-subsidy matters and investigate the harm such acts have brought to industries.②

(22) Ministry of Culture

The Ministry of Culture is a ministry of the government of the People's Republic of China which is responsible for culture policy and activities in the country.

The ministry has such major responsibilities as to study and formulate policies, guidelines and regulations on culture and art and supervise their implementation, study and map out development strategies and plans of cultural undertakings, provide guidance to the reform of the cultural system, take charge of literary and art undertakings, offer guidance to artistic creation, and production, give assistance to representative, demonstrative and experimental artistic forms, take charge of overall management of major national cultural activities, plan and guide the construction of key national cultural facilities, take overall responsibility of administering the cultural market, formulate development plans for the cultural market, manage libraries, and oversee the State Cultural Relics Bureau.③

(23) National Health and Family Planning Commission

National Health and Family Planning Commission (NHFPC) of the People's Republic of China is the executive agency under the State Council which is responsible for providing information, raising health awareness and education, family planning, ensuring the accessibility of health services, monitoring the quality of health services provided to citizens and visitors in the mainland, population and family planning in the People's Republic of China.

---

① China.org.cn. Ministry of Agriculture [EB/OL]. [2013-10-11]. http://wiki.china.org.cn/wiki/index.php/Ministry_of_Agriculture.

② China.org.cn. Ministry of Agriculture [EB/OL]. [2013-10-11]. http://wiki.china.org.cn/wiki/index.php/Ministry_of_Commerce.

③ China.org.cn. Ministry of Culture [EB/OL]. [2013-10-11]. http://wiki.china.org.cn/wiki/index.php/Ministry_of_Culture.

The ministry is created from the former Ministry of Health and National Population and Family Planning Commission. This was announced at the 2013 National People's Congress.

The commission reports directly to the State Council. Its functions include: drafting laws, regulations, plans and policies related to public health; formulating policies for maternity and child-care programs; overseeing disease prevention and treatment; controlling the spread of epidemics; supervising blood collection; reforming medical institutions; overseeing state hospitals; drawing up medical science and technology development projects; setting quality standards for foods and cosmetics; overseeing medical education and setting related standards; managing the Beijing Medical College and the Chinese Academy of Medical Sciences; overseeing the State Administration of Traditional Chinese Medicine; population control and family planning. [1]

(24) People's Bank of China

The People's Bank of China (PBC or PBOC) is the central bank of the People's Republic of China with the power to control monetary policy and regulate financial institutions in mainland China. The People's Bank of China has the most financial assets of any single public finance institution ever.

The top management of the PBC is composed of the governor and a certain number of deputy governors. The governor of the PBC is appointed into or removed from office by the President of the People's Republic of China. The candidate for the governor of the PBC is nominated by the Premier of the State Council and approved by the National People's Congress. When the National People's Congress is in adjournment, the Standing Committee of the National People's Congress sanctions the candidacy for the governor of the PBC. The deputy governors of the PBC are appointed into or removed from office by the Premier of the State Council.

The PBC adopts a governor responsibility system under which the governor supervises the overall work of the PBC while the deputy governors provide assistance to the governor to fulfill his or her responsibility.

(25) National Audit Office

The National Audit Office is the supreme audit institution in the People's Republic of China. It was established in 1983 according to the Constitution. It is a ministry under the State Council and under the leadership of the Prime Minister.

The National Audit Office scrutinizes public spending on behalf of Parliament.

The Office has two main aims. By reporting the results of the audits to Parliament, it holds

---

[1]　Wikipedia. National Health and Family Planning Commission [EB/OL]. [2013-10-11]. http://en.wikipedia.org/wiki/National_Health_and_Family_Planning_Commission.

government departments and bodies to account for the way they use public money, thereby safeguarding the interests of taxpayers. In addition, the Office aims to help public service managers improve performance and service delivery.[①]

2) Special Organization directly under the State Council

The State-owned Assets Supervision and Administration Commission of the State Council (abbreviation SASAC) is a special commission of the People's Republic of China, directly under the State Council. It is responsible for managing China's state-owned enterprises, including appointing top executives and approving any mergers or sales of stock or assets, as well as drafting laws related to state-owned enterprises.

3) Organizations directly under the State Council

The organizations directly under the State Council include:

General Administration of Customs

State Administration of Taxation

State Administration for Industry and Commerce

General Administration of Quality Supervision, Inspection and Quarantine

General Administration of Food and Drug

State General Administration of Press, Publication, Radio, Film and Television (National Copyright Administration)

General Administration of Sport

State Administration of Work Safety

National Bureau of Statistics

State Forestry Administration

State Intellectual Property Office

National Tourism Administration

State Administration for Religious Affairs

Counselors Office of the State Council

Government Offices Administration of the State Council

National Bureau of Corruption Prevention

4) Administrative Offices under the State Council

The Administrative Offices under the State Council include:

Overseas Chinese Affairs Office of the State Council

Hong Kong and Macao Affairs Office of the State Council

---

① 中华人民共和国审计署官方网站. [EB/OL]. [2012-04-11]. http://www.nao.org.uk/about_us.aspx.

Legislative Affairs Office of the State Council

Research Office of the State Council

5) Institutions Directly under the State Council

The institutions directly under the State Council include:

Xinhua News Agency

Chinese Academy of Sciences

Chinese Academy of Social Sciences

Chinese Academy of Engineering

Development Research Center of the State Council

China National School of Administration

China Earthquake Administration

China Meteorological Administration

China Banking Regulatory Commission

China Securities Regulatory Commission

China Insurance Regulatory Commission

National Council for Social Security Fund

National Natural Science Foundation

6) Administrations and Bureaus under the Ministries & Commissions

The Administrations and Bureaus under the Ministries & Commissions include:

State Bureau for Letters and Calls

State Administration of Grain

National Bureau of Energy

State Administration of Science, Technology and Industry for National Defense

State Tobacco Monopoly Administration

State Administration of Foreign Experts Affairs

State Bureau of Civil Servants

State Oceanic Administration

State Bureau of Surveying and Mapping

Civil Aviation Administration of China

State Post Bureau

State Administration of Cultural Heritage

State Administration of Traditional Chinese Medicine

State Administration of Foreign Exchange

State Administration of Coal Mine Safety

2. Local Governments

Local people's governments at various levels are the executive bodies of local organs of state power as well as the local organs of state administration at the corresponding levels. Governors, mayors and heads of counties, districts, townships and towns assume overall responsibility for local people's governments at various levels.

1) Terms

The term of office of local people's governments at various levels is the same as that of the people's congresses at the corresponding levels.

2) Powers

Local people's governments at and above the county level, within the limits of their authority as prescribed by law, conduct administrative work concerning the economy, education, science, culture, public health, physical culture, urban and rural development, finance, civil affairs, public security, nationalities affairs, judicial administration, supervision and family planning in their respective administrative areas, issue decisions and orders; appoint or remove administrative functionaries, train them, appraise their performance and reward or punish them.

People's governments of townships, nationality townships, and towns execute the resolutions of the people's congress at the corresponding level as well as the decisions and orders of the state administrative organs at the next higher level and conduct administrative work in their respective administrative areas.

3) Hierarchy of Government

Local people's governments at and above the county level direct the work of their subordinate departments and of people's governments at lower levels, and have the power to alter or annul inappropriate decisions of their subordinate departments and of people's governments at lower levels.

4) Auditing

Auditing bodies are established by local people's governments at and above the county level. Local auditing bodies at various levels independently exercise their power of supervision through auditing in accordance with the law and are responsible to the people's government at the corresponding level and to the auditing body at the next higher level. [1]

 **Vocabulary**

State Council   国务院

---

[1]   U.S. Constitution Online. Constitution of the People's Republic of China [2013-09-12]. http://www.usconstitution. net/china.html#Article85.

prefecture	地级行政区、自治区
premier	总理
State councilor	国务委员
minister	部长
auditor-general	审计长
incumbent	现任的、在职者
entrust	委托
diplomacy	外交
national defense	国防
administrative legislation	行政立法
proposal	提案、建议
grant	授予、允许
plenary meeting	全体会议
foreign affairs	外交事务
negotiate	谈判、商议
bilateral	双边的
multilateral	多边的
inter-governmental	政府间的
subordinate	从属的
recruitment	征募新兵
remuneration	薪酬、报酬
macroeconomic	宏观经济的
restructure	调整、重建
civil servant	国家公务员
compulsory basic education	基础义务教育
vocational education	职业教育
tertiary education	高等教育
draft	起草、设计
postal service	邮政
knowledge economy	知识经济
ethnic minority	少数民族
function	功能、职责
oversight	监督
paramilitary	准军事的

counterintelligence	反情报，反间谍活动
subversion	颠覆、破坏
sabotage	破坏、破坏活动
counterrevolutionary	反革命的、反动的
civil affairs	民政事务
jurisdiction	管辖权
prosecution	起诉、检举
attorney general	司法部长，首席检察官
fiscal policy	财政政策
interest rate	利率
financial crisis	金融危机
staff reduction	裁员
labor-intensive	劳动密集型的
exploitation	开发、开采
merge	合并
announce	宣布、公布
empower	授权
synonymous	同义的
rural economy	农村经济
circulation system	流通制度、流通体系
anti-dumping	反倾销
anti-subsidy	反补贴
map out	筹划、制订
health service	卫生服务
non-partisan	无党派的
adjournment	休会、休会期间
sanction	批准
candidacy	候选资格
scrutinize	详细检查
public spending	政府开支
taxpayer	纳税人
state-owned assets	国有资产
monetary policy	货币政策
state-owned enterprises	国有企业

customs	海关
quality supervision, inspection and quarantine	质量监督检验检疫
intellectual property	知识产权
assume responsibility	承担责任
corresponding	相应的
public health	公共卫生
functionary	官员、公务员
annul	废除、宣告无效
inappropriate	不适当的
township and town	乡镇
prescribe	规定
physical culture	体育
public security	公共安全
nationalities affair	民族事务
performance	绩效
nationality township	民族乡
auditing	审计
exercise power	行使权力

👤☰ FURTHER READING

Local Government in the United States

Local government in the United States is structured in accordance with the laws of the various individual states, territories, and the District of Columbia. Typically each state has at least two separate tiers of local government: counties and municipalities. Some states further have their counties divided into townships. There are several different types of local government at the municipal level, generally reflecting the needs of different levels of population densities; typical examples include the city, town, borough, and village. The types and nature of these municipal entities varies from state to state. Many rural areas and even some suburban areas of many states have no municipal government below the county level, while others do not operate under a distinct county government at all. In other places the different tiers are merged, for example as a consolidated city–county in which city and county functions are managed by a single municipal government, or in the case of towns in New England, which in some states have completely replaced the county as the unit of local government.

The local governments described above are classified general purpose local governments by the United States Census Bureau. In addition, there are also often local or regional special purpose local governments. Special purpose governments include special districts that exist for specific purposes, such as to provide fire protection, sewer service, transit service or to manage water resources, and in particular school districts to manage schools. Such special purpose districts often encompass areas in multiple municipalities.

The Tenth Amendment to the United States Constitution makes local government a matter of state rather than federal law, with special cases for territories and the District of Columbia. As a result, the states have adopted a wide variety of systems of local government. The United States Census Bureau conducts the Census of Governments every five years to compile statistics on government organization, public employment, and government finances. The category of local government established in this Census of Governments is a convenient basis for understanding local government in the United States. The categories are as follows:

- County Governments
- Town or Township Governments
- Municipal Governments
- Special-Purpose Local Governments

County governments are organized local governments authorized in state constitutions and statutes. Counties and county-equivalents form the first-tier administrative division of the states. All the states are divided into counties or county-equivalents for administrative purposes, although not all counties or county-equivalents have an organized county government. Connecticut and Rhode Island have completely eliminated county government, as have portions of Massachusetts. The Unorganized Borough in Alaska also does not operate under a county level government. Additionally, a number of independent cities and consolidated city-counties operate under a municipal government that serves the functions of both city and county. In areas lacking a county government, services are provided either by lower level townships or municipalities, or the state.

Town or township governments are organized local governments authorized in the state constitutions and statutes of 20 Northeastern and Midwestern states, established to provide general government for a defined area, generally based on the geographic subdivision of a county. Depending on state law and local circumstance, a township may or may not be incorporated, and the degree of authority over local government services may vary greatly.

Municipal governments are organized local governments authorized in state constitutions and statutes, established to provide general government for a defined area, generally corresponding to a population center rather than one of a set of areas into which a county is divided. The category includes those governments designated as cities, boroughs (except in Alaska), towns (except in Minnesota and Wisconsin), and villages.

This concept corresponds roughly to the "incorporated places" that are recognized in Census Bureau reporting of population and housing statistics, although the Census Bureau excludes New England towns from their statistics for this category, and the count of municipal governments excludes places that are currently governmentally inactive. Municipalities range in size from the very small (e.g., the Village of Lazy Lake, Florida, with 38 residents), to the very large (e.g., New York City, with about 8 million people), and this is reflected in the range of types of municipal governments that exist in different areas.

Special-purpose local governments include school districts and special districts. School districts are organized local entities providing public elementary, secondary, and/or higher education which, under state law, have sufficient administrative and fiscal autonomy to qualify as separate governments. The category excludes dependent public school systems of county, municipal, township, or state governments. Special districts are all organized local entities other than the four categories listed above, authorized by state law to provide only one or a limited number of designated functions, and with sufficient administrative and fiscal autonomy to qualify as separate governments; known by a variety of titles, including districts, authorities, boards, commissions, etc., as specified in the enabling state legislation. A special district may serve areas of multiple states if established by an interstate compact. Special districts are widely popular, have enjoyed "phenomenal growth" and "nearly tripled in number" from 1957 to 2007.

Discussion:

> Are local governments in the United States similarly structured in different states?

> What categories of local government established in the United States Census Bureau?

> Which states have completely eliminated county government?

> What are school districts and special districts respectively in the United States?

Source: 2002 Census of Governments, Individual State Descriptions, available at http://www.census.gov/prod/2005pubs/gc021x2.pdf;

Local government in the United States, available at http://en.wikipedia.org/wiki/Local_government_in_the_United_States.

4.2.5 Judicial Branch

The judicial branch is one of three branches of government in the People's Republic of

China, along with the executive and legislative branches. Strictly speaking, it refers to the activities of the People's Court system. According to Criminal Procedure Law of PRC, during the criminal proceeding, people's court, people's procuratorate and public security organ shall perform their task respectively as well as cooperate. In this meaning, people's procuratorate and public security organ both execute judicial power, although their judicial function are limited in a relatively narrow scope. Thus broadly speaking, China's judicial system institutionally comprises of three parts: people's court system, the people's procuratorate system, the public security system. Corresponding to this, judicial structure in the Chinese broad sense does not only refer to courts, but also to procuratorates and public security organs.[①]

The security organ is one branch in the administrative system; the other two branches are created by the people's congress and, in the legal sense, are on an equal footing with the administrative branch. The presidents of courts and the procurator-generals of procuratorates are selected and appointed by the people's congresses on the same levels. The judges and procurators are selected and appointed by the standing committees of the respective people's congresses, and assistant judges and assistant procurators are appointed by the respective courts and procuratorates.

Constitutionally, the court system is intended to exercise judicial power independently and free of interference from administrative organs, public organizations, and individuals. Yet the constitution simultaneously emphasizes the principle of the "leadership of the Communist Party".

1. People's Courts

The people's courts are judicial organs exercising judicial power on behalf of the state. According to the Constitution of the People's Republic of China of 1982 and the Organic Law of the People's Courts of 1979 as amended in 1983, China practices a system of courts characterized by "four levels and two-instance of trials". The judicial authority of the PRC is exercised by the following people's courts: local people's courts at various levels; military courts and other special people's courts and the Supreme People's Courts. The local people's courts are divided into basic people's courts, intermediate people's courts and higher people's courts. The organizational structure of the court system in China is shown in Figure 4.3.

1) The Supreme People's Court

The Supreme People's Court is the highest judicial organ of the State. The president of the

---

① The University of Mississippi. China's Judicial System: People's Courts, Procuratorates, and Public Security [EB/OL]. [2012-03-08]. http://www.olemiss.edu/courses/pol324/chnjudic.htm.

Supreme People's Court is elected by the NPC and its standing committee. His term of office is five years and he may serve for no more than two consecutive terms. The NPC standing committee appoints or dismisses vice-presidents, head and associate heads of divisions, and judges.

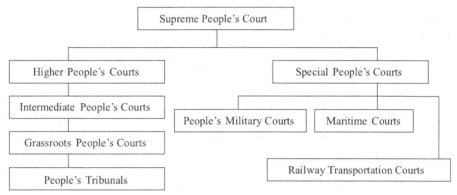

Figure 4.3　Organizational structure of the court system in China

The Supreme People's Court has a criminal division, a civil division, and an economic division. It may have such other divisions, as it deems necessary.

The Supreme People's Court supervises the work of the local people's courts at various levels as well as the special courts. "The Supreme People's court gives interpretation on questions concerning specific application of laws and decrees in judicial proceedings." In reality, the practice of interpreting laws and decrees by the Supreme People's Court has developed in recent years to an extent that is called "judicial legislation". This was not previously defined in the Constitutional Law. However, the legislation does require guidance in order to fill gaps and to solve conflicts and some vagueness among the laws so that effective enforcement can be carried out by the judicial branch.[1]

2) The Higher People's Courts

The Higher People's Courts are courts of provinces, autonomous regions and municipalities directly under the Central Government. The internal structure is almost the same as that of the Supreme People's Court according to the definition of the organic Law.

A higher people's court deals with cases of the first instance assigned by laws and decrees, cases of the first instance transferred from people's courts at the next lower level, cases of appeals and of protests lodged against judgments and orders of people's courts at the next lower level, and cases of protests lodged by people's procuratorates.[2]

---

[1]　The University of Mississippi. China's Judicial System: People's Courts, Procuratorates, and Public Security [EB/OL]. [2012-03-08]. http://www.olemiss.edu/courses/pol324/chnjudic.htm.

[2]　Ibid.

3) The Intermediate People's Courts

They are the courts established in capitals or prefectures in the provincial level. The scope of jurisdiction by an intermediate people's court covers cases of first instance assigned by laws and decrees, cases of first instance transferred from the basic people's courts, and appealed and protested cases from the lower court.[①]

4) The Basic People's Courts

The basic courts or the grassroots people's courts, as the lowest level, are normally located at the county, municipal districts and autonomous counties. A basic people's court may set up a number of people's tribunal according to the conditions of the locality, population and cases involved. A people's tribunal is a component of the basic people's court, and its judgments and orders are considered as judgments and orders of the basic people's court with the same legal effects. In practice, a tribunal of this nature is often set up in big town or townships where there is a concentrated population. As defined in the Organic Law, the basic people's court adjudicates all criminal and civil cases of the first instance except where the law provides otherwise. Besides trying cases, a basic people's court is also responsible for settling civil disputes, handling minor criminal cases that do not require formal handling, and directing the work of the people's mediation committees.[②]

5) The Special Courts

The special courts include military courts, railway courts and maritime courts. The military court that is established within the PLA is in charge of hearing criminal cases involving servicemen. This is a relatively closed system.

The railway and transport court deals with criminal cases and economic disputes relating to railways and transportation.

Ten maritime courts have been established by the Supreme People's Court at the cities of Beihai, Guangzhou, Shanghai, Qingdao, Tianjin, Haikou, Ningbo, Dalian, Wuhan and Xiamen. These courts have jurisdiction over maritime cases and maritime trade cases of the first instance, including any other disputes of this category taking place between Chinese and foreign citizens, organizations, and enterprises. Nevertheless, they have no jurisdiction over criminal cases and other civil cases belonging to the ordinary courts. The higher people's court in the locality where a maritime court is located shall have jurisdiction over appeals against the judgment and orders of

① The University of Mississippi. China's Judicial System: People's Courts, Procuratorates, and Public Security [EB/OL]. [2012-03-08]. http://www.olemiss.edu/courses/pol324/chnjudic.htm.

② The University of Mississippi. China's Judicial System: People's Courts, Procuratorates, and Public Security [EB/OL]. [2012-03-08]. http://www.olemiss.edu/courses/pol324/chnjudic.htm.

the maritime court.①

2. People's Procuratorates

The people's procuratorates in China are state organs of legal supervision. Their organization corresponds to that of the people's courts.

As is the case with the people's courts, the people's procuratorates exercise their own authority according to law, independent of interference from any administrative organ, civic organization or individual. All citizens are equal regarding the application of the law in this regard.②

1) Nature and Tasks

Article 129 of the Constitution of the People's Republic of China states that the people's procuratorates are state organs for legal supervision. By exercising their procuratorial authority, the people's procuratorates suppress all treason, attempts to split the country or other counterrevolutionary activities, and prosecute counterrevolutionaries and other criminals. Their purpose is to safeguard the unity of the country, the people's democratic dictatorship and the socialist legal system; to maintain public order, including order in production and other work, in education and scientific research, and in the daily life of the people; to protect the socialist property owned by the whole people and by collectives and the private property lawfully owned by individuals; to protect the citizens' rights of the person and their democratic and other rights; and to ensure the smooth progress of socialist modernization. The people's procuratorates also educate the citizens, encouraging them to be loyal to their socialist motherland, to conscientiously observe the Constitution and the laws and to combat illegal activities.③

2) Organizational Structure

Article 130 of the Constitution of the People's Republic of China provides that the PRC establishes the Supreme People's Procuratorate, local people's procuratorates at different levels, the military procuratorates and other special people's procuratorates.

(1) The Supreme People's Procuratorate

The Supreme People's Procuratorate is the highest agency at the national level responsible for both prosecution and investigation in the People's Republic of China.

The procurator-general of the Supreme People's Procuratorate shall be elected and

---

① The University of Mississippi. China's Judicial System: People's Courts, Procuratorates, and Public Security [EB/OL]. [2012-03-08]. http://www.olemiss.edu/courses/pol324/chnjudic.htm.

② China.org.cn. People's Procuratorates [EB/OL]. [2013-04-18]. http://www.china.org.cn/english/features/China2005/142017.htm.

③ 中国法院网. Introduction to the People's Procuratorates of the PRC [EB/OL]. [2014-03-08]. http://en.chinacourt.org/public/detail.php?id=44.

removed by the NPC. The deputy procurator-general, members of the procuratorial committee and procurators of the Supreme People's Procuratorate shall be appointed and removed by the Standing Committee of the NPC upon the recommendation of the procurator-general. The Supreme People's Procuratorate is responsible to the NPC and its Standing Committee. The Supreme People's Procuratorate may establish a number of procuratorial departments and other professional departments as needed.

According to the Organic Law, if the Supreme People's Procuratorate discovers some errors in a legally effective judgment or order of a people's court at any level, it shall file a protest in accordance with the procedure of judicial supervision. [①]

(2) The Local People's Procuratorates

These include:

People's procuratorates of provinces, autonomous regions and municipalities directly under the Central Government;

Branches of the above, and people's procuratorates of autonomous prefectures and cities directly under the provincial governments; and

People's procuratorates of counties, cities, autonomous counties and municipal districts.

If their work requires it, people's procuratorates at provincial or county level, with the approval of the standing committee of the people's congress at the corresponding level, may set up branches in industrial and mining areas, agricultural reclamation areas, forest zones, etc. [②]

(3) Special People's Procuratorates

There are two types of special people's procuratorates:

The military procuratorates are special organs for legal supervision in the Chinese People's Liberation Army. They exercise procuratorial authority in cases of dereliction of duty and other criminal offenses committed by active servicemen.

Railway procuratorates include branches in all regional railway bureaus and sub-bureaus. [③]

⚙ Vocabulary

criminal	刑事的
criminal proceeding	刑事诉讼
procuratorate	检察院

---

① The University of Mississippi. China's Judicial System: People's Courts, Procuratorates, and Public Security [EB/OL]. [2012-03-08]. http://www.olemiss.edu/courses/pol324/chnjudic.htm.

② 中国法院网. Introduction to the People's Procuratorates of the PRC [EB/OL]. [2014-03-08]. http://en.chinacourt.org/public/detail.php?id=44.

③ Ibid.

corresponding to	相应，与……相一致
procurator-general	检察长
interference	干扰、干涉
two-instance of trials	两审终审
term of office	任期
dismiss	解雇、开除
judicial legislation	司法立法
the first instance	一审
decree	法令
appeal	上诉
lodge a protest against	提出抗议
grassroots people's courts	基层人民法院
tribunal	法庭
adjudicate	裁定、宣判
civil case	民事案件
try cases	审理案件
settle dispute	解决争端
minor criminal case	轻微刑事案件
mediation	调解、仲裁
maritime	海事的
hear cases	审理案件
suppress	抑制、镇压
treason	叛国罪
prosecute	检举
democratic dictatorship	人民民主专政
property	财产
conscientiously	认真地
observe	遵守
judicial interpretation	司法解释
agricultural reclamation	农垦
dereliction of duty	失职、玩忽职守

🕮 FURTHER READING

U. S. Supreme Court—A Brief History

Other than establishing it, Article III of the U.S. Constitution spells out neither the specific duties, powers nor organization of the Supreme Court.

"[t]he judicial Power of the United States, shall be vested in one Supreme Court, and in such inferior Courts as the Congress may from time to time ordain and establish."

Instead, the Constitution left it to Congress and to the Justices of the Court itself to develop the authorities and operations of the entire Judicial Branch of government.

The very first bill introduced in the United States Senate was the Judiciary Act of 1789. It divided the country into 13 judicial districts, which were further organized into the Eastern, Middle, and Southern "circuits". The 1789 Act called for the Supreme Court to consist of a Chief Justice and only five Associate Justices, and for the Court to meet, or "sit" in the Nation's Capital. For the first 101 years of its service, Supreme Court Justices were required to "ride circuit", holding court twice a year in each of the 13 judicial districts. The Act also created the position of U.S. Attorney General and assigned the power to nominate Supreme Court justices to the President of the United States with the approval of the Senate.

The Supreme Court was first called to assemble on Feb. 1st, 1790, in the Merchants Exchange Building in New York City, then the Nation's Capital. The first Supreme Court was made up of:

Chief Justice:

John Jay, from New York

Associate Justices:

John Rutledge, from South Carolina

William Cushing, from Massachusetts

James Wilson, from Pennsylvania

John Blair, from Virginia

James Iredell, from North Carolina

Due to transportation problems, Chief Justice Jay had to postpone the first actual meeting of the Supreme Court until the next day, Feb. 2nd, 1790.

The Supreme Court spent its first session organizing itself and determining its own powers and duties. The new Justices heard and decided their first actual case in 1792.

Lacking any specific direction from the Constitution, the new U.S. Judiciary spent its first decade as the weakest of the three branches of government. Early federal courts failed to issue strong opinions or even take on controversial cases. The Supreme Court was not even sure if it had the power to consider the constitutionality of laws passed by Congress. This situation changed drastically in 1801 when President John Adams appointed John Marshall of Virginia to be the fourth Chief Justice. Confident that nobody would tell him not to, Marshall took clear and firm steps to define the role and powers of both the Supreme Court and the judiciary system.

The Supreme Court, under John Marshall, defined itself with its historic 1803 decision in the case of Marbury v. Madison. In this single landmark case, the Supreme Court established its power to interpret the U.S. Constitution and to determine the constitutionality of laws passed by congress and the state legislatures.

John Marshall went on to serve as Chief Justice for a record 34 years, along with several Associate Justices who served for over 20 years. During his time on the bench, Marshall succeeded in molding the federal judicial system into what many consider to be today's most powerful branch of government.

Supreme Court Justices are nominated by the President of the United States. The nomination must be approved by a majority vote of the Senate. The Justices serve until they either retire, die or are impeached. The average tenure for Justices is about 15 years, with a new Justice being appointed to the Court about every 22 months. Presidents appointing the most Supreme Court Justices include George Washington, with ten appointments and Franklin D. Roosevelt, who appointed eight Justices.

Table 4.1 below shows the current Justices of the Supreme Court.

Table 4.1　The current Justices of the Supreme Court

Justice	Appointed In	Appointed By
John G. Roberts (Chief Justice)	2005	G. W. Bush
Elena Kagan	2010	Obama
Samuel A. Alito, Jr.	2006	G. W. Bush
Antonin Scalia	1986	Reagan
Anthony Kennedy	1988	Reagan
Sonia Sotomayor	2009	Obama
Clarence Thomas	1991	Bush
Ruth Bader Ginsburg	1993	Clinton
Stephen Breyer	1994	Clinton

Discussion:

➤ Which act assigned the power to nominate Supreme Court justices to the President of the United States?

➤ When was the U.S. Supreme Court first called to assemble?

➤ What made the situation for U.S. Supreme Court changed drastically in 1801?

➤ Do U.S. Supreme Court justices have life tenure?

Source: Available at http://usgovinfo.about.com/library/weekly/aa081400a.htm.

4.2.6 Military Branch

The Central Military Commission (CMC) refers to the parallel national defense organizations of the Communist Party of China and the People's Republic of China: the Central Military Commission of the People's Republic of China (a state organ) and the Central Military Commission of the Communist Party of China (a party organ).

The command and control of the People's Liberation Army (Chinese armed forces) is exercised in name by the "State CMC", supervised by the Standing Committee of the National People's Congress. The State CMC is nominally considered the supreme military policy-making body and its chairman, elected by the National People's Congress, is the commander-in-chief of the armed forces. In reality, command and control of the PLA, however, still resides with the Central Military Commission of the Chinese Communist Party Central Committee—the "Party CMC". [1]

Both commissions are identical in membership, thus actually forming one identical institution under two different names, in order to fit in both state government and party systems.

1. Organizations [2]

1) Headquarters

The Headquarters of the General Staff, General Political Department, General Logistics Department, and General Armament Department, which are not only working organs of the CMC, but also leading organs for military, political, logistics and armament affairs of the entire army. They undertake the primary tasks of ensuring the implementation and realization of strategic decisions, policies and principles of the CMC on military warfare and army building.

---

① Wikipedia. Central Military Commission of CPC [EB/OL]. [2013-12-18]. http://en.wikipedia.org/wiki/Central_Military_Commission_of_CPC.

② 中国政府网. [EB/OL]. [2013-10-08]. http://english.gov.cn/2005-09/02/content_28477.htm.

2) Ministry of Defense

It is the organ for military affairs in the State Council. The Ministry of Defense does not command the armed forces. Exchanges in the military field with foreign institutions are usually conducted in the name of the Ministry of Defense.

3) Headquarters of the various branches of the armed forces

(1) Headquarters of the Navy

The headquarters of the Navy was established in December 1949, as an organ of the CMC for the administration of the navy as well as a leading body for the naval force, its scientific research, logistics and armament affairs.

(2) Headquarters of the Air Force

The headquarters of the Air Force was established in July 1949, as an organ of the CMC for the administration of the air force as well as a leading body for the air force, its scientific research, logistics and armament affairs.

(3) Headquarters of the 2nd Artillery Corps

The headquarters of the 2nd Artillery Corps was established in July 1966, which was then made up of the commanding headquarters, political department and logistics department. In December 1975, a scientific research department was added. The headquarters underwent a major reform in June 1985, as overlapping organizations were dismissed and commanding control and automation control departments established.

4) Area military commands

Headquarters of the various area military commands are the highest commanding bodies of consolidated military forces in each strategic region. Usually they are made up of the commanding headquarters, political departments, logistics departments and armament departments.

The primary jobs of the headquarters of the area military commands are: being responsible for the commanding of the war operations of the army, navy and air force in the areas under their jurisdiction as well as the military, political, logistic and armament affairs of the forces under their command. They are also responsible for the militia, military service, mobilization and construction of military facilities and sites in areas under their respective jurisdiction.

2. Membership

The CMC is composed of the chairman, vice-chairmen and other members. The Chairman of the CMC is elected by the NPC. The NPC decides other members according to the nomination of the Chairman of the CMC. The NPC has the power to remove from office the Chairman of the CMC and other members of the CMC. When the NPC is not in session, its Standing

Committee may decide other members of the CMC upon the nomination of the Chairman of the CMC.

The Chairman of the CMC assumes overall responsibility for the work of the CMC and is responsible to the NPC and has the power to make final decisions on matters within the functions and powers of the CMC. The term of office of the CMC is five years, the same as that of the NPC.[①]

3. Command structure

Unlike in most countries, the Central Military Commission is not considered as just another ministry. Although China does have a Ministry of National Defense, headed by a Minister of National Defense, it exists solely for liaison with foreign militaries and does not have command authority.

The most important chain of command runs from the CMC to the four General Headquarters (General Staff Department, General Political Department, General Logistic Department, General Armament Department) and, in turn, to each of the service branches (ground, navy and air forces) and military regions. In addition, the CMC also has direct control over the Second Artillery Corps (strategic missile force), the National Defense University, and the Academy of Military Science. As stipulated in the 1997 National Defense Law, the CMC also controls the paramilitary People's Armed Police (PAP).

Although in theory the CMC has the highest military command authority, in reality the ultimate decision making power concerning war, armed forces, and national defense resides with the Communist Party's Politburo. The CMC is usually chaired by the General Secretary of CPC, who is supported by two to three Vice Chairmen.

✿ Vocabulary

nominally	名义上地
commander-in-chief	总司令
armed forces	武装部队，陆海空三军
logistics	后勤
armament	武器、军备
naval force	海军
air force	空军
militia	民兵组织

---

① 中国文化网. Central Military Commission [EB/OL]. [2013-01-18]. http://www.chinaculture.org/gb/en_aboutchina/2003-09/24/content_22324.htm.

nomination	提名
in session	在开会
paramilitary	准军事的

👤≡ FURTHER READING

The United States Secretary of Defense

The United States Department of Defense (DoD) is responsible for providing the military forces needed to deter war and protect the security of the United States (U.S.). The major elements of these forces are the Army, Navy, Air Force, and Marine Corps. The President is the Commander-in-Chief, while the Secretary of Defense exercises authority, direction, and control over the Department. This includes the Office of the Secretary of Defense, Organization of the Chairman of the Joint Chiefs of Staff, the three Military Departments, the Combatant Commands, the Office of the Inspector General, 18 Defense Agencies, 10 DoD Field Activities, and other organizations, such as the National Guard Bureau (NGB) and the Joint Improvised Explosive Device Defeat Organization (JIEDDO).

The United States Secretary of Defense is the civilian head of the Department of Defense, a sprawling government agency which deals with military matters. As head of the Department of Defense, the US Secretary of Defense advises the President of the United States on policy matters, and he or she also works with the Joint Chiefs of Staff, who command the branches of the United States military.

This position in the United States government is widely regarded as critical, because the Secretary of Defense has a huge influence on the direction of American military policy.

This is a Cabinet position, which means that the President appoints the US Secretary of Defense, and the United States Congress must confirm the appointment. The Undersecretaries who assist the Secretary of Defense are also subject to confirmation hearings. As with other Cabinet positions, the US Secretary of Defense is part of the line of succession to the Presidency; in the unlikely event that the President, Vice-President, Speaker of the House, President Pro Tempore of the Senate, Secretary of State, and Secretary of the Treasury were all incapacitated, the Secretary of Defense would become the President of the United States.

As a Cabinet member, the US Secretary of Defense must keep the President advised about important issues which may affect the security and well-being of the United States. Together with the President, the Secretary of Defense comprises the National Command Authority, which has the ability to launch nuclear weapons in the event that the President and the US Secretary of Defense agree on such an action. The Secretary of Defense also oversees research and development, training, policies, spending, and other key aspects of the American military.

Policy is one of the most important facets of the work of the US Secretary of Defense. In addition to formulating sound policies for the American military, the Secretary of Defense must also be able to enforce policy, and to demonstrate the importance of such policy to the world. Policies handled by the Department of Defense can range from mundane issues, like proper haircuts for members of the armed forces, to critical decisions like how to handle nuclear weapons.

The position was created in 1947, and, by law, the Secretary of Defense must be a civilian who has not served in the military for at least a decade. Many Secretaries of Defense have had military service, although it is not required, and as of 2008, only one former General, George Marshall, had served in this position. Because the US Secretary of Defense or SecDef holds so much power, the position is considered to be among the "Big Four" on the Presidential Cabinet. (The Secretary of Defense, Secretary of State, the Attorney General and the Secretary of the Treasury, are generally regarded as the four most important cabinet officials because of the importance of their departments.)

Discussion:

➢ Why is the position of Secretary of Defense critical in the United States?

➢ Who are in the line of succession to the U.S. Presidency?

➢ What are the requirements for a person to be the U.S. Secretary of Defense?

➢ What are the "Big Four" on the U.S. Presidential Cabinet?

Source: 美国国防部网站, available at http://www.defense.gov/osd/.

Available at http://www.wisegeek.com/what-is-the-us-secretary-of-defense.htm.

4.3
Official Positions in the Communist Party of China and State Organs of People's Republic of China

4.3.1　Official Positions in the Communist Party of China

1. General Secretary of the CPC Central Committee

The General Secretary of the Communist Party of China, officially General Secretary of the

Central Committee of the Communist Party of China, is the highest ranking official within the Communist Party of China, a standing member of the Politburo and head of the Secretariat. Also the post holders are usually the de facto leaders of the People's Republic of China.

Since its founding, the most important position in the PRC has been the General Secretary (as Chairman before 1982). The Communist party and its leader hold ultimate power and authority over state and government.

2. Standing Member of the CPC Politburo

The Central Politburo Standing Committee of the Communist Party of China (PSC) is a committee consisting of the top leadership of the Communist Party of China. Its members are closely watched by both the national media and the political watchers abroad.

3. Members of the CPC Politburo

The Central Politburo of the Communist Party of China or Political Bureau of the CPC Central Committee is a group of 25 members who oversee the Communist Party of China. Most of the members are top-ranked officials in the Chinese central or provincial governments.

4. Secretary of the CPC Central Commission for Discipline Inspection

The Secretary of the CPC Central Commission for Discipline Inspection is the chief of the Central Commission for Discipline Inspection of the Communist Party of China, which is an organization run under the central committee of the Communist Party of China and in charged of rooting out corruption and malfeasance among party cadres.

5. Secretary of the CPC Secretariat

Secretaries of the CPC Secretariat are members of the Secretariat of the Communist Party of China Central Committee, which is the permanent bureaucracy of the Communist Party of China and forms a parallel structure to state organizations in the People's Republic of China.

6. Secretary of Political and Legislative Affairs Committee of the CPC Central Committee

The Secretary of Political and Legislative Affairs Committee of the CPC Central Committee is the head of the Central Political and Legislative Affairs Committee of the CPC, also called Central Politics and Law Commission of the CPC, which is the organization under the CPC Central Committee responsible for political and legal affairs.

7. Head of the CPC Propaganda Department

The Head of the CPC Propaganda Department, also called the CPC Propaganda chief, is the head of Propaganda Department of the Communist Party of China (later officially called the Publicity Department of the CPC), which is an internal division of the Communist Party of China in charge of ideology-related work, as well as its propaganda system.

8. Head of the Organization Department of the CPC Central Committee

The Head of the Organization Department of the CPC Central Committee is the chief of the CPC Organization Department which controls staffing positions within the CPC.

9. Party Chief of the Communist Party of China

In the Politics of the People's Republic of China, a party chief, variously called a party boss, and officially termed the Communist Party Committee Secretary for a certain region, is the leader of the local Communist Party of China division, and in most cases, the de facto first-in-charge of its area of jurisdiction. Aside from the regional or municipal affix, the title does not change regardless of the size of the jurisdiction.

Beginning at the provincial level, China's party-government dual administrative system arranges a hierarchy by which the party chief is in charge of determining the direction of policy as well as personnel changes, and the corresponding government leader is responsible for implementing party policy and arranging the annual budget, as well as other everyday government matters and ceremonial tasks. The list of party chief levels is as follows:

- At the central level, the party chief is known as CPC Central Committee General Secretary, while the corresponding government position is known as Premier.
- At the provincial level, the party chief is known as CPC Provincial Committee Secretary, while the corresponding government position is known as Governor.
- At the prefecture or municipal level, the party chief is known as CPC Municipal Committee Secretary, while the corresponding government position is known as Mayor.
- At the county level, the party chief is known as CPC County Committee Secretary, while the corresponding government position is known as the County Governor.
- At the township level, the party chief is known as CPC Township/town Committee Secretary, while the corresponding government position is known as the Magistrate.
- At the village level, the local party chief, known as the Village Party Branch Secretary, heads a committee of around ten people to make executive decisions related to the village. The process is not entirely formal, and therefore the party chief at this level is not considered part of the Chinese civil service.

Generally, a party chief may concurrently hold the corresponding deputy government position, while a top government official (the mayor, governor) also holds the first deputy party chief position.[1]

---

[1] Wikipedia. Party Chief of the Communist Party of China [EB/OL]. [2014-11-08]. http://en.wikipedia.org/wiki/Party_chief_of_the_Communist_Party_of_China.

⚙ Vocabulary

standing	长期的、固定的
leadership	领导阶层
top-ranked	第一级的，名列第一的
commission	委员会
inspection	检查，视察
root out	根除
corruption	贪污，腐败
malfeasance	渎职，违法行为
cadre	干部
secretariat	书记处，秘书处
bureaucracy	官僚机构
propaganda	宣传
publicity	宣传
ideology	意识形态
party chief	党委书记
central level	中央级
provincial level	省级
governor	省长
prefecture level	地级
municipal level	市级
mayor	市长
county level	县级
county governor	县长
township level	乡级
magistrate	乡长，镇长
village level	村级
party branch	党支部
civil service	公务员，行政部门

👤 FURTHER READING

Chinese Communist Party Chief Stresses Inner-party Democracy

Hu Jintao, former chief of the Communist Party of China (CPC), has called for a vigorous improvement of inner-party democracy in order to enhance the Party's ruling capacity and leadership in the development of China.

Hu, former General Secretary of the CPC Central Committee, presided over a meeting of the Political Bureau of the CPC Central Committee on Monday. The digest of his speech at the meeting was published on Tuesday, one day ahead of the party's 88th birthday.

Hu said the CPC must pay greater attention to inner-party democracy and actively promote it, because this will help the CPC perform its duty as the ruling party in more scientific and democratic ways and in accordance with the law.

"We must converge the wisdom and strength of the Party to an utmost level; we must fully inspire the creativity and vigor of the Party, and we must spare no efforts to consolidate the unity of the Party," so that the Chinese people can be united under the CPC leadership to carry forward the cause of socialism with Chinese characteristics, Hu said.

The realization of inner-party democracy must rely on the guarantee of all Party members' democratic rights to know, to participate, to vote and to supervise in all internal affairs of the Party, Hu said.

CPC members, nearly 76 million out of the 1.3 billion Chinese population, should be encouraged to supervise and suggest on all matters concerning inner-party democracy, such as the work to fight corruption inside the Party.

Hu said mechanisms to ensure the inner-party democracy must be improved, such as the CPC congresses at all levels, and the system to elect, supervise, evaluate and promote officials.

The CPC Central Committee Political Bureau decided on Monday that the Party will reform its appraisal system on officials on the basis of merit and transparency.

The assessment system will put more emphasis on achievements made in "coordinating economic and social development, maintaining social stability, and improving people's livelihoods".

Discussion:

➢ Why did Hu Jintao call for a vigorous improvement of inner-party democracy?

➢ What must the realization of inner-party democracy rely on, according to Hu?

➢ What will the party assessment system put more emphasis on?

Source: 人民网, available at http://english.people.com.cn/90001/90776/90785/6690198.html [2009-06-30].

4.3.2 Official Positions in the Legislative Branch

1. Chairman of the Standing Committee of the National People's Congress

The Chairman of the Standing Committee of the National People's Congress is the chairman and/or speaker of the Standing Committee of the National People's Congress of the People's Republic of China, which is considered China's top legislative body. In the political order of precedence, the Chairman ranks below the CPC General Secretary and President, but above the Premier.

The position holds reserve constitutional powers under the 1978 revision of the Constitution of the People's Republic of China. As stipulated in Article 84 of the Constitution, should both the President and Vice-President become incapacitated, and the National People's Congress is unable to elect a timely replacement, the Chairman of the NPC will act as President.

2. Vice Chairman of the Standing Committee of the National People's Congress

The Vice Chairmen of the Standing Committee of the National People's Congress are all elected by the NPC from its deputies for a term of five years, the same term as an NPC. The Chairman of the NPC Standing Committee directs the work of the Standing Committee. The Vice Chairmen and the Secretary-General assist the Chairman in his work.

3. Secretary-General of the Standing Committee of the National People's Congress

The Chairman, Vice Chairmen and Secretary-General constitute the Chairmen's Council, which handles the important day-to-day work of the Standing Committee.

4. Member of Standing Committee of the National People's Congress

The Standing Committee of the National People's Congress is a committee of about 150 members of the National People's Congress (NPC) of the People's Republic of China (PRC), which is convened between plenary sessions of the NPC.

⚙ Vocabulary

incapacitate	使无能力，使不能
vice	副的
secretary-general	秘书长
convene	召开，开会
plenary session	全体会议

4.3.3　Official Positions in the Presidency

1. President of the People's Republic of China

The President of the People's Republic of China, formerly called Chairman of the People's Republic of China from 1954 to 1975, is a ceremonial office and a part of State Organs under the National People's Congress. In combination with the NPC Standing Committee, the president of the PRC exercises his or her functions and powers as the head of state.

2. Vice President of the People's Republic of China

The Vice President of the People's Republic of China, formerly called Vice Chairman of the People's Republic of China from 1954 to 1975, is a senior position in the government of the People's Republic of China.

The office was created by the 1982 Constitution. Formally, the Vice President is elected by the National People's Congress in accordance with Article 62 of the Constitution. The candidate is recommended by the Presidium of the National People's Congress, which also theoretically has the power to recall the Vice President.

The Vice President's duties include assisting the President, and replacing him should he resign or die in office.

✿ Vocabulary

ceremonial	仪式的，礼仪的
vice president	副总统，副主席
presidium	主席团
recall	撤销，召回
resign	辞职
in office	执政，在位

4.3.4   Official Positions in the Executive Branch

1. Official Positions in the Central Government

(1) Premier of the People's Republic of China

The Premier of the State Council of the People's Republic of China, sometimes also refers to as the "Prime Minister" informally, is the Leader of the State Council of the People's Republic of China, who is the head of government and holds the highest-ranking (Level 1) of the civil service of the People's Republic of China. This position was originally known as Premier of the Government Administration Council of the Central People's Government and changed to its current name in 1954. The Premier is formally approved by the National People's Congress upon the apparent nomination of the President. The Premier has always been a member of the powerful Politburo Standing Committee of the Communist Party of China.[1]

(2) Vice Premier of the People's Republic of China

The Vice Premier of the State Council of the People's Republic of China is a high-ranking

---

[1]   Wikipedia. Premier of the People's Republic of China [EB/OL]. [2013-01-18]. http://en.wikipedia.org/wiki/Premier_ of_the_People%27s_Republic_of_China.

executive assistant to the Premier. Generally, the title is held by multiple individuals at one time, with each Vice-Premier holding a broad portfolio of responsibilities. The highest-ranked office holder is informally called the Executive Vice Premier (EVP). The EVP takes over duties of the Premier at the time of the latter's incapacity.

(3) State Councilor of the People's Republic of China

The State Councilor is a powerful position within the State Council of the People's Republic of China, i.e. the executive organ of China's central government (comparable to a cabinet). It ranks immediately below the Vice-Premiers and above the Ministers of various departments.[①]

In theory, State Councilors are to assist the Premier and Vice-Premiers to oversee various government portfolios. They can also represent the State Council on foreign visits. State Councilors are part of a Standing Committee of the State Council, alongside the Premier, Vice-Premiers, and the Secretary General of the State Council.

(4) Ministers in charge of ministries and commissions

The ministers in charge of ministries and commissions of the State Council are the heads of the various ministries and commissions of the People's Republic of China. They are important cabinet posts.

According to the Constitution of the People's Republic of China, the ministers are nominated by the Premier and confirmed by the National People's Congress or its Standing Committee.

(5) Auditor-general of National Audit Office of the People's Republic of China

The auditor-general of National Audit Office of the People's Republic of China is the head of the National Audit Office, which is the supreme audit institution in the People's Republic of China.

(6) Governor of People's Bank of China

The governor of People's Bank of China is the head of People's Bank of China. The governor is appointed into or removed from office by the President of the People's Republic of China. The candidate for the governor of the PBC is nominated by the Premier of the State Council and approved by the National People's Congress.

(7) Secretary General of the State Council of the People's Republic of China

The Secretary General of the State Council is an executive position within the State Council of the People's Republic of China. It subordinates below the Premier and above the Ministers of various ministries and departments. The Secretary General is responsible for the day to day work of the State Council and is in charge of the general office of the State Council.

---

① www.gov.cn. Laws on the Composition of the State Council [EB/OL]. [2013-05-13]. http://www.gov.cn/gjjg/2005-06/10/content_5548.htm.

2. Official Positions in the Local Government

(1) Governors of Provinces of the People's Republic of China

The governors of various provinces in the People's Republic of China are the highest ranking officials in the provincial People's Government. However, in the province's governing system, the Governor has less power than the Communist Party of China Provincial Committee Secretary, colloquially termed the "CPC Provincial Party Chief".

(2) Mayors of Municipal Governments of the People's Republic of China

The Mayors are the highest ranking officials in the municipal People's Governments of People's Republic of China. In the city's dual party-government governing system, the mayor has less power than the Communist Party of China Municipal Committee Secretary.

(3) County Governors of the People's Republic of China

The county governors are the highest ranking officials in the county level People's Governments of People's Republic of China.

(4) Magistrate of Township Level Governments of the People's Republic of China

The magistrate is the highest ranking official in the township level governments of the People's Republic of China.

(5) (Deputy) Head of a Department under a Provincial Government

(6) (Deputy) Director-general

(7) (Deputy) Chief of a Subministry Department/(Deputy) Head of a Subministry Department

(8) (Deputy) Division Chief/(Deputy) Division Head

(9) (Deputy) Office Director/(Deputy) Office Administrator

⚙ Vocabulary

prime minister	首相，总理
Government Administration Council	政务院
Executive Vice Premier	常务副总理
incapacity	无能力，无能
auditor-general	审计长
colloquially	口语地，用通俗语
deputy	副的

👤≣ FURTHER READING

Role and Powers of the Governors in the United States

The United States Constitution preserves the notion that the country is a federation of semisovereign states and that powers not specifically granted to the federal government are retained by the states. States, therefore, are not merely provinces or subdivisions of federal administration. State governments in the U.S. are relatively powerful; each state has its own independent criminal and civil law codes, and each state manages its internal government.

The governor thus heads the executive branch in each state or territory and, depending on the individual jurisdiction, may have considerable control over government budgeting, the power of appointment of many officials (including many judges), and a considerable role in legislation. The governor may also have additional roles, such as that of commander-in-chief of the state's National Guard (when not federalized), and in many states and territories the governor has partial or absolute power to commute or pardon a criminal sentence. All U.S. governors serve four-year terms except those in New Hampshire and Vermont, who serve two-year terms.

In all states, the governor is directly elected, and in most cases has considerable practical powers, though this may be moderated by the state legislature and in some cases by other elected executive officials. In the five extant U.S. territories, all governors are now directly elected as well, though in the past many territorial governors were historically appointed by the President of the United States. Governors can veto state bills, and in all but seven states they have the power of the line-item veto on appropriations bills (a power the President does not have).

In some cases legislatures can override a gubernatorial veto by a two-thirds vote, in others by three-fifths. In Alabama, Indiana, Kentucky, and Tennessee, the governor's veto can be overridden by a simple majority vote, making it virtually useless. In Arkansas, a gubernatorial veto may be overridden by an absolute majority. The Governor of North Carolina had no veto power until a 1996 referendum. In 47 states, whenever there is a vacancy of one of the state's U.S. Senate seats, that state's governor has the power to appoint someone to fill the vacancy until a special election is held; the governors of Oregon, Alaska, and Wisconsin do not have this power.

A state governor may give an annual State of the State address in order to satisfy a constitutional stipulation that a governor must report annually (or in older constitutions described as being "from time to time") on the state or condition of the state. Governors of states may also perform ceremonial roles, such as greeting dignitaries, conferring state decorations, issuing symbolic proclamations or attending the state fair. The governor may also have an official residence.

Discussion:

➢ Are governors in the United States directly or indirectly elected?

➢ Which power do governors have while the President has not?

➢ What kind of the ceremonial roles do governors of states in the United States perform?

Source: Available at http://en.wikipedia.org/wiki/Governor_(United_States)#Role_and_powers.

4.3.5　Official Positions in the Judicial Branch

1. President of the Supreme People's Court of the People's Republic of China

The president of the Supreme People's Court is elected by the NPC and remains in office for no more than two successive terms with each term of five years. The deputy presidents of the Supreme People's Court, members of the judicial committee, presiding judges of affiliated courts and their deputies, and judicial officers are appointed and recalled by the Standing Committee of the NPC.[①]

2. Vice/Deputy President of the Supreme People's Court of the People's Republic of China

3. Chief Grand Justice

4. Senior Judge

5. Procurator-General of Supreme People's Procuratorate of People's Republic of China

6. Deputy Procurator-General of Supreme People's Procuratorate of People's Republic of China

7. Chief Grand Procuratorate

8. Senior Procurator

⚙ Vocabulary

presiding judge	审判长，法庭庭长
judicial committee	审判委员会
affiliated	附属的
procurator	检察官

4.3.6　Official Positions in the Military Branch

1. Chairman of the Central Military Commission of the People's Republic of China

The Chairman of the Central Military Commission of the People's Republic of China has overall responsibility for the Central Military Commission. According to Chapter 3, Section 4 of the Constitution of the People's Republic of China, "The Central Military Commission of the People's Republic of China directs the armed forces of the country. The Central Military Commission is composed of the following: The Chairman, The Vice-Chairmen, and Members.

---

① 人民网. The Supreme People's Court [EB/OL]. [2013-06-03]. http://english.people.com.cn/data/organs/court.html.

The term of office of the Central Military Commission is the same as that of the National People's Congress."

2. Vice Chairman of the Central Military Commission of the People's Republic of China

vice-chairman   副主席

term of office   任期

👥 FURTHER READING

Duties of the Chief Justice of the United States

Often incorrectly called the "Chief Justice of the Supreme Court", the Chief Justice of the United States not only presides over the Supreme Court, he or she serves as the head of the judicial branch of the federal government.

The other eight members of the Supreme Court are called "Associate Justices of the Supreme Court". In addition to the duties of the Associate Justices, the Chief Justice has the following additional duties:

The Chief Justice enters the courtroom first and casts the first vote when the justices deliberate. The Chief Justice's vote carries no more influence than the votes of the Associate Justices.

If the Chief Justice votes with the majority in a case decided by the Supreme Court, he or she may choose to write the Court's opinion, or to assign the task to one of the Associate Justices.

The Chief Justice sits as the judge in impeachments of the President of the United States. Only two Chief Justices have ever served this role: Chief Justices, Salmon P. Chase presided over the Senate trial of President Andrew Johnson in 1868, and the late William H. Rehnquist presided over the trial of President William Clinton in 1999.

The Chief Justice presides over the impeachment trial of the Vice President if the Vice President is serving as Acting President (a Senate rule, not provided for by the Constitution).

The Chief Justice swears in the President of the United States at inaugurations. This is a purely traditional role. According to law, any federal or state judge, even a notary-public, is empowered to administer oaths of office.

The Chief Justice serves as Chancellor of the Smithsonian Institution, and sits on the boards of the National Gallery of Art and the Hirshorn Museum.

The Chief Justice writes an annual report to Congress about the state of the federal court system.

The Chief Justice serves as the head of the Judicial Conference of the United States, the chief administrative body of the U.S. federal courts. The Judicial Conference is empowered by the Rules Enabling Act to promulgate rules to ensure the smooth operation of the federal courts.

Just like the Associate Justices, the Chief Justice of the United States is nominated by the President of the United States and must be confirmed by a majority vote of the U.S. Senate. Also like the Associate Justices, the Chief Justice serves until retirement, death or impeachment.

The Chief Justice is also paid more than the Associate Justices. In 2009, the yearly salary of the Chief Justice was set at $217,400, while the salary of an Associate Justice was $208,100.

Discussion:

➢ Who is the head of the judicial branch of the federal government in the United States?

➢ How many Justices in the Supreme Court of the United States?

➢ Does the Chief Justice's vote have more influence than the votes of the Associate Justices in the United States?

➢ Who nominates the Chief Justice of the United States?

Source: Robert Longley. Duties of the Chief Justice of the United States, available at http:// usgovinfo.about.com/od/uscourtsystem/a/chiefduties.htm.

Chapter 5
Academic English

5.1

Conducting an Effective English Literature Search

"I just join as new graduate students and I am not sure how to do a literature search, especially an English literature research."

"I have been into research for sometimes now but I spend a lot of time getting the English articles I want."

"I wanted to start a new research work, how can I get the right English literature in the shortest possible time?"

If you experience similar issues, this section may help you to do an effective English literature search.

5.1.1 Definition of English Literature Search

An English literature search is a study of information and publications on a specific topic in English. If you want to write a research paper, it is important that you are aware of all the English literature that exists around your specific topic.

The English literature search is an important part of your research. As you can see in Figure 5.1, it consists of many different tasks and you need to manage several skills to complete a good English literature search.

To start a good English literature search, you have to know how and where you can find all the relevant sources. After you found them, set up a system to organize all the literature you have read. Once you have selected all the relevant literature, use it to ground your research. The final step is to review what you have done, making sure your search is efficient and the outcome of your writing is purposeful.

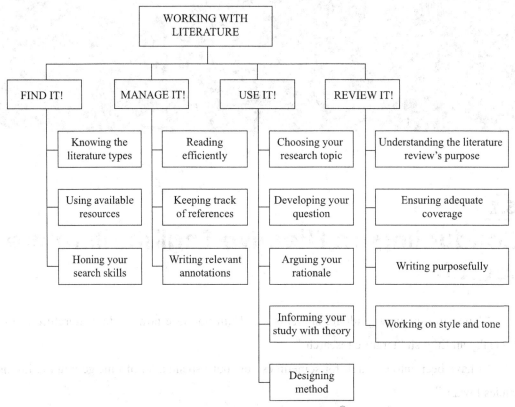

Figure 5.1　Working with literature[①]

5.1.2　Reasons for Doing English Literature Search

The process of conducting an English literature search familiarizes you with the body of work in English related to your research topic. Using the published literature is a core part of the academic communication process. It connects your work to the great scholarly chain of knowledge, and in more immediate terms it demonstrates your understanding and puts the work you have done in a wider context.

The reasons that an English literature search should be done are as followed:

◆ You will know what research on your topic is already done. You might find gaps in existing knowledge, so your research will be unique.

◆ You will find variations in terminology, you will acquire the subject vocabulary and you will be able to define your own terminology.

◆ You will establish the context of your topic.

◆ You can gain a new perspective by synthesizing the literature.

◆ You can learn from existing research: for example methodologies and research techniques

---

① Zina O'Leary. The Essential Guide to Doing Research [M]. London, Thousand Oaks, New Delhi: Sage, 2004.

that have been used, errors that have been made.[1]

5.1.3　Rules and Steps to Do Academic English Literature Search

In order to analyze the published body of knowledge on a subject, you will first need to do a literature search to identify relevant and appropriate material. Remember that the information you find in your literature search does not just slot into the "literature review" section of a dissertation or other piece of work: it should inform and underpin everything you write.

This can be a confusing and time-consuming process but there are some simple rules which make the process work much more effectively.

1. Identify Sources for Academic English Literature Search

1) Know What Type of Literature is Required for Sources

If writing a paper on public administration, peer-reviewed public administration journals or books should be key sources. Relevant peer-reviewed law, political science and management journals should also be consulted, since the three disciplines form the underlying foundation of the field of public administration.[2]

2) Determine the Accessibility of Search Engines and Library Resources

Many university and some high school library systems maintain a large database of scientific or peer-reviewed journals available at no cost to their faculty and the students, provided they are logged into the system. Check with the universities or schools to see if they have access to these resources. Some universities partner with others to offer more for their students, so ask about that as well.

If they provide free access to a list of relevant peer-reviewed journals, learn how to use a search engine. Most libraries offer informational sessions or private guidance for navigating scholarly search engines. When used correctly, search engines can make the literature search process a snap.[3]

3) Know What Counts as Academic Sources

Peer-reviewed or scholarly sources are sometimes difficult to identify if a student is

---

① Chris Hart. Doing a Literature Review: Releasing the Social Science Research Imagination [M]. London,Thousand, Oaks, New Delhi: Sage, 2000.

② Andrew Booth, Mary Dixon-Woods. How to Do a Literature Search [EB/OL]. [2012-07-02].http://www.ccsr.ac.uk/ methods/festival2004/programme/Sat/pm/D/Documents/Booth_000.ppt#363,75,Evaluation.

③ Bradley E. Wright. Public Administration as an Interdisciplinary Field: Assessing Its Relationship with the Fields of Law, Management, and Political Science [J]. Public Administration Review, 2011, (1): 96.

unfamiliar with the search process and the standards[1] for academic sources. Though there are many tips for identifying peer-reviewed references, it basically means sticking to academic journals, sources on Google Scholar, books from reputable publishers, and government or university web pages.

Avoid just doing a general internet search for the paper topic, as most of the ".com" websites to come up in the results will be inappropriate for citations in an academic paper.

2. Important Steps to Start Academic English Literature Search

1) Decide on Your Topic and Its Boundaries

You need to decide what exactly you want to find out. A precise question usually works better than a vague one, so if you are looking for the impact of television advertising on children, you might want to think about what exactly you want to find out. A more precise question might be:

"Does television advertising have any influence on children's eating habits?"

Also what are the limits to your investigation? Are you going to be restricted by:

Time: only current issues, rather than historic trends?

Country: USA only or international as well?

Discipline: are you approaching this from a Media Studies, Health, Psychology, Marketing, Politics perspective?

Gender: are you interested in children or just boys or only girls?

Age: are you interested in children or particular age groups like the under 5s or 8-12s?

Type of material: are you interested in research material or popular and practitioner/trade publications?

It is a good idea to think about boundaries. Until you have started your literature search you do not necessarily know whether there will be enough/too much/too little relevant material. Analyzing the topic and its boundaries can help you later if you get bogged down.[2]

TIP: Reading a general text or doing some browsing on the Internet can be a helpful way of clarifying your thoughts at this stage, and ensuring you focus on exactly what you want to research.

2) Choose the Key Words and Their Synonyms

This is a really important stage. Search engines and library databases do not look for your

---

[1] Amour K. How to Perform a Literature Search: Successfully Find Peer-Reviewed Articles for Research Papers [EB/OL]. [2013-11-12]. http://suite101.com/article/how-to-perform-a-literature-search-a123069.

[2] De Montfort University. How to Undertake a Literature Search and Review for Dissertations and Final Year Projects [EB/OL]. [2012-06-13]. http://www.library.dmu.ac.uk/Images/Howto/LiteratureSearch.pdf.

ideas; they just try to match up the words that you use. Write a paragraph which outlines your research interest. Note words or phrases which define your topic. Often a topic will have several key concepts. Generate a list of synonyms and other words that might be used in discussion of each concept. Be creative! When you start searching, you can use the synonyms in keyword searching.

Here are some important principles to consider when selecting search words[①]:

Be specific: Start your search by using the words that really define your research topic.

Similar and related terms: Are there other words with similar meanings? List them.

Spellings and terminology: Can your search term be spelt in different ways? Behaviour or behavior for example? Many databases and search engines don't automatically call up the US spelling or terminology.

Singulars and plurals: Try both. Usually people and things are plural, ideas are expressed as singular.

Combining terms: Remember you can search for phrases or combine terms using AND, OR and NOT. It is often a good idea to split up a phrase and link it by AND if you aren't getting enough results.

Truncating terms: Most databases will allow you to search for terms that begin with the same stem. By using * $ or ? at the end of, for example, politi. A database will search for politic, politics and political. The symbol used will vary between databases so do check the help screens to find out which one to use.

Table 5.1 demonstrates an example of using synonyms in keyword searching.

Table 5.1　Using synonyms in keyword searching

Topic: What effect does health have on literacy learners' success?

Concept 1	Concept 2
Learner success	Health
Learning outcome	Wellbeing
Learner progress	Illness
Goal achievement	Sickness
Learner assessment	Disease
	Medical condition

3) Plan Your Search

(1) Finding Books

---

① De Montfort University. How to Undertake a Literature Search and Review for Dissertations and Final Year Projects [EB/OL]. [2012-06-13]. http://www.library.dmu.ac.uk/Images/Howto/LiteratureSearch.pdf.

A book is often a good starting point. A textbook summarizes key theories and more specialized texts which often present research findings in a clear and comprehensive way. To be sure you have traced the relevant books; you need to look in two different places:

The library catalogue-lists, what are available in university libraries or the National Library of China.

Internet booksellers, like Amazon.com and dangdang.com—list recently published books titles.

(2) Tracing Journals

On many subjects, journals are the key resource for any literature search. This may be because your topic is so specialized or new that no books have been published on it. It is also because journals are the principal publications where research and practice are discussed and new work presented.

The university libraries list the most useful databases for searching the journal and report literature on your subjects.

You will need to use databases to find relevant journal articles. The frequently used databases for public administration research available in many university libraries in China include:

ASP (Academic Search Premier EBSCO的学术期刊数据库)

Elsevier SD (荷兰Elsevier Science出版)

Springer LINK (德国施普林格出版的全文期刊数据库)

PRL (ProQuest Research Library) 学术期刊图书馆(原：ARL)

JSTOR (Journal Storage 全文数据库)

ProQuest Dissertations & Theses (PQDT)

You can take a number of approaches in this stage:

Systematic—you try to find all relevant material.

Retrospective—you find the most recent material and work backwards.

Citation—you follow leads from useful articles, books and reading lists.

Targeted—you restrict your topic and focus on a narrow area of the literature.

In practice, everyone tends to use a mixture of approaches. For example you might:

Be systematic in looking at everything relevant in the library.

Adopt a retrospective approach when looking at journal articles.

Use citation searching to get useful leads if your topic crosses several disciplines.

Be more targeted when you have a clear picture of what you need to find out.

TIP: Don't forget the reference books and reference articles listed at the end of the articles that you have read. You will find more articles relevant to your research from there.

4) Start the Search

When you're searching literature, ask yourself the following questions[①]:

Are you consulting different sources? Many electronic search engines exist, are you using them?

Are you consulting a primary, a secondary or an alternative source?

How relevant is the source to your needs?

How detailed is the treatment of your subject in this source?

Is your topic the major focus of this source?

How current is your source?

Have recent developments made any parts of your source date? Does your source cite information from earlier work? Is this information still sound?

How reliable is your source?

5) Review and Repeat the Search Again

Literature searching is a cycle and you will need to go through several stages before it is complete (see Figure 5.2).

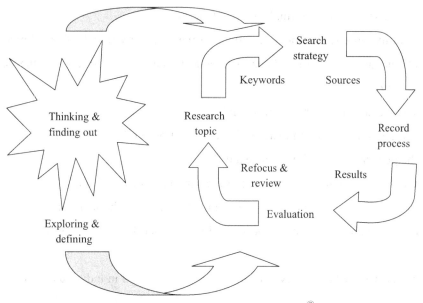

Figure 5.2   The literature searching cycle[②]

①   Catholic Theological Union. [EB/OL]. [2013-05-13]. http://www.ctu.edu.vn/guidelines/scientific/scientific/2.1howlit eraturesearch.htm.

②   De Montfort University. How to Undertake a Literature Search and Review for Dissertations and Final Year Projects [EB/OL]. [2012-06-13]. http://www.library.dmu.ac.uk/Images/Howto/LiteratureSearch.pdf.

You may find that you need to modify your search because you are finding too many or too few references. Here are some suggestions:

(1) Finding Too Many

Sometimes you will find that there is just too much information. This might be because:

Lots has been written on your main topic.

Your topic has links with many other subject areas.

It is up to you to decide how you will set the boundaries.

(2) Finding Too Few

This can be just as worrying. Try to refocus your topic, perhaps by carrying on reading while you are doing the primary research.

You will need to think of ways of broadening the scope of your project. In particular you can think about:

Making the project (or just your keywords) more general.

Comparative or related information that might be helpful.

Don't forget to speak to your tutor. Sometimes it just happens that very little is written on the subject you have chosen.[①]

3. Example of an Academic English Literature Search[②]

1) Define Your Topic and Formulate Good Questions

We would like to write a scientific article on the inequality of school enrollment in China. Children in China do not share equal access to education and we need to know the main reasons for this inequality.

What questions could we be interested in?

Is there a difference between in accessing to education rural areas and cities?

Does the gender of the children make a difference?

Does the socio-economic status (SES) of the parents make a difference?

Does the education of the parents have an influence on the school enrollment of children?

Is there a difference between first born children and their brothers or sisters?

…

As you can see, we have many questions. We are interested in individual, family and school

---

① De Montfort University. How to Undertake a Literature Search and Review for Dissertations and Final Year Projects [EB/OL]. [2012-06-13]. http://www.library.dmu.ac.uk/Images/Howto/LiteratureSearch.pdf.

② We got the inspiration for this example from this article: Nguyen, P. Effects of Social Class and School Conditions on Educational Enrollment and Achievement of Boys and Girls in Rural Vietnam [J]. International Journal of Educational Research, 2006, 45 (3), 153-175. And we change Vietnam to China.

characteristics so we will select the questions that tell us most about these items:

Does the socio-economic status (SES) of the parents make a difference?

Does the education of the parents have an influence on the school enrollment of children?

Of course it is possible to have more questions, but try to limit them.

2) Choose Your Keywords

Now we have our questions, which keywords will help us find information about our topic?

The first keywords we think of are education, SES, school results, education parents, inequality, …

In the end, we decide to combine the words "education" and "equality", so we will search for "educational inequality". We can try "school results", but "student achievement" could be an even better option. For our first search, we decide to try the keywords "educational inequality" and "SES".

3) Limit Your Search

You can set limits for the subject, publication date, geographic restrictions and publication type.

You can also use Boolean terms when you're searching: if you put "AND" between two keywords, the search engine will only give you the results of the combination of those two words. "OR" between keywords will give you the results of all the keywords, "NOT" will leave out the results of a keyword.

Our research will be about China, but information about other countries can be useful, so we decide not to set geographic restrictions.

We will use Boolean terms because different combinations of keywords will give us more results.

4) Decide About the Type of Information You Want and the Information Resources You Will Use

You can use "for example" books, journal articles and government papers.

Which libraries, online search engines, online journal databases, … will you use to find information?

We will search for scientific articles, books and government data about school enrollment. Our first search will be using Google Scholar.

5) Search the Literature

We search with Google Scholar (http://scholar.google.com/) for "educational inequality" AND "SES". These are the first results we get, as shown in Figure 5.3.

Figure 5.3 "educational inequality" AND "SES"

We search again with Google Scholar and this time we try "educational inequality" OR "SES". These are our first results now, as shown in Figure 5.4.

Figure 5.4 "educational inequality" OR "SES"

As you can see, the results of our two searches are different.

When you check the dates of the articles, you notice that they are out of date. So we decide to do an advanced search, and select articles written in the year 2000 or later. The search result is shown in Figure 5.5.

Educational Inequality: Mapping Race, Class and Gender. A Synthesis of Research Evidence
D Gillborn, HS Mirza - 2000 - eric.ed.gov
Abstract: This document synthesizes research on educational inequality in the United
Kingdom, examining the significance of race, ethnicity, gender, and social class. It analyzes
data from the Department of Education and Employment and from the ongoing Youth ...
被引用次数：396 - 相关文章 - 网页快照

[图书] Why segregation matters: Poverty and educational inequality　　　　bsdvt.org 中的 [PDF]
G Orfield, C Lee... - 2005 - bsdweb.bsdvt.org
Much of the discussion about school reform in the US in the past two decades has been
about racial inequality. President Bush has promised that the No Child Left Behind Act and
the forthcoming expansion of high stakes testing to high schools can end the "soft racism ...
被引用次数：247 - 相关文章 - HTML 版 - 所有 15 个版本

Educational inequality and the expansion of UK higher education　　　　lse.ac.uk 中的 [PDF]
J Blanden... - Scottish Journal of Political Economy, 2004 - Wiley Online Library
In this paper we explore changes over time in higher education (HE) participation and
attainment between people from richer and poorer family backgrounds during a time period
when the UK higher education system expanded at a rapid rate. We use longitudinal data ...
被引用次数：161 - 相关文章 - 所有 17 个版本

American schooling and educational inequality: A forecast for the 21st century　　icsd.k12.ny.us 中的 [PDF]
A Gamoran - Sociology of Education, 2001 - JSTOR
Inequality among different socioeconomic and racial groups was a salient subject for
sociology of education in the 20th century. What will happen to educational inequality in the
21st century? On the basis of past trends and the assumption that the American ...
被引用次数：161 - 相关文章 - 所有 46 个版本

Figure 5.5　"educational inequality" OR "SES" with written in the year 2000 or later

The first and second items look relevant to our topic and we decide to download them.

If we change the keyword "educational inequality" to "education inequality" and all other

things being the same, the above three searching results are as followed in Figure 5.6, Figure 5.7,

Figure 5.8.

Secondary school tracking and educational inequality: Compensation, reinforcement, or neutrality?　wisc.edu 中的 [PDF]
A Gamoran... - American journal of Sociology, 1989 - JSTOR
... Those who view tracking as having little to do with educational outcomes base their ... Inequality
interest in the success of schools in producing graduates, we code students who ... His- panics,
and males (and zero otherwise), and an index of socioeconomic status (SES), which is an ...
被引用次数：477 - 相关文章 - 所有 7 个版本

Socioeconomic status and health: how education, income, and occupation contribute to risk factors　nih.gov 中的 [PDF]
for cardiovascular discaso.
MA Winkleby, DE Jatulis... - American journal of ... 1992 - ajph.aphapublications.org
... Suinrnai There can be no SES measure that is universally valid and suitable for all pop- ulations. ...
and if the research hypothesis does not dictate otherwise, this study suggests that higher education,
rather than ... 2. Blaxter M. Evidence on inequality in health from a national survey ...
被引用次数：912 - 相关文章 - 所有 12 个版本

Race, cultural capital, and educational resources: Persistent inequalities and achievement returns　umich.edu 中的 [PDF]
VJ Roscigno - Sociology of education, 1999 - JSTOR
... Page 8. Inequalities and Achievement Returns 165 ... The analyses proceed in two steps.
First, we examine the extent to which racial differences in cultural capital and household
educational resources are a function of family SES and structure. ...
被引用次数：317 - 相关文章 - 所有 9 个版本

[图书] Inequality at the starting gate: Social background differences in achievement as children begin
school.
VE Lee... - 2002 - eric.ed.gov
... same disadvantaged children are then placed in low-resource schools, magnifying the initial
inequality. ... are based on analysis of the US Department of Education's Early Childhood ... scores
in literacy and mathematics by race, ethnicity, and socioeconomic status (SES) as they ...
被引用次数：521 - 相关文章 - 网页快照 - 所有 13 个版本

Figure 5.6　"education inequality" AND "SES"

[图书] High stakes education: Inequality, globalization, and urban school reform
P Lipman - 2004 - books.google.com
dr-rhythm.com 中的 [PDF]
What are the implications of education accountability reforms, particularly in urban schools, in a political, economic, and cultural context of intensifying globalization and increasing social inequality and marginalization along lines of race and class? High ...
被引用次数：403 - 相关文章 - 所有 5 个版本

[图书] Measuring education inequality: Gini coefficients of education
V Thomas, Y Wang... - 2001 - books.google.com
google.com 中的 [HTML]
Equal access to education is a basic human right. But in many countries gaps in education between various groups are staggering. An education Gini index--a new indicator for the distribution of human capital and welfare--facilitates comparison of education inequality ...
被引用次数：181 - 相关文章 - 所有 17 个版本

Measuring education inequality: Gini coefficients of education
V Thomas, Y Wang... - Research Working papers, 1999 - ingentaconnect.com
Abstract: January 2001Equal access to education is a basic human right. But in many countries gaps in education between various groups are staggering. An education Gini index—a new indicator for the distribution of human capital and welfare—facilitates ...
被引用次数：64 - 相关文章 - 所有 2 个版本

As America Becomes More Diverse: The Impact of State Higher Education Inequality.
PJ Kelly - National Center for Higher Education Management ..., 2005 - eric.ed.gov
Abstract: At a time when many states are becoming increasingly diverse, the need for more complete and useful measures of educational equality among ethnic and gender groups is critical. This study--funded by the Lumina Foundation for Education--examines disparities ...
被引用次数：65 - 网页快照

Figure 5.7 "education inequality" OR "SES"

[图书] High stakes education: Inequality, globalization, and urban school reform
P Lipman - 2004 - books.google.com
dr-rhythm.com 中的 [PDF]
What are the implications of education accountability reforms, particularly in urban schools, in a political, economic, and cultural context of intensifying globalization and increasing social inequality and marginalization along lines of race and class? High ...
被引用次数：403 - 相关文章 - 所有 5 个版本

[图书] Measuring education inequality: Gini coefficients of education
V Thomas, Y Wang... - 2001 - books.google.com
google.com 中的 [HTML]
Equal access to education is a basic human right. But in many countries gaps in education between various groups are staggering. An education Gini index--a new indicator for the distribution of human capital and welfare--facilitates comparison of education inequality ...
被引用次数：181 - 相关文章 - 所有 17 个版本

As America Becomes More Diverse: The Impact of State Higher Education Inequality.
PJ Kelly - National Center for Higher Education Management ..., 2005 - eric.ed.gov
Abstract: At a time when many states are becoming increasingly diverse, the need for more complete and useful measures of educational equality among ethnic and gender groups is critical. This study--funded by the Lumina Foundation for Education--examines disparities ...
被引用次数：65 - 网页快照

Precautionary demand for education, inequality, and technological progress
ED Gould, O Moav... - Journal of Economic Growth, 2001 - Springer
huji.ac.il 中的 [PDF]
This paper offers an explanation for the evolution of wage inequality within and between industries and education groups over the past several decades. The model is based on the disproportionate depreciation of technology-specific skills versus general skills due to ...
被引用次数：120 - 相关文章 - 所有 21 个版本

Figure 5.8 "education inequality" OR "SES" with published date from 2000 to 2012

As you can see, different keywords result in different searching results. So we should try as many relevant keywords as possible in the academic English literature search.

⚙️ Vocabulary

literature search	文献检索
literature review	文献综述
peer-reviewed	同行评议，同行审阅
accessibility	可达性，可及性
search engine	搜索引擎
synonym	同义词
terminology	术语，术语学

5.2 Performing an Academic English Literature Review

5.2.1　Definition of a Literature Review

A review of the literature is:

It is literally that: a "re" view or "look again" at what has already been written about the topic. It is not a literary review, which usually is a review of a literary work such as a play, novel, book of poems or a review that has some artistic merit.

A compilation of the research that has been published on a topic by recognized scholars and researchers.

Defined by a guiding concept (e.g., your research objective, the problem or issue you are discussing or your argumentative thesis). It is not just a descriptive list of the material available, or a set of summaries.

Provide background for the problem the students are attacking or put the problem into historical perspective and, at times, show how others handled similar problems in the past.[①]

A literature review is not:

An Annotated Bibliography: An annotated bibliography is a list of citations to books, articles, and documents. Each citation is followed by a brief (usually about 150 words) descriptive and evaluative paragraph, the annotation. The purpose of the annotation is to inform the reader of the relevance, accuracy, and quality of the sources cited.

Literary Review: A literary review is a brief critical discussion about the merits and weaknesses of a literary work such as a play, novel or a book of poems.

A Book Review: A book review is a brief critical discussion about the merits and weaknesses of a particular book. Book reviews of creative works are sometimes called literary reviews. Scholarly books are also reviewed by other scholars. Scholarly book reviews are often published in scholarly journals.

A good literature review:
- clearly delimits the subject matter to be reviewed.
- covers all important relevant literature.
- is up-to-date.

---

① 美国大学图书馆网站. [2012-07-13]. http://www.library.american.edu/Help/tutorials/lit_review/it_is.html.

- provides an insightful analysis of the ideas and conclusions in the literature.

- points out similarities and differences, strengths and weaknesses in the literature.

- identifies gaps in the literature for future research.

- identifies the context for which the literature is important.[①]

⚙ Vocabulary

artistic	艺术的，风雅的
compilation	编辑，编译
argumentative	好辩的，辩论的，争辩的
annotated	有注释的，带注解的
bibliography	参考书目，文献目录

5.2.2 Contents of a Literature Review[②]

A literature review should contain: an introduction, a middle (body) and a conclusion.

In the Introduction:

- define the topic, providing an appropriate context for reviewing the literature.

- establish writer's reasons (point of view) for reviewing the literature.

- explain the organization of the review (sequence).

- state what literature is and is not included (scope).

In the Body:

- group the literature according to common themes.

- provide insight into relationship between central topic and a larger area (i.e. discipline).

- proceed from the general, wider view of the research under review to the specific problem.

In the Conclusion:

- summarize major contributions of the literature.

- evaluate the current "state of the art" literature reviewed.

- point out major flaws, or gaps in research.

- outline issues pertinent to future study.

Some points to remember as the writer of a literature review:

- it is not a descriptive list of the information gathered.

---

① Source: available at http://www.asb.unsw.edu.au/learningandteaching/Documents/writingaliteraturereview.pdf.

② RMRT University. Library Guide to Literature Review [EB/OL]. [2014-05-05]. http://www.rmit.edu.au/browse/Current%20students%2FLibrary%2FGuides,%20tutorials%20and%20classes%2FLibrary%20guide%20to%20literature%20review/.

- it is not a summary of one piece of literature after another.
- the review must be defined by a guiding concept (e.g. essay question, research objective, etc.).
- your purpose is to convey to the reader what knowledge and ideas have been established on a topic—what are the strengths and weaknesses.
- do not attempt to list all published material, but rather synthesize and evaluate the literature according to your guiding concept.[①]

5.2.3 Steps to Do an Academic English Literature Review

1. Analyze the Literature[②]

Once you have identified and located the articles for your review, you need to analyze them and organize them before you begin writing:

(1) Overview the articles: skim the articles to get an idea of the general purpose and content of the articles (focus your reading here on the abstract, introduction and first few paragraphs, and the conclusion of each article).

(2) Group the articles into categories (e.g. into topics and subtopics and chronologically within each subtopic).

(3) Take notes:

- Define key terms: look for differences in the way key terms are defined (note these differences).
- Note key statistics that you may want to use in the introduction to your review.
- Select useful quotes that you may want to include in your review. Important tips: If you copy the exact words from an article, be sure to cite the page number, as direct quotes must always be accompanied by page references.
- Note emphases, strengths & weaknesses: since different research studies focus on different aspects of the issue being studied, each article that you read will have different emphases, strengths, and weaknesses. Your role as a reviewer is to evaluate what you read, so that your review is not a mere description of different articles, but rather a critical analysis that makes sense of the collection of articles that you are reviewing. Critique the research methodologies used in the studies, and distinguish between assertions (the author's opinion) and actual research findings (derived from empirical evidence).

---

① Source: Library guide to literature review, available at http://www.rmit.edu.au/browse/Current%20 students%2FLibrary%2FGuides,%20tutorials%20and%20classes%2FLibrary%20guide%20to%20literature%20review/.

② Helen Mongan-Rallis. Guidelines for Writing a Literature Review [EB/OL]. [2014-11-21]. http://www.duluth.umn. edu/~hrallis/guides/researching/litreview.html.

- Identify major trends or patterns: as you read a range of articles on your topic, you should make note of trends and patterns over time as reported in the literature. This step requires you to synthesize and make sense of what you read, since these patterns and trends may not be spelled out in the literature, but rather become apparent to you as you review the big picture that has emerged over time. Your analysis can make generalizations across a majority of studies, but you should also note inconsistencies across studies and over time.

- Identify gaps in the literature, and reflect on why these might exist (based on the understandings that you have gained by reading literature in this field of study). These gaps will be important for you to address as you plan and write your review.

- Identify relationships among studies: note relationships among studies, such as which studies were landmark ones that led to subsequent studies in the same area.

2. Write the Review[①]

- Identify the broad problem area.

- Early in the review, indicate why the topic being reviewed is important.

- Indicate why certain studies are important.

- If you are commenting on the timeliness of a topic, be specific in describing the time frame.

- If citing a classic or landmark study, identify it as such.

- If a landmark study was replicated, mention that and indicate the results of the replication.

- Discuss other literature reviews on your topic.

- Justify comments such as, "no studies were found."

- Avoid long lists of nonspecific references.

- Cite all relevant references in the review section of thesis, dissertation, or journal article.

⚙ Vocabulary

chronologically	按年代地
synthesize	合成，综合
inconsistency	不一致，易变
timeliness	及时，时间性，好时机

---

① Jose L. Galvan. Writing Literature Reviews: A Guide for Students of the Behavioral Sciences (3rd ed.) [M]. Glendale, CA: Pyrczak Publishing, 2006: 81-90.

⬚ FURTHER READING

Example of Bad and Good Literature Review

Bad Review

Sexual harassment has many consequences. Adams, Kottke, and Padgitt (1983) found that some women students said they avoided taking a class or working with certain professors because of the risk of harassment. They also found that men and women students reacted differently. Their research was a survey of 1,000 men and women graduate and undergraduate students. Benson and Thomson's study in Social Problems (1982) lists many problems created by sexual harassment. In their excellent book, The Lecherous Professor, Dziech and Weiner (1990) give a long list of difficulties that victims have suffered.

Good Review

The victims of sexual harassment suffer a range of consequences, from lowered self-esteem and loss of self-confidence to withdrawal from social interaction, changed career goals, and depression (Adams, Kottke, and Padgitt, 1983; Benson and Thomson, 1982; Dziech and Weiner, 1990). For example, Adams, Kottke, and Padgitt (1983) noted that 13 percent of women students said they avoided taking a class or working with certain professors because of the risk of harassment.

Source: Neuman, W. Lawrence. (2003). Social research methods: qualitative and quantitative approaches, 5th ed, Allyn and Bacon, Boston.

5.3
English Language Skills in Thesis and Dissertation Writing

5.3.1　Title of Thesis and Dissertation in English

The English title is usually comprised of noun phrases, including nouns and their pre-attribute or post-attribute. Therefore, there are generally nouns, adjectives, prepositions, conjunctions and articles in the English titles. If there are verbs, they should be in the forms of present participle, past participle or gerund.

It should be noted that if the title is an interrogation, there should be a question mark at the end of the title. However, if the title is a complete narrative sentence, there is no period at the end.

1. Three Common Problems in Writing English Titles of Thesis and Dissertation

(1) The position of the words including research, study and report, and the omission of the

sentence-initial article.

The words, such as A Study of/on，A Report of/on, The Survey of/on, and The Research on, are usually put at the beginning of the English title. In contrast, these words in Chinese are normally placed at the end of the Chinese title. For example, the Chinese title is "公众参与环境政策制定研究". Its corresponding English title is "A Study of Public Participation in Environmental Policymaking".

In recent years, English titles of theses and dissertations tend to be concise. The sentence-initial articles including "The, An, and A" are usually omitted. In addition, the words such as "A Study of, Report of, Research on, The Survey of, Design of, and The Observation on" at the beginning of the English title are also frequently omitted, if the omissions do not affect the meaning of the title. We can hardly find any articles published in English academic journals using "Research, Study or Report" in their titles or using "The, An, A" at the beginning of the titles. Therefore, it is better to translate the Chinese title "公众参与环境政策制定研究" to "Public Participation in Environmental Policymaking".

(2) Using translation software to translate Chinese titles directly into English.

Many students in China often use translation software including Kingsoft Powerword and Google Translate, and professional translation websites such as Youdao online translation, to translate Chinese titles of theses and dissertations directly into English. However, most of these translation software and translation websites just translate the Chinese titles word by word into English. Because of the different word orders, the meaning of the translated English title is usually different from its Chinese counterpart. For example, the Chinese title "高科技文化产业发展的影响因素研究" is translated into "High-tech culture industry development influence" by Youdao online translation. This translated English title cannot reflect the meaning of the Chinese title. The correct translation is "Factors Affecting the Development of High-tech Culture Industry" or "Determinants of the Development of High-tech Culture Industry".

Furthermore, the translations of some single words by professional translation software or translation website are not accurate enough. For example, almost all of the translation software translate the word "对策" in the Chinese title "高科技文化产业发展的对策研究" into "countermeasure". But the meaning of "countermeasure" in Chinese is "反措施、反抗手段" or "抵消另一行动所采取的行动", not "解决对策". "对策" in the title "高科技文化产业发展的对策研究" should be translated into "solution".

(3) Rules of writing uppercase and lowercase letters in English titles.

The content words in English consist of nouns, verbs, pronouns, adjectives, adverbs and numerals. The function words include articles, prepositions, conjunctions and interjections.

The rules of writing uppercase and lowercase letters in English titles are as follows:

● The content words should be uppercase while the function words should be lowercase.

● The function word at the beginning of the title should be uppercase.

● The word at the beginning of the subtitle should be uppercase, for example, Public Participation in Environmental Policymaking in China: A Case Study.

● The initials of each single content word in compound words should be uppercase, for example, The English-Speaking People in China.

2. Examples for English Titles of Theses and Dissertations

Example 1: 我国依法行政工作的问题及强化对策研究——基于我国司法权与行政权现存关系的考察

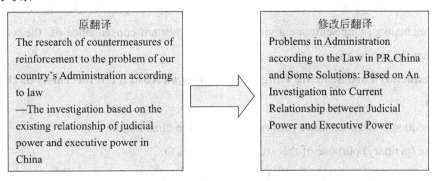

Example 2: 沈阳市养老服务体系建设中的政府职能研究

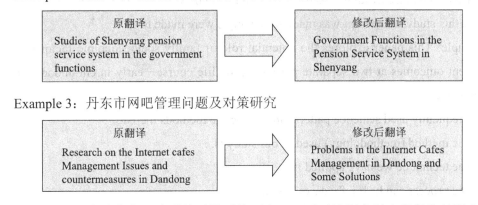

Example 3：丹东市网吧管理问题及对策研究

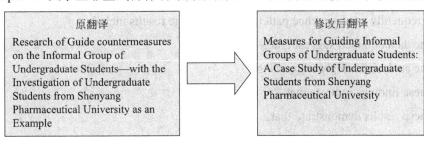

Example 4：大学生非正式群体引导对策研究——以对沈阳药科大学学生的调查为例

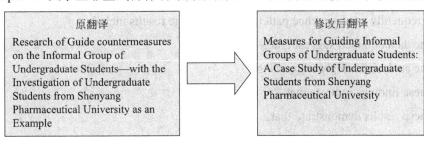

5.3.2 Abstract of Thesis and Dissertation in English

1. Five Essential Elements of the Abstract

Abstracts are short statements that briefly summarize an article or an academic paper.

Abstracts are similar to the blurbs on the back covers of novels. They entice someone to read further. In the abstract, you have to prove that it is worthwhile reading your work.

There are five essential elements of the abstract, which are shown below:

- Background: One or two simple opening sentences offering the context for the work.

- Aims: One or two sentences giving the purpose of the work.

- Method(s): One or two sentences explaining what has been done. (Described as it is unusual)

- Results: One or two sentences summarizing the main discovery. (Absolutely essential)

- Conclusions: One sentence giving the most important consequence of the work(Telling what the results mean).

2. Frequently Used Sentence Patterns in Writing an Abstract of the Thesis or Dissertation in English

(1) Frequently used sentence patterns in writing the aims include:

- The (primary) purpose of this study (paper) was to...

- The object (aim) of this study (the present research) was to...

- This (The present) study was designed (undertaken) to...

- In this study, an attempt was made to (attempts were made to)...

Example: This paper explores the potential role of family socioeconomic factor in school achievement outcomes at two separate periods in the life course—early in childhood or during late adolescence.

(2) Frequently used sentence patterns in writing the methods include:

- The method (methodology) used in our study is...

- The technique we have applied is...

- The process can be briefly described as...

- The field survey, consisted of three steps, is described in...

(3) Frequently used sentence patterns in writing the results include:

- The data obtained suggest that...

- The analysis strongly suggests that...

- These findings indicate that...

- These results demonstrate that...

- We conclude that...

- In conclusion, we state that...

(4) Frequently used sentence patterns in writing the conclusion include:

- It is concluded that...

- We conclude that...

- The study suggests that...

3. Hints for Writing an Abstract of Thesis or Dissertation in English

(1) Voice

- The abstract of an academic article is mainly to describe facts. Therefore, it is preferred to use the passive voice rather than utilize the active voice in an abstract.

(2) Tense

- If the background are general facts, which could not be changed by time, it should use the present tense to describe it.

- In describing the research purpose or activities, mostly, the present tense is used in "paper-oriented" abstract (e.g. This paper presents...), while the past tense is mostly used in "research-oriented" abstract (e.g. We investigated...).

- In describing the research process, methods, and results, normally, the past tense is used.

- In the conclusion and discussion part, the present tense is generally used.

(3) Personal Pronouns

Generally, it had better use the third personal pronouns, such as "the author", to replace the first personal pronouns, such as "I" or "we".

Warning:

Due to the significant difference between the Chinese and English, such as the word order, the verbalism etc, the students should not translate the Chinese abstract into English word by word, to the contrary, they should write the abstract in English utilizing the English thinking.

Chapter 6
English at Work

6.1
English in the Interview

6.1.1   Personal Information

Personal information is the basic information for an interview, here are some questions and answers for personal information in the interview.

(1) How would you describe yourself?

I sincerely believe that I'm the best person for the job. I bring an unique quality that makes me the very best person for the job—my attitude for excellence. Not just giving lip service to excellence, but putting every part of myself into achieving it. In college and at my previous jobs, I have consistently reached for becoming the very best I can become. I think my leadership awards from my college, and my management positions are the result of possessing the qualities you're looking for in an employee.

(2) How would you describe your leadership skills?

I am a leader who likes to take everyone's opinion into consideration and be willing to listen to what they want to say. I think my job as a leader is to organize things and keep them in order. Being the leader does not mean I know everything there is to know because I can not possibly know more than everyone else about every topic. It is just not plausible.

(3) What is your most rewarding accomplishment?

The most rewarding accomplishment that I've had was that I got my bachelor degree. Because, I was able to share the fruits of my triumphs with my family, especially my parents. I compensated all their hard works and sacrifices in order for me to finish my studies.

(4) Given the investment our company will make in hiring and training you, can you give us a reason to hire you?

My background to date has been centered around preparing myself to become the very best financial consultant I can become. Let me tell you specifically how I've prepared myself. I am an undergraduate student in finance and accounting at Peking University. My past experiences have been in retail and higher education. Both aspects have prepared me well for this career.

(5) What quality or attribute do you feel will most contribute to your career success?

My greatest strength is my flexibility. I have learned that work conditions change from day to day and throughout the day, as well, no matter where I have worked in the past. I also have realized that certain projects require individual attention and others involve a teamwork approach. These are just a few examples of the changes that happen in the financial consulting field, as you are well aware. My flexibility to adapt to the different demands of the job has allowed me to surpass my supervisor's expectations.

(6) What personal weakness has caused you the greatest difficulty in school or on the job?

My greatest weakness had been delegation. I would take it upon myself to do many small projects throughout my shift as a manager that could have been done by others in an attempt to improve my workers' efficiency. Once I realized that I was doing more work than the other assistant managers, and they were achieving better results, I reevaluated what I was doing. I quickly realized that if I assigned each person just one small project at the beginning of their shift, clearly state expectations for the project, and then follow up that everything would get done, and I could manage much more efficiently and actually accomplish much more.

(7) What is the biggest mistake you've made?

The biggest mistake in my life that I have made is taking for granted the sacrifices my parents endured for me. I look back and realize that everything they did was for me so that I could succeed in life. I am thankful now and do everything to my best ability to make them proud because I am so thankful that they have been there for me so that I can give back to society and to my job the opportunities that they never had.

(8) What have you learned from your experiences outside the workplace/classroom?

I have learned that the real world is much different from what you learn in the classroom, that some things you learn are similar to what you were taught, but for the most part, learning is achieved through the process of doing. In the world of health-care marketing, things happen at a fast pace, and you must take everything one day at a time while still keeping an eye on the future.

(9) When given an important assignment, how do you approach it?

I like to make a list, a timeline of how and by when things need to be done. I really like to get started on the assignment immediately because I've found that once I get started on a project I tend to get gradually more excited about it and involved in it, and I want to expand the project more and more as I go on. By getting started earlier, I can get the most out of the project and maximize it as much as possible while providing time to give it that extra review.

(10) What specific goals, including those related to your occupation, have you established for your life?

I want to be working for an excellent company like yours in a job in which I am managing information. I plan to contribute my leadership, interpersonal, and technical skills. My long-range career goal is to be the best information systems technician I can for the company I work for.

6.1.2　Education Background

Education background is a common inquiring aspect in the interview. Here are some questions and answers about education background.

(1) How has your college experience prepared you for a business career?

I have prepared myself to transition into the work force through real-world experience involving travel abroad, internship, and entrepreneurial opportunities. While interning with a private organization, I developed a 15-page marketing plan that recommended more effective ways the company could promote its services. As you can see from my academic, extracurricular, and experiential background, I have unconditionally committed myself to success as a marketing professional.

(2) What were your reasons for selecting your college or university?

My college has always had a reputation as having an excellent accounting department, so I knew that if I enrolled there, I would achieve first-class preparation for my chosen career field. It is also a highly accredited school known for satisfying employers with the preparation of its graduates—that's why companies like yours recruit at my school—the school produces top graduates. The school offers an excellent liberal-arts background, which research shows equips graduates with numerous qualities, such as versatility and strong critical-thinking skills. Finally, having visited the campus before enrolling, I knew that the business school emphasized group projects. During my four years in the school, I participated in more than 35 group projects, which taught me invaluable teamwork, communication, and interpersonal skills.

(3) Which college classes or subjects did you like best? Why?

My favorite classes have been the ones pertaining to my major, which is marketing. These classes have laid the groundwork for my career in marketing. They have also taught me skills that I can bring to my employer, ranging from communication skills to interacting with others.

(4) Describe the type of professor that has created the most beneficial learning experience for you.

My favorite professors were the ones who gave me hands-on learning experiences that I can apply to my career. Any person can make you memorize the quadratic equation, but someone who can show you how to use it, and why, were the professors I liked. I liked teachers who realized that sometimes there is more than one answer and everyone thinks differently.

6.1.3　Experiences and Potentialities in Work

The questions about working experiences and potentialities in the future are always in the questions list in the interview. Here are some examples.

(1) Please describe the ideal job for you following graduation.

My ideal job is one that incorporates both my education and practical work skills to be the best I can be. Namely combining my education in finance with my working knowledge of customer service operations, entrepreneurial abilities, computer skills, and administrative skills. I want to utilize my analytical expertise to help people meet their financial goals. This is exactly why I am convinced that I would be a very valuable member in your company.

(2) What influenced you to choose this career?

My past experiences have shown me that I enjoy facing and overcoming the challenge of making a sale. Without a doubt, once I have practiced my presentation and prepared myself for objections, I feel very confident approaching people I don't know and convincing them that they need my product. Lastly, I like sales because my potential for success is limited only by how much of myself I dedicate toward my goal. If any profession is founded on self-determinism, it surely must be sales.

(3) What do you expect to be doing in five years?

Although it is hard to predict the future, I sincerely believe that I will become a very good financial consultant. I believe that my abilities will allow me to excel to the point that I can seek other opportunities as a portfolio manager (the next step) and possibly even higher. My ultimate goal continues to be—and will always be—to be the best at whatever level I am working at in your company.

(4) Describe the characteristics of a successful manager.

A successful manager should have the vision and capabilities to formulate strategies to reach his or her objectives and communicate these ideas to his or her team members. In addition to serving as a positive role model for co-workers, successful managers must also be capable of inspiring others to recognize, develop, and apply their talents to their utmost potential to reach a common goal. These are the traits I hope to demonstrate when I'm a manager.

(5) Why did you decide to seek a position in this field?

I want to work in the marketing and PR industry because ever since I took my first marketing course in college, I have felt very passionate toward the industry and cannot imagine myself doing anything else.

(6) Why did you decide to seek a position in this company?

I am convinced that there would be no better place to work than Alliance PKU. You are the top consulting firm in China. You provide your employees with the tools they need to stay competitive and sharpen their skills while working in an open, team-based environment. I am also aware that you provide a mentor for all new employees, and I would embrace any opportunity to work with a mentor and eventually become one myself.

(7) Which is more important to you, the job itself or your salary?

A salary commensurate with my experience and skills is important, but it's only one piece of the package. Many other elements go into making up a compensation package, but more importantly, it's critical to me to enjoy what I'm doing, fit into the corporate culture, and feel I'm making a genuine contribution.

(8) Which two or three things are most important to you in your job?

I want to be happy. I want to work in a job that I am passionate about, and for a company that respects and rewards my contributions. I want to have co-workers whom I like and respect. I think these things all work together for a positive work environment—which increases productivity—resulting in happy employees and a happy employer.

I also seek fulfillment. I don't want to work in a job that I feel is below what I am capable of doing. I seek a job that will challenge me to perform at the highest levels and seek ongoing professional development so that I can be even better at my job, making an even stronger contribution to my employer. From everything I've researched and seen, this job that I'm interviewing for meets all my criteria.

(9) How do you determine priorities in scheduling your time? Give examples.

I took a time-management course in which I learned to prioritize all tasks on A, B, or C lists. I always try to tackle the A list first. In every working situation, co-workers have always complimented me on how well I manage my time. I enjoy the social atmosphere of the office, but I make it a point not to waste much time on chitchat with colleagues. I've also learned that the average office worker spends about an hour a day handling e-mail. I make it a point not to deal with my e-mail more than once or twice a day and I filter my messages into folders so I can prioritize the way I deal with them.

(10) Describe a situation in which you had to arrive at a compromise or guide others to a compromise.

My first semester in college, I was a political-science major. My introductory government class professor had a differing political view than I. We disagreed on everything, and many classes were filled with criticizing each others' view. However, on one test I answered a question with the view I believe in, and she marked it wrong. So I asked her how an opinion can be wrong, and she said because her opinion is the way she taught it in class. I pointed out that my answer showed I understood the concepts of the question. She agreed, and I also agreed not be so combative in answers on tests. Compromise is the key to problem solution.

(11) Tell me about a time when you failed to meet a deadline. What things did you fail to do? What were the repercussions? What did you learn?

I recently failed to meet a deadline in my communications course with a project I had to do on the Internet. I did not meet the deadline because I underestimated the amount of time the assignment would cost me to complete. Therefore, the assignment was incomplete when I turned it in. As a result I lost points on my final grade. I learned the importance of examining tasks more carefully so I can better estimate the amount of time required to complete them. I also learned to build some flexible time into projects so that if my estimates are wrong, I'll still have time to complete the tasks.

(12) What, in your opinion, are the key ingredients in guiding and maintaining successful business relationships?

Communication is the key ingredient in guiding and maintaining successful business relationships. Being able to clearly communicate your ideas to others allows you to build and maintain a relationship with others. It is also very important to be an active listener and address any concerns or questions the other party might have. Also, to maintain a successful business relationship, you have to be able to compromise and do what is the best for both parties involved.

(13) What would you do if the work of a subordinate or team member was not up to expectations?

Luckily, I have quite a bit of previous team experience, and have faced this situation a few times in the past—so let me tell you how I've learned to handle the issue. The most important principle in dealing with an underperforming subordinate or team member is honest communications—talking with the person can lead to some surprising discoveries, such as the person not understanding the assigned tasks or being overwhelmed with the assignment. Once I discovered the problem, I could then figure out a solution that usually solved the problem and allowed the work to move forward. So often in situations like this, the problem is some combination of miscommunication and unrealistic expectations.

(14) What would you do if the priorities on a project you were working on changed

suddenly?

I would notify everyone working on the project of the changes. I would then want to know why the priorities have changed, and if there is risk of them changing again in the future, I would then meet with everyone involved with a new strategy to address the new priorities.

(15) You disagree with the way your supervisor says to handle a problem. What would you do?

I would evaluate why I disagreed with my supervisor and come up with a different way that I think the situation should be handled. I would then sit down with my supervisor—in private—and discuss with him what I had a problem with and how I think it should have been done.

(16) As a supervisor, you've made an unpopular decision. What action would you take so that morale in the department is not negatively affected?

I would call for a meeting to let my employees know that their opinions about my decision are valued, however, I would also explain to them why the decision needed to be made. Sometimes people are more empathetic once they know the reasons for a certain action. I would also ensure employees that positives are to come from this decision and reinforce that their opinions and ideas are valued, but that this was a decision that needed to be made.

(17) Give me an example of a time you had to persuade other people to take action. Were you successful?

I was the leader of my macroeconomics group in college. As a leader, I had to delegate parts of the assignment to other group members. Not only did I do a written part for each paper, but also I gathered all of the props we needed for our oral presentation, and I typed all of the five papers assigned. I was also taking four other classes at the time. By the fourth paper, I decided to persuade some of the other group members to edit and finalize it. I learned a lot about delegation and leadership when I discovered that they were happy to help out.

(18) Describe a time when you got co-workers or classmates who dislike each other to work together. How did you accomplish this? What was the outcome?

When I worked for a law firm, my co-workers and I had a huge mailing to complete. We had the choice of working more efficiently as a team—or individually in a much more time-consuming manner. My two co-workers did not care for each other and they wanted to complete the mail-out on an individual level. When I presented them with the evidence that we would finish at least an hour earlier by working together, they decided that working together was the right path to take. As a result, we finished the mail-out in a short period of time and could work on other tasks that day.

(19) Everyone has made some poor decisions or has done something that just did not turn

out right. Give an example of when this has happened to you.

In my psychology class, we had to do a group project and presentation, and we got to pick our group members. I was a freshman, and inexperienced with group projects, so I picked two of my friends, even though I knew that they were not hard workers and didn't care about their grades. I just wanted to be comfortable with the people I was working with. I ended up doing most of the project very last minute and by myself because I couldn't get them to work on it with me. The project and presentation were both really bad, So all three of our final grades were almost 10 points lower. Needless to say, I never picked a friend as a group member, again.

⚙ Vocabulary

unique	独一无二的，独特的
plausible	貌似真实的
rewarding	值得的，有报酬的
accomplishment	成就，技能
undergraduate student	本科生
flexibility	柔韧性，灵活性
teamwork	配合，团队工作
surpass	超过
sacrifice	牺牲
interpersonal	人际的
extracurricular	课外的
passionate	狂热的，充满激情的
genuine	真正的
prioritize	优先处理
accredited	可信任的，委任
versatility	多才多艺
delegation	代表，授权

👤 FURTHER READING

Interviewers' Tough Questions

Hiring managers are known to create a tough interviewing experience in order to challenge candidates and test their thinking abilities under pressure. To find out which companies have the toughest interviews, we turned to Glassdoor.com, which put together a list of the 25 most difficult companies to interview with. The site looked through 80,000 interview reviews, ranking companies based on a 5-point interview difficulty scale. Glassdoor also included a "negative interview experience" and "employee satisfaction" rating, to see if employees were ultimately satisfied with their jobs.

The First Three—Difficulty Doesn't Match Popularity

No.3 Oliver Wyman

Interview difficulty rating: 3.7

Negative interview experience rating: 9%

Employee satisfaction: 3.6

Tough interview question: "What is the profit potential of offering wireless Internet service on planes?"

No.2 Boston Consulting Group

Interview difficulty rating: 3.8

Negative interview experience rating: 10%

Employee satisfaction: 4.1

Tough interview question: "How many people would use a drug that prevents baldness?"

No.1 McKinsey & Company

Interview difficulty rating: 3.9

Negative interview experience rating: 13%

Employee satisfaction: 4.1

Tough interview question: "There are 3 products: tomatoes, luxury cars, T-shirts. What value added-tax is applied to each product type?"

The Famous Ones, Not Easy Ones

No.9 Google

Interview difficulty rating: 3.5

Negative interview experience rating: 18%

Employee satisfaction: 4.1

Tough interview question: "How many hotels are there in the US?"

No.24 Facebook

Interview difficulty rating: 3.3

Negative interview experience rating: 19%

Employee satisfaction: 4.6

Tough interview question: "It's 6 p.m. and your work day is over, what happened during the day that made it awesome?"

No.25 Amazon

Interview difficulty rating: 3.3

Negative interview experience rating: 18%

Employee satisfaction: 3.3

Tough interview question: "If you were to rank quality, customer satisfaction, and safety in order of importance, how would you rank them? Discuss."

Source: English Salon, 2012,(11):14-15.

6.2
How to Write E-mail

The ability to write an e-mail to foreign researchers appropriately is an essential professional skill. In this sector, we will cover the basic format for a formal e-mail used for professional communication as well as the basic grammar for polite requests in English.

Most formal e-mails contain a three or four paragraphs structure that includes the following:

- Subject header
- Salutation
- Titles and greetings
- Introducing yourself
- Start the letter
- Closing sentence

6.2.1　Subject Header

The subject header is very important because it tells the reader what your e-mail is about. When people receive an e-mail from senders they don't know, they look to the subject header for clues. Based on subject header alone, they may delete mail that looks unimportant to them. So, the subject header is the only hint that the e-mail is important and should be read immediately. If your subject header is vague—or even worse, if it's blank—you have missed your first opportunity to inform or persuade your reader.

Basically the subject header = goal of the email.

Good subject headers are short, clear and to the point. They reflect the purpose of your message.

Examples:

"Homework assignment"

"Question about today's lecture"

"I will be absent for your_____class[1] tomorrow"

"Request for a space in your_____class"

"I'd like to enroll in your_____class"

6.2.2 Salutation

The salutation you use will depend on your relationship with the recipient as well as the formality of the letter. Here are some possibilities:

If you're writing a formal letter and you do know the contact person, the safest salutation to use is "Dear". "Dear" is the correct formal greeting for all types of e-mail and letters. If you're writing a semiformal letter, you might use "Dear" or "Hello" as a salutation. If you're writing an informal letter, you can use "Dear" or "Hello", as well as more informal greetings such as "Hi".[2]

Avoid "Hey"—no one we queried likes that one.

6.2.3 Titles and Greetings

If you are sending an e-mail to a faculty member, then use title and family/last name.

There are actually very few titles in English. They are Professor, Dr., Mr., Ms., Mrs., and some military and political titles.

1. Professor/Dr.

Generally speaking, you should use "Dear Professor + Last name". If he/she has a doctor degree, you can also call him/her "Dear Dr. + Last name".

Use only one title with a last name, and not both Dr. and Prof. together.

Do not use the professor's first name unless you have been explicitly invited to do so. If she or he signs the reply with a first name, it is still best to address her/him as "Professor" in an e-mail.

Examples:

Wrong: Prof. Dr. Dong-guk Lee

Right: Professor Jones

Right: Dr. Jones

The abbreviation Prof. is usually only used with the full name, not with family name only. The abbreviation Dr. is used with family name only, except for very formal introductions such as introducing a guest speaker.

You should always try to find the name of the person you are sending applications to, but if

---

[1] Be sure to include the name or number of the course you are writing about. The more specific you can be, the easier you make it for your professor.

[2] "Hi" should only be used for personal e-mails, or if you know the recipient of the e-mail well.

you can't, then you should use either of these two examples:

"Dear Sir or Madam,"

"To Whom It May Concern,"

2. Mr./Ms./Mrs.

Ms. is the most commonly used salution for women today as the equivalent to Mr., because it does not show whether a woman is married or not.

Only use Mrs. or Miss if a woman asks you to do so.

Do not use "Mr. Last-name", especially when the professor has a Ph.D., where the only alternative honorific is "Dr.".

6.2.4 Introducing Yourself

Pay attention to the difference between undergraduate and graduate students when introducing yourself.

1. Undergraduate Students

These examples are appropriate for introducing undergraduate students.

Examples:

● My name is Ki-Hyun Seol, and I am a senior in the Department of Civil Engineering at Hanyang University in Seoul, Korea.

● I am studying civil engineering at Hanyang University.

● My major is civil engineering. I go to Hanyang University.

Major is used only for undergraduate students. Major is a type of student; it is not a field of study. If you introduce yourself at a conference and say, "My major is mechanical engineering", then people might think that you are an undergraduate student who is helping to move tables and giving directions at the conference, not a presenter!

2. Graduate Students

These examples are appropriate for introducing graduate students.

Examples:

● My name is Ji-Sung Park. I am a master's student in the Department of Chemical Engineering at Hanyang University in Seoul, Korea. I am currently researching hybrid materials.

● My name is Hong-Mahn Choi. I am a Ph.D. student in the Department of Chemical Engineering at Hanyang University in Seoul, Korea. I am currently researching self-assembling molecules and nanoparticles.

Any of these structures are correct for talking about your student status. Master's candidate is not as common, but it is not wrong.

When you are introducing yourself, don't just mention that you are a graduate student. Say what kind of student you are, master's or doctoral.

- master's student
- master's candidate
- doctoral student
- doctoral candidate
- Ph.D. student
- Ph.D. candidate

3. Common Mistakes When Introducing Yourself

(1) Ph.D. student/ Ph.D. Candidate

There is an official difference between Ph.D. student and Ph.D. candidate. A Ph.D. candidate is considered to have finished taking courses, and is currently researching or writing a dissertation whereas a Ph.D. student is still taking classes.

(2) Ph.D/ PhD/ Ph.D.

For doctoral degrees, use either periods after both "h" and "D" or no periods at all, not just one period. It is an abbreviation of Doctor of Philosophy from the Latin, Philosophiae Doctor, or D.Phil., so the "h" is not a full word. The modern trend is to write it without periods.

Examples:

Wrong: She is a Ph.D student.

Right: She is a PhD student.

Right: She is a Ph.D. student.

(3) Univ./ U./ University

Don't use an abbreviation for the word "university" in normal writing unless you are filling out an application form or you lack space to write in a document like a brochure.

Examples:

Wrong: I graduated from Hanyang Univ.

Wrong: I graduated from Hanyang U.

Right: I study at Hanyang University.

Right: I am studying at Hanyang University in Seoul, Korea.

(4) Research Part/ Researching about/ Research Field

Do not use "about" or "part" to describe your research.

Examples:

Wrong: I am currently researching about fuel cells.

Wrong: My research part is nanoparticles.

Right: I am currently researching fuel cells.

Right: My research field is nanoparticles.

Right: My area of research is hydrogen storage materials.

(5) Receive a Degree in Subject/From Department

You receive a degree in a subject or from a university, but not from a department or a division.

Examples:

Wrong: He has a M.S. in the Department of Materials Science and Engineering.

Wrong: He has a M.S. in the Division of Materials Science and Engineering.

Right: Hc has a M.S. in Materials Science and Engineering from Hanyang University.

Right: He is a master's student in the Division of Materials Science and Engineering at Hanyang University.

6.2.5　Start the Letter

Now you can start your letter. Get straight to the point. Time is money, and you don't want to waste the recipient's time. State your request clearly and seek for his help.

1. Be Specific

Think of your audience. Give them the complete information to solve the problem, answer your question, or complete the task. Give them exact page references of articles, product numbers, or shipping orders that they might need to do a job or fix a problem without looking up the information. For example, if you are requesting an appointment, state your purpose and name the time that you could come in your initial message. Your respondent may then be able to answer you with only one additional message. If necessary, quote selectively and briefly from any prior messages to provide context and background.

Examples:

Wrong: It would be very helpful if you could send me some image data that is mentioned on your website.

The recipient might ask: Which website? What data? What section or page? Which article?

Right: Your paper entitled, "_____" has been essential for my work on _____. Would it be possible for you to explain the method for _____ on page 23 of that article. How does your proposed algorithm…?

2. Suggest a Solution

If you are e-mailing with a problem, suggest a solution. Be considerate of how your solution might create additional work for the professor. If you can accomplish this important step, you can help your professor take action immediately after reading your e-mail. And not only will you get a quick response from them, but you'll also get into that wait listed class much sooner.

3. Be Respectful

Think about what kinds of things might sound odd or offensive to your professor. Many professors advise that you think about why you are sending an e-mail message. Are you asking something that could easily be checked if you took a few extra steps yourself? For example, e-mailing a professor simply to ask when her office hours are can be annoying when the office hours have been clearly announced on the syllabus already. On the other hand, e-mailing for an appointment is just fine. Are you asking a question privately that might be better asked on the course conference, where all the students might usefully see the response? Are you e-mailing to lodge a complaint or to ask for a letter of recommendation or to seek help with a problem set? In these cases, personal contact and an office visit might be much better.

4. Keep It Short

Write short paragraphs, separated by blank lines. Ideally, you don't want more than three to four sentences in a paragraph. And you don't want to stuff one message with too many paragraphs. Keep most messages to under a screen in length; Unless, that is, you're sharing feedback or a personal story that will help your professor get to know you and better understand how they can help you out. Lots of readers will simply defer reading long messages, and then may never come back to them.

5. Keep the Message Focused

Often recipients only read partway through a long message, hit "reply" as soon as they have something to contribute, and forget to keep reading. This is part of human nature.

If your e-mail contains multiple messages that are only loosely related, in order to avoid the risk that your reader will reply only to the first item that grabs his or her fancy, you could number your points to ensure they are all read (adding an introductory line that states how many parts there are to the message). If the points are substantial enough, split them up into separate messages so your recipient can delete, respond, file, or forward each item individually.

6.2.6 Closing Sentence

A closing sentence ends your letter on a good note and establishes a connection with the recipient. Make two hard returns after the last paragraph of the letter, and then write the closing sentence. For formal letters, stick to "Sincerely yours", "Kindest regards", or "Best wishes".

👤≡ FURTHER READING

Basic Guidelines for Writing E-mail

There are several things you can do to improve your chances of gaining admission. Contacting a faculty member is critical, since they make decisions on who is admitted. However, when contacting a faculty member, there are several key points to remember:

1. English Expression Must Be Perfect

It is better to proofread very important documents on paper before sending them. Read it over. Show a draft to a close associate, in order to see whether it actually makes sense. It is a good idea to write the first draft of an important e-mail in a word processing program to allow you to check the grammar and spelling. You can then copy and paste the text into your e-mail program. A faculty wants to bring in students who will make less work for me, not more.

2. Make Sure Your Letters Arrive on Time

The recommendation letters are critically important to your case. Make sure they arrive on time. Letters from academic sources are preferable to those from industry, and a letter from an advisor on a research project is the best, so long as it directly addresses your performance on the research project, and your skills as a researcher.

3. Make Your Point Fast

In the preliminary review of files, the typical application receives 2-8 minutes of consideration by each faculty member that reviews it. Follow-on reviews are typically more detailed, since there are fewer files at this point. Personal statements are first scanned, then carefully read if they seem interesting. Your personal statement should ensure that the most important points are made in the first 1-2 paragraphs.

Because the faculty may receive many hundreds of applications, and must make rapid decisions on them. In order to provide timely response to applicants, each application cannot be reviewed for very long. Second, after reviewing hundreds of applications, faculty get very good at making rapid assessments of academic records.

4. Use Your Professional E-mail Address, Not Your Personal One

If you have a university account, try to use your real name, not a nickname for your ID if possible. Don't use an account like toughguy@ihanyang.ac.kr for a formal email or job applications. It is a good idea to have one e-mail for your professional purposes and another one for your school or job related mail. You can add some numbers if you have a common family name as I have done, adamturner7@gmail.com.

5. Don't Demand or Ask for A Positive Result

Don't demand or ask for a positive result, whether it is for a job or a journal article.

Examples:

Wrong: Please send e-mail to me, I hope with good news.

Also, don't say that you are waiting for an answer, but instead give a specific reason why they should contact you by a specific time.

Wrong: I look forward to your positive reply.

Wrong: I am waiting for your answer soon.

Wrong: I expect that I get help from you.

Right: Thank you for considering my application.

Right: I would really appreciate any advice you could give me.

Right: I look forward to your reply.

Right: If you have any questions or require further information, please do not hesitate to contact me at …

Right:I would really appreciate it if you could review this article this week. The deadline is next Tuesday.

6. Don't Use Smiley Faces or Other Emoticons in Formal E-mails

Don't use smiley faces or other emoticons when e-mailing professors, and don't use all those internet acronyms, abbreviations, and shortened spellings (e.g., LOL, or "U" for "you"). Similarly, don't confuse e-mail style with txt style. All of that electronic shorthand signals a level of intimacy (and perhaps of age) that is inappropriate for exchanges with your professors.

Example:

An Instant-delete E-mail

"Dear Professor Kelsky,

I am a student at XXX College and I'm thinking about graduate school on xxx and I'm getting in touch to ask if you can give me any advice or direction about that.

Sincerely,

student X"

Here is what an e-mail to a professor should look like:

Dear Professor XXX,

I am a student at XXX College with a major in xxx. I am a [junior] and will be graduating next May. I have a [4.0 GPA] and experience in our college's [summer program in xxx/internship program in xxx/Honors College/etc.].

I am planning to attend graduate school in xxx, with a focus on xxx. In one of my classes, "xxx," which was taught by Professor XXX, I had the chance to read your article, "xxxx."

I really enjoyed it, and it gave me many ideas for my future research. I have been exploring graduate programs where I can work on this topic. My specific project will likely focus on xxxx, and I am particularly interested in exploring the question of xxxxx.

I hope you don't mind my getting in touch, but I'd like to inquire whether you are currently accepting graduate students. If you are, are you willing to talk to me a bit more, by e-mail or on the phone, or in person if I can arrange a campus visit, about my graduate school plans? I have explored your department's graduate school website in detail, and it seems like an excellent fit for me because of its emphasis on xx and xx, but I still have a few specific questions about xx and xxx that I'd like to talk to you about.

I know you're very busy so I appreciate any time you can give me. Thanks very much,

Sincerely,

XX XXX

Why is this email good? Because it shows that you are serious and well qualified. It shows that you have done thorough research and utilized all the freely available information on the website. It shows that you have specific plans which have yielded specific questions. It shows that you are familiar with the professor's work. It shows that you respect the professor's time.

All of these attributes will make your e-mail and your name stand out, and exponentially increase your chances of getting a timely, thorough, and friendly response, and potentially building the kind of relationship that leads to a strong mentoring relationship.

Source: available at

http://wenku.baidu.com/link?url=S_YaPD94qsBJU0zdeSOTV5N5j_NgHB1ZOBmoEpXYQK72g4dzXZJ4j5MDdl2-z40IjT2Y4JT6Obbe26S31zwEvQvGUs302TkJ1lRaiQxDO5C

How to Write a Successful CV

6.3.1 What Is a CV?

Curriculum Vitae is an outline of a person's educational and professional history, usually prepared for job applications. It conveys your personal details in the best way. You can "sell" your skills, abilities, qualifications and experience to employers. So it is the most flexible and convenient way to make applications.

6.3.2　When Should a CV Be Used?

- When an employer asks for applications to be received in this format.
- When an employer simply states "apply to ..." without specifying the format.
- When making speculative applications (when writing to an employer who has not advertised a vacancy but who you hope might have one).

6.3.3　What Information Should a CV Include?

Here are the key headings and pointers that you should include:

1. Personal Details

Normally these would be your name, address, date of birth, telephone number and e-mail.

2. Education

This section should include your education. It is important to put the title of each educational institution and the date that you attended. If you have not graduated, then you can list an expected grade and include your yearly average if you know them.

3. Work Experience

You should start off with your most recent employment, as with your education. You should include paid work, voluntary work and shadowing roles. It is important to state the dates that you worked at each place，for example (Dec. 2009-Dec. 2010).

List some examples under the headings. They can show what skills you have gained from each place along with your key responsibilities.

- Even work in a shop, bar or restaurant will involve working in a team, providing a quality service to customers, and dealing tactfully with complaints. Don't mention the routine, non-person tasks (cleaning the tables) unless you are applying for a casual summer job in a restaurant or similar.

- Try to relate the skills to the job. A finance job will involve numeracy, analytical and problem solving skills, so focus on these. If for a marketing role, you would place a bit more emphasis on persuading and negotiating skills.

- Use action words such as developed, planned and organized.

4. Awards

This section, although optional, can be extremely important to set you apart from the next candidate. It is important to make these achievements relevant to the employer and show off your skills.

5. Interests

This section is your opportunity to show what you do outside of work and give the employer an insight into your qualities. It is important as it can show that you are a social person or are good in a team etc. But how to write about your interests can be very tricky. Here are some examples.

This could be the same individual as in the first example, but the impression is completely the opposite: an outgoing proactive individual who helps others.

- Don't put many passive, solitary hobbies (reading, watching TV, stamp collecting) or you may be perceived as lacking people skills. If you do put these, then say what you read or watch: *"I particularly enjoy Dickens, for the vivid insights you get into life in Victorian times."*
- Show a range of interests to avoid coming across as narrow: if everything centers around sport, they may wonder if you could hold a conversation with a client who wasn't interested in sport.
- Hobbies that are a little out of the ordinary can help you to stand out from the crowd: skydiving or mountaineering can show a sense of wanting to stretch yourself and an ability to rely on yourself in demanding situations.

Anything showing evidence of employ ability skills such as leadership, team working, organizing, planning, persuading, negotiating etc. is important to mention.

6. Skills

It is important to think of what skills your prospective employer is looking for. Be sure to do some research into the kind of qualities and skills that they want you to have. They will be specific. Research the company's website, the job advert or current employees of the company.

More generally, all employers will value certain traits in a candidate. Whilst relevant job experience can often land you a job, there are a number of key personal qualities and skills that employers are always hunting for. Nail a few of these and your chances of getting the job are looking much better.

6.3.4   What Makes a Good CV?

There is no single "correct" way to write and present a CV but the following general rules apply:

(1) CVs tend to be two pages in length so try your best to cut it down to this size. Also do not print it back to back. If you can summarize your career history comfortably on a single side, this is fine. However, you should not leave out important items, or crowd your text too closely together in order to fit it onto that single side.

(2) Always remember to back up your skills with relevant experiences and vice-versa. At the

same time, try not to be too vague.

(3) Use key words to emphasize your points and do not use the same words over and over again.

(4) Make sure that you always proofread and spell-check the document a few times over and if possible, get a friend to check it for you. There is nothing worse than a spelling or grammar mistake on a CV.

(5) There is not a set out format, so do not worry if yours looks too different. However do not go too over the top as using things such as watermarks, colored fonts and elaborate borders which can look unprofessional.

(6) Keep all of your sentences and paragraphs short as you do not want to bore the reader.

Here is an example of CV.

Bill Smith	
20 North road	
West Didsbury	0161 440 8998
Manchester M20 1PP	Email: Bill@physics.org

Education

2009-present	University of Kent
2007-2009	Zhongshan High School

Work experience

Administrative Assistant(2011-2012)

　Handled incoming telephone calls

　Organized and maintained the Manager's filing system.

　Solved co-workers' PC problems

　Organized games for people attending in the afternoons

Sales Assistant (2010-2011)

　Provided excellent customer service and dealt with enquiries and orders.

　Stocked shelves and updated stock system.

　Administered deliveries and dealt with suppliers.

Awards

Excellent Student Cadre Scholarship

First Prize of Excellent Undergraduate Scholarship

Third-grade Scholarship

Excellent Cadre of Students

Guanghua Scholarship

College English Test (Band 6)

Skills

Languages　Good conversational English, basic French

Driving　Full clean driving license

Computer　Proficient in Office applications, use of internet and e-mail.

Interests

Travel: travelled through Europe by train this summer in a group of four people, visiting historic sites and practicing my French and Italian.

⚙ Vocabulary

appropriately	适当地
subject header	主题，标题
salutation	称呼语
recipient	接收者
formality	礼节，形式
graduate students	研究生
dissertation	学位论文
stuff	材料，塞满
intimacy	亲密，亲近
Curriculum Vitae	履历
proactive	主动的，先发制人的

👤 FURTHER READING

Top 10 Ways to Rock Your Resume

Whether you're looking for a new job or just pruning up your paperwork, one of the keys to nabbing the job you want is creating a successful resume. Here are our top 10 ways to make sure yours stands out.

10. Start with a Big List, and Then Shorten It

We know keeping your resume brief is important, but one of the best ways to make sure your resume is as good as possible is to start long. Make a plain text document of all the possible information you might include, and then pare it down from there. You're less likely to forget anything important, and it will also come in handy if you ever need to tweak it for different job opportunities.

9. Know What Not to Include

When it comes time to narrow down your giant list of accomplishments, you'll want to make sure you're including the most important stuff. You definitely want to get rid of not-so-no-table accomplishments, and anything outdated can probably go too. There are also a lot of phrases that are just wasting ink on the page, and you should get rid of those too.

8. Avoid Overused Phrases

If you want to make your resume stand out, you're going to want to avoid canned phrases like "team player", "strong work ethic", and "innovative". We've gone through lists of tired phrases on more than one occasion, so make sure you check out every list to clean out the cliches.

7. Quantify Your Accomplishments

Instead of filling your resume with the aforementioned canned phrases, pick something quantifiable. Anything you can describe with numbers demonstrates something real and tangible that your potential employers can see. Saying you "increased sales by 300 percent" (and mentioning how you did so) is much better than saying you "exceeded expectations". Always be on the lookout for ways you can put your accomplishments into numbers.

6. Find the Keywords Your Employer is Looking for and Use Them

Nowadays, so many people are passing their resumes around that sometimes they don't even get read. Instead, HR folks are scanning them for relevant keywords, like names of computer programs you know. Making sure these are somewhere on your resume increase its chances of getting seen and actually read.

5. Strategically Tweak Your Dates of Employment

Employers aren't usually too fond of job-hoppers, so if you've had a few recent jobs instead of a steady one, you might want to try and pull attention away from that fact. One of the best ways to do that is strategically format your resume to highlight the jobs, not the dates. Using only years to describe employment terms, for example, looks better than the more specific month-and-year approach.

4. Try a Visual Slideshow or Video Resume

While many employers will prefer the simple, single-page list of accomplishments, lots of others would prefer to see your personality and accomplishments more in-depth through a slideshow or video resume. Make sure you make it worth their while, of course, if your slideshow is just as boring as your text-based resume would be, you're not doing yourself any favors. And of course, check with the HR department before sending something like this in to make sure it's okay.

3. Don't Use It Until the End of the Interview Process

Some employers may request your resume at the beginning, but if they don't, consider holding off. It's too easy for a potential employer to scan your resume and reject you. If you wait to hand in your resume until the end, you'll be forced to show yourself off in other ways, and keep your potential employers thinking about something else beyond the dull checklist of accomplishments.

2. Use Multiple Resumes for Different Potential Jobs

If you're applying for multiple jobs, even if they're in the same field, you may not want to use the same resume for each job. Tailor your resume to each specific job you apply for, and send a unique resume out for each one.

1. Proofread from the Bottom Up

When you're done and ready to send your resume in, you will want to proofread it for errors. There are a lot of ways to make sure you proofread it well (like printing it out), but one of the more interesting ways we've seen is to read it from the bottom up. This way, you'll make sure you don't skip over any sections, and will also help you see things from an angle other than the one you've already written and proofread it fifteen times.

Source: available at http://m.lifehacker.com

Appendix

Words & Phrases with Chinese Characteristics

1. 经济类

社会主义市场经济　the socialist market economy

非公有制经济　non-public sector

高度集中的计划经济　highly centralized planned economy

新型工业化道路　new path of industrialization

转变经济发展方式　transformation of the mode of economic development

产业结构优化升级　upgrading of the industrial structure

扩大国内需求　boost domestic demand

生产要素　factors of production

全面振兴东北地区等老工业基地　rejuvenate northeast China and other old industrial bases

国有企业改革　reform of state-owned enterprises

加工贸易　processing trade

综合国力　overall national strength

下岗职工再就业　re-employment of laid-off workers

西部大开发战略　develop-the-west strategy / go-west strategy

扩大中等收入者比重　raise the proportion of the middle-income group

收入分配制度　income distribution system

转移支付　transfer payments

初次分配　primary distribution

再次分配　redistribution

绝对贫困　absolute poverty

低收入群体　low-income groups

社会公平　social equity

基本公共服务均等化　equal access to basic public services

最低工资　minimum wage

"引进来"和"走出去"　"bring in" and "go global"

企业职工工资正常增长　regular pay increases for enterprise employees

保护合法收入，调节过高收入，取缔非法收入　to protect lawful incomes, regulate excessively high incomes and ban illegal gains

公有制为主体、多种所有制经济共同发展　public ownership is dominant and different economic sectors develop side by side

2. 科技类

创新型国家　innovative country

国家创新体制　national innovation system

自主创新能力　capacity for independent innovation

科技进步　scientific and technological advance

科教兴国　rejuvenating the country through science and technology

人才强国　strengthen the nation with trained personnel

前沿技术研究　research in frontier technology

社会公益性技术研究　technological research for public welfare

促进科技成果向现实生产力转化　promoting the translation of scientific and technological advances into practical productive forces

科技成果产业化　application of scientific and technological achievements in production

激励机制　incentive mechanism

一线的创新人才　innovative personnel in the frontline of production

劳动者素质提高　improvement in the quality of work force

可再生能源　renewable energy resources

资源节约型、环保型社会　a resource-conserving, environment-friendly society

循环经济　circular economy

国家中长期科学和技术发展规划纲要　Outline of the National Program for Long-and Medium-Term Scientific and Technological Development

把科学成果转化成生产力　transform scientific research results into productive forces

3. 教育类

教育公平　equal access to education

育人为本、德育为先　educating students with top priority given to cultivating their moral integrity

高中阶段教育　senior secondary education

学前教育　pre-school education

减轻学习负担　ease the study load

规范教育收费　regulate the collection of education-related fees

资助制度　system of financial aid to students

远程教育　distance learning

继续教育　continuing education

终身学习　lifelong learning

高校毕业生　college graduates

学有所教、劳有所得、病有所医、老有所养、住有居所

all people enjoy their rights to education, employment, medical and old-age care, and housing

爱国守法、明礼诚信、团结友善、勤俭自强、敬业奉献

patriotism and observance of law; courtesy and honesty; solidarity and friendship; diligence, frugality and self-improvement; and devotion and contribution

爱国主义教育基地

site for patriotic education/site rich in patriotic significance

4. 卫生医疗类

把社会效益放在首位　give prime consideration to social effects

社会保障体系　social security system

社会保险、社会救助、社会福利　social insurance, assistance and welfare

合作医疗制度　cooperative medical care system

重大疾病防控　prevent and control the outbreak of major diseases

完善失业、工伤、生育保险制度　improve the system of unemployment, workers' compensation and maternity insurances

人道主义精神　humanitarian spirit

基本医疗卫生制度　a basic medical and health care system

政事分开、管办分开、医药分开、营利性和非营利性分开　separate government administration from medical institutions, management from operation, medical care from pharmaceuticals, and for-profit from nonprofit operations

公共卫生服务体系、医疗服务体系、医疗保障体系、药品供应保障体系　systems of public health services, medical services, medical security, medical supply

5. 政治类

中国特色社会主义伟大旗帜

the great banner of socialism with Chinese characteristics

三个代表重要思想　the important thought of Three Represents

(The party must always represent the requirements of the development of China's advanced productive forces, the orientation of the development of China's advanced culture, and the fundamental interests of the overwhelming majority of the people in China.)

科学发展观　scientific outlook on development

马克思主义中国化　adapting Marxism to conditions in China

社会主义初级阶段　the primary stage of socialism

全面协调可持续发展　comprehensive, balanced and sustainable development

统筹兼顾　overall consideration

推进各方面体制改革创新　to promote institutional reform and innovation in various sectors

改革开放　reform and opening-up

全面建设小康社会　to build a moderately prosperous society in all respects

和谐社会　harmonious society

解放思想、实事求是　emancipate the mind, seek truth from facts

勇于变革、勇于创新　to make bold changes and innovations

永不僵化、永不停滞　to stay away from rigidity or stagnation

与时俱进　advancing with time

缩小城乡地区间发展差距　narrow the urban-rural and interregional gaps in development

以人为本　putting people first

邓小平理论　Deng Xiaoping Theory

第一代中央领导集体　first generation of the central collective leadership

社会主义建设规律　laws governing socialist construction

新民主主义革命　new-democratic revolution

全心全意为人民服务　serving the people wholeheartedly

出发点和落脚点　the aim and outcome

发展为了人民、发展依靠人民、发展成果由人民共享

Development is for the people, by the people and with the people sharing in its fruits

"一个中心、两个基本点"的基本路线　taking economic development as the central task and upholding the Four Cardinal Principles and the reform and opening up policy, known as "one central task and two basic points"

社会主义民主政治　socialist democracy

人民代表大会制度　system of people's congress

中国共产党领导的多党合作和政治协商制度　system of multiparty cooperation and political consultation under the leadership of the CPC

民族区域自治制度　system of regional ethnic autonomy

多党合作及政治协商制度　system of multi-party cooperation and political consultation

长期共存、互相监督、肝胆相照、荣辱与共　long-term coexistence, mutual oversight, sincere treatment of each other and the sharing of weal and woe

政治体制改革　political restructuring

人民当家作主的地位　the position of the people as the masters of the country

基层群众自治制度　system of self-governance at the primary level of society

调动人民积极性　arouse the initiative of the people

社会主义法治国家　socialist country under the rule of law

社会主义政治文明　socialist political civilization

知情权、参与权、表达权、监督权　rights to be informed, to participate, be heard, and to oversee

民主监督　democratic oversight

参政议政　participation in the deliberation and administration of state affairs

职工代表大会　workers' conferences

企事业单位　enterprises and public institutions

法律面前一律平等　all citizens are equal before the law

审判机关、检察机关　courts and procuratorates

爱国统一战线　patriotic united front

增进团结、凝聚力量　enhance unity and pool strengths

党外干部　Non-CPC persons

海外侨胞　overseas Chinese nationals

人大代表依法行使职权　deputies to people's congresses exercise their functions and powers in accordance with the law

民主集中制　democratic centralism

改善民主制度　improve institutions for democracy

民主选举　democratic election

6. 党建类

两大历史性课题(提高党的执政能力和领导水平、提高拒腐防变和抵御风险能力)

the two major historic subjects of enhancing the abilities of administration and art of leadership and resisting corruption, guarding against degeneration and warding off risks.

全面推进党的建设的新的伟大工程　forge ahead with the new great project of party building

职务终身制　life-long tenure

论资排辈　to assign priority according to seniority

公务员制度　civil service

竞聘上岗　compete for the post

立党为公、执政为民　Party that is built for public interests and exercises governance for the people

艰苦奋斗、清正廉洁　hardworking and clean

学习型政党　a party committed to learning

票决制　system of voting

选举制度　electoral system

候选人提名制度　system for nominating candidates

政令畅通　ensure its resolutions and decisions are carried out effectively

公开选拔、竞争上岗、差额选举　open selection, competition for position and multi-candidate election

任期、回避、交流制度　tenure system, recusal system, system for transferring leading cadres between different posts

干部双重管理体制　system of dual administration of cadres

德才兼备、注重实绩、群众公认　political integrity, professional competence and outstanding performance and enjoy popular support

党政领导机关　party and government leading organs

各级党组织　party organizations at all levels

维护宪法和法律的尊严　to uphold the authority of the Constitution and laws

基层党组织　grass-roots Party organizations

特邀代表　specially invited delegates

提高党内事务透明度　to increase transparency in Party affairs

反对、阻止个人或少数人的武断决策　to oppose and prevent arbitrary decision-making by an individual or a minority of people

党外人士　non-Communists

无党派人士　person with no political affiliation

党章　Party Constitution

建立党员党性定期分析制度　introduce the practice of regularly reviewing Party members' compliance with the Party spirit

群众路线　the mass line

权为民所用、情为民所系、利为民所谋　exercising power for the people, showing concern for them and working for their interests

学风和文风　styles of study and writing

讲党性、重品行、做表率　uphold the Party spirit, be impeccable in moral standard and play an exemplary role in society

批评和自我批评　criticism and self-criticism

党纪国法　Party discipline and state laws

标本兼治　address both its symptoms and root cause

惩防并举　combine punishment with prevention

拒腐防变　resist corruption and decadence

廉政建设　clean government building

权钱交易　trade power for money

以权谋私　abuse of power for personal gains

扫黑　to sweep away the "black" (i.e., secret societies)

反贪　anti-embezzlement

党要管党、从严治党　Party exercise self-discipline and is strict with its members

反腐倡廉　fight corruption and uphold integrity

巡视制度　system of inspection tours

不正之风　unhealthy practices

违纪违法案件　all cases involving violation of law and discipline

腐败分子　corruptionist

居安思危　stay prepared for adversities in time of peace

忧患意识　be mindful of potential dangers

戒骄戒躁　guard against arrogance and rashness

顾全大局　bear the overall interests in mind

人才辈出、人尽其才　capable people come forth in great numbers and put their talents to best use

八个坚持、八个反对

eight do's and eight don'ts (1.Emancipate the mind and seek truth from facts; do not keep doing things the old way. 2.Combine theory with practice; do not copy mechanically or worship books. 3.Keep close ties with the people; do not be formal or bureaucratic. 4.Adhere to the principle of democratic centralism; do not act arbitrarily or be feeble and lax. 5.Abide by Party discipline; do not act pursue liberalism.6.Be honest and up right; do not abuse power for personal gains.7.Work hard; do not be hedonistic.8.Appoint people on their merits; do not practice favoritism in personnel.)

保证中央的政令畅通　ensure the Central Committee's decisions are carried out without fail

7. 机构改革类

依法治国　rule of law

政治体制改革　political restructuring

党政机关　Party and government organs

事业单位　public institutions

政企分开、政资分开、政事分开、政府与市场中介组织分开

the separation of the functions of the government from those of enterprises, state assets management authorities, public institutions and market-based intermediaries

减少和规范行政审批　to reduce the number of matters requiring administrative examination and approval and standardize such procedures

制约及监督机制　mechanism of restraint and supervision

让权力在阳光下运行　power must be exercised in the sunshine

服务型政府　service-oriented government

电子政务　e-government

行政执法部门　administrative law-enforcement agencies

垂直管理部门　local departments directly under central government organs

机构重叠、职责交叉、政出多门　overlapping organization and functions and conflicting policies from different departments

完善制约和监督机制　improve the mechanism of restraint and oversight

决策权、执行权、监督权　decision-making, enforcing and oversight powers

引咎辞职　resignation

科学执政、民主执政、依法执政　scientific, democratic and law-based governance

合法权益　legitimate rights and interests

制度化、规范化、程序化　define institutions, standards and procedures

行政管理体制　administration system

舆论监督　the oversight role of public opinion

保证人民当家作主　ensure that they are masters of the country

科学及民主决策　scientific and democratic decision-making

公众听证会　public hearings

行使民主权利　exercise democratic rights

自我管理、自我服务、自我教育、自我监督　practice self-management, self-service, self-education and self-oversight

8. 文化类

社会主义先进文化　advanced socialist culture

社会主义荣辱观　socialist maxims of honors and disgraces

马克思主义理论研究和建设工程　project to Study and Develop Marxist Theory

精神文明建设　cultural and ethical progress

引领社会思潮　guide the trends of thought

尊重差异、包容多样　respect divergence and allow diversity

新闻出版、广播影视、文学艺术事业　press, publishing, radio, film, television, literature and act

弘扬社会正气　foster healthy social trends

诚信意识　awareness of integrity

社会公德　social ethics

职业道德　professional codes of conduct

家庭美德　family virtues

个人品德　individual morality

思想政治工作　ideological and political work

思想活动的独立性、选择性、多变性、差异性

People have become more independent, selective, changeable and diverse in thinking.

社会志愿服务体系　system of voluntary public services

男女平等　gender equality

尊老爱幼　respecting the elderly and caring for the young

互爱互助　showing concern for and helping each other

见义勇为　coming to the rescue of others even at the risk of oneself

取其精华、去其糟粕　keep its essence and discard its dross

文物和非物质文化遗产　cultural relics and intangible cultural heritage

百花齐放、百家争鸣的方针　The principle of "let a hundred flowers blossom and a hundred schools of thoughts contend"

贴近实际　maintain close contact with reality

公益性文化事业　nonprofit cultural programs

出精品、出人才、出效益　produce fine works, outstanding personnel and good results

公民道德建设　citizen's ethical construction

保障公民的基本文化权益　to guarantee the people's basic cultural rights and interests

给予正确导向，弘扬社会正气　to give correct guidance to the public and foster healthy social trend

发展和管理网络文化　to develop and manage Internet culture

培育良好的网络环境　to foster a good cyber environment

公益文化活动　nonprofit cultural programs

文化设施　cultural facilities

大力发展文化产业　to vigorously develop the cultural industry

富有地方特色的文化产业　cultural industries with regional features

百花奖　Hundred Flowers Award

唱响社会主义文化的旋律　highlight the main theme of socialist culture

9. 军事类

加快中国特色军事变革　to accelerate the revolution in military affairs with Chinese characteristics

应对多种安全威胁　respond to various security threats

完成多样化军事任务　accomplish diverse military tasks

党对军队绝对领导　the Party exercising absolute leadership over the armed forces

人民军队的根本宗旨　the fundamental purpose of the armed forces serving the people

建设信息化军队　to build computerized armed forces

高素质新型军事人才　high-caliber military personnel

转变战斗力生成模式　to change the mode of generating combat capabilities

中国特色军民融合式发展　development with Chinese characteristics featuring military and civilian integration

听党指挥　following the Party's orders

英勇善战　fight valiantly and skillfully

从严治军　enforce strict discipline on the armed forces

军民结合　integrate military with civilian purpose

寓军于民　combine military efforts with civilian support

拥军优属　support the military and give preferential treatment to the families of servicemen and martyrs

拥政爱民　the military supports the government and cherishes the people

10. 外交类

持久和平、共同繁荣　lasting peace and common prosperity

均衡、普惠、共赢　balanced development, shared benefits and win-win progress

求同存异　seeking common ground while shelving differences

世界多样性　the diversity of the world

以和平方式解决国际争端　to settle international disputes by peaceful means

高举和平、发展、合作旗帜　to hold high the banner of peace, development and cooperation

奉行独立自主的和平外交政策　pursue an independent foreign policy of peace

维护国家主权、安全、发展利益　safeguard China's interests in terms of sovereignty, security and development

恪守维护世界和平、促进共同发展的外交政策宗旨　uphold its foreign policy purposes of maintaining world peace and promoting common development

军备竞赛　arms race

损人利己、以邻为壑　to seek benefits for itself at the expense of other countries or shift its troubles onto others

"台独"势力　the forces of "Taiwan independence"

分裂活动　secessionist activities

维护中国的主权和领土完整　to safeguard China's sovereignty and territorial unity

构建两岸关系和平发展框架　to construct a framework for peaceful development of cross-Straits relations

和平统一　peaceful reunification

一个中国原则　one-China principle

两岸敌对状态　the state of hostility across the Taiwan Straits

两岸关系和平发展新局面　a new phase of peaceful development

霸权主义强权政治　hegemonism and power politics

防御性的国防政策　a national defense policy that is defensive in nature

互利共赢的开放战略　a win-win strategy of opening-up

通行的国际经贸规则　internationally recognized economic and trade rules

贸易和投资自由化便利化　the liberalization and facilitation of trade and financial systems

经贸摩擦　economic and trade frictions

永远不称霸　never seek hegemony

永远不搞扩张　never engage in expansion

防御性的国防政策　a national defense policy that is defensive in nature

反对一切形式的恐怖主义　to oppose terrorism in any form

推动国际和地区安全合作　to promote international and regional security cooperation

港人治港、澳人治澳　Hong Kong people administer Hong Kong and Macao people administer Macao

爱国爱港、爱国爱澳　love for the motherland and devotion to their respective regions

三通　direct links of mail, transport and trade

霸权主义　hegemonism

强权政治　power politics

局部冲突　local conflicts

热点问题　hotspot issues

南北差距拉大　the North-South gap is widening

国际关系准则　norms of international relations

秉持公道，伸张正义　stand for fairness and justice

和平共处五项原则　Five Principles of Peaceful Coexistence

睦邻友好　good-neighborly relations

以邻为善、以邻为伴的外交方针　follow the foreign policy of friendship and partnership

References

[1] Herbert A. Simon, Victor A. Thompson, Donald W. Smithburg. Public Administration[M]. New Jersey: Transaction Publishers,1991.

[2] Luther Gulick, L. Urwick. Papers on the Science of Administration[M]. New York: Institute of Public Administration, 1937.

[3] Jay Shafritz, Albert Hyde.Classics of Public Administration[M]. //Dwight Waldo. What Is Public Administration?.Oak Park, Ill.: Moore, 1978.

[4] Fritz Morstein Marx, Henry Reining. The Tasks of Middle Management. Elements of Public Administration[M]. Englewood Cliffs: Prentice-Hall,1959.

[5] Woodrow Wilson. The Study of Administration[J]. Political Science Quarterly, 1887, (2).197-211.

[6] Leonard D. White. Introduction to the Study of Public Administration[M]. New York: Macmillan, 1926.

[7] Frank J. Goodnow. Politics and Administration: A Study in Government[M]. Russell & Russell, 1900.

[8] David H. Rosenbloom. Public Administration: Understanding Management, Politics, and Law in the Public Sector[M]. Fifth ed. New York: McGraw-Hill Company, INC., 2002.

[9] Frederick Winslow Taylor. The Principles of Scientific Management[M]. New York, USA and London, UK: Harper & Brothers, 1911.

[10] Henri Fayol. General and Industrial Management[M]. Translated by C. Storrs. London: Sir Isaac Pitman & Sons,1949.

[11] Charles E. Lindblom. The Science of Muddling Through[J]. Public Administration Review, 1959,(2):79-88.

[12] David Osborne, Ted Gaebler. Reinventing Government: How the Entrepreneurial Spirit Is Transforming the Public Sector[M]. Boston, USA: Addison-Wesley Publishing Company, Inc., 1992.

[13] Encyclopedia Britannica. Britannica Concise Encyclopedia[M]. London: Encyclopedia Britannica Incorporated, 2007.

[14] Anonymous. The E-Government Act of 2002[EB/OL]. http://www.whitehouse.gov/ omb/e-gov, 2002-12-17/2014-06-08.

[15] Sinrod E. J. A Look at the Pros and Cons of E-government[EB/OL]. http://usatoday30. usatoday.com/tech/columnist/ericjsinrod/2004-06-30-sinrod_x.htm, 2004-06-30/2014-06-07.

[16] Schhrer B. How Web 2.0 will Transform Local Government[EB/OL]. http://www. govtech.com/e-government/102472664.html, 2008-10-16/2014-06-09.

[17] Thorpe S. J. Facilitating Effective Online Participation in E-government[EB/OL]. https://cdt.org/, 2008-06-23/2014-07-06.

[18] Anonymous. The Office of Management and Budget. Report to Congress on the Benefits of the President's E-Government Initiatives[EB/OL]. http://www.whitehouse.gov/sites/ default/files/omb/assets/egov_docs/fy13_e-gov_benefits_report_final_20130509.pdf, 2013-05-09/2014-07-08.

[19] Satyanarayana J. E-Government: The Science of the Possible[M]. New Delhi: Prentice Hall of India Pvt. Ltd., 2004.

[20] Bohlen M. et al. E-Government: Towards Electronic Democracy[M]. Berlin: Springer, 2005.

[21] Becker S. A. Bridging Literacy, Language, and Cultural Divides to Promote Universal Usability of E-government Websites[D]. Northern Arizona University,2009.

[22] Denhardt R. B., Denhardt J. V. The New Public Service: Serving rather than Steering[J]. Public Administration Review, 2000,60 (6), 549-559.